Praise for John Douglas Marshall's

Reconciliation Road

"This is a remarkable story that threads a man's search for the truth about his grandfather into a call for reconciliation between individuals and generations, between history and our own lives, between the men who fought the Vietnam war and all the rest of us for whose sins they suffered . . . . Read this for the peace offering it is."
Bill Moyers

"This poignant book . . . an important contribution to the rich literature of the Vietnam War."
David Halberstam, *The Washington Post Book World* (cover review)

"A modest and searching memoir of self-discovery . . . often moving, aiming unerringly for political and personal reconciliation in the still-unsettled aftermath of the war in Vietnam."
The New York Times Book Review

"Marshall gives us the painful process of a family finally coming back together. This book is both soul-searching and compelling, one that could help other families heal long-festering wounds . . ."
Rocky Mountain News

"*Reconciliation Road* is one of those rare books that purports to tell a straightforward tale but in its own subversive way tackles issues of major import . . . . This book succeeds on several levels . . . leaves indelible marks upon the reader."
Chicago Tribune

"A fascinating portrait of General Marshall emerges, interwoven with events from the turbulent Sixties and the author's yearning for reconciliation; highly recommended."
Library Journal

Reconciliation Road

A Family Odyssey

Road

John Douglas Marshall

Hungry Mind Press

For Anne
True friend, true partner, true love

JOHN DOUGLAS MARSHALL, the grandson of author S. L. A. Marshall, grew up in Detroit and Cleveland. He graduated from the University of Virginia and served as an Army lieutenant during the Vietnam War era before winning honorable discharge as a conscientious objector. He later received a master's in journalism from the University of Missouri. For the past two decades, he has worked on newspapers in the Pacific Northwest and now writes for the *Seattle Post-Intelligencer*. He is coauthor of *Volcano: The Eruption of Mount St. Helens*, a national best seller, and is the recipient of a fellowship from the National Endowment for the Humanities, as well as numerous journalism prizes. He now lives in Seattle with his wife and their two children. *Reconciliation Road* is his first book on his own.

Contents

Illustrations

Acknowledgments

THIS ACCOUNT OF MY JOURNEY would never have been possible without the kindness and assistance of many people, from family and friends to absolute strangers. Many of their names appear in the narrative, some do not.

I want to express particular gratitude to all the people who so graciously agreed to be interviewed. I was often touched by the reception I received from former military officers and Vietnam veterans despite my stand as a conscientious objector. I certainly had not expected this reception, which is one of the main reasons why this book's title includes "reconciliation." It is my great hope that more of us who went through the agonizing period of Vietnam will experience similar reconciliation, in order to finally end what writer Larry Heinemann calls this "unfinished business." A problem underscored once more when President Bill Clinton made his controversial visit to the Vietnam "Wall" on Memorial Day 1993.

This book also could not have been completed without the guidance and patience of people at the various archives I visited. These archivists are unsung keepers of history's attic. I owe the most to Thomas F. Burdett, curator of the S. L. A. Marshall Military History Collection at the University of Texas at El Paso; he was unfailingly helpful in providing the materials on my grandfather that form the foundation for this book. Other archivists who provided needed research materials included: Rich Boylan at the National Archives Washington National Records Center in Suitland, Maryland;

Will Mahoney at the National Archives in Washington, D.C.; and David Keough at the U.S. Army Military History Institute at Carlisle Barracks, Pennsylvania. I also received assistance in the libraries of the U.S. Army Infantry School at Fort Benning, Georgia, the University of Virginia in Charlottesville, the Seattle Public Library and the U.S. Army's Chief of Military History in Washington.

I took an unpaid leave of absence from the *Seattle Post-Intelligencer* to write this book, which meant that any financial support from others was a precious gift. The Kaltenborn Foundation of Palm Beach, Florida, supported this project even before I set out on the road. The David Busch family of Scottsdale, Arizona, provided crucial support along the way. The Centrum Foundation of Port Townsend, Washington, provided a residency in a perfect setting to write this particular book, a former military fort converted to peaceful use as a state park and arts center. And the Evans Wyckoff family of Bainbridge Island, Washington, provided a remarkable place to work on revisions.

Many other people supported this project in ways I will never forget. Pat and Susan Dunn threw a neighborhood party to salute my departure. On the road, many people welcomed me into their homes, often on short notice, and I appreciated the hospitality of: John and Elouise Westover, Lois and Buddy Greene, John and Marilyn Campbell, Bobby and Alex Miles, Ralph and Jane Roughton, Dick and Jann Klinger, Robert and Susan Rosen, Sarah Detmer, Burt and Betty Marshall, Jackson and Karen Lears, Chuck Adams and Jane Hennessey, Susan and Sanford Sacks, Paul and Gay Larsen, Janet and Jim O'Hara, Tom and Janet Matrka, Larry and Edie Heinemann, and Dick Young.

Some friends spent many hours reading the voluminous original manuscript ("the book in the box") and their suggestions aided my revisions: Anne Bugge, Casey Corr, William Downing, Pat Dunn, William Arnold, David Horsey, Richard Tuggle, Susan Sacks, David Schooler, and Kristin Webb.

Many fellow writers provided support and counsel and I salute the generosity of: Bill Moyers, Tim O'Brien, Terry Tempest Williams, Gay Talese, Richard Ford, Mona Simpson, Tess Gallagher, David Shields, John Gregory Dunne, William Least Heat-Moon, James Salter, and Tobias Wolff. Other artists who provided inspiration to me were: Gail Grinnell, Sandy Silva, Robert Priest, Richard Yates, and Norie Sato.

I also owe thanks to J. D. Alexander, executive editor of the *Seattle Post-Intelligencer*, who sent me on my initial research mission into the S. L. A. Marshall controversy. He believed in this story from the start.

Two people provided extraordinary support during this lengthy project: Russell Galen, my agent, who demonstrated dogged persistence; and William Arnold, my newspaper colleague, good friend, and neighbor who has written two books and always had welcome words of encouragement about mine.

The members of the Marshall family all deserve special thanks. Charles Burton Marshall and S. L. A. Marshall, Jr., offered important insights into my grandfather, became subjects in this narrative, critiqued the manuscript, and never once tried to censor my observations, no matter how painful.

My greatest debt is to my wife, Anne, who supported this project with untold sacrifices, encouragement, patience, computer work, plus a caring editor's eye. I dare anyone to even attempt what Anne managed—to give birth to a new business and a new baby, while her spouse was trying to give birth to a first book. We must have been crazy, or in love, or both.

That this book is dedicated to Anne is only a small token of my admiration, appreciation, and especially my love.

Reconciliation Road

It is hard to know what to do with all the detail that rises out of a fire. It rises out of a fire as thick as smoke and threatens to blot out everything—some of it is true but doesn't make any difference, some is just plain wrong, and some doesn't even exist, except in your mind, as you slowly discover long afterwards. Some of it, though, is true—and makes all the difference.

—Norman Maclean, *Young Men and Fire*

Prologue

THE WEST TEXAS SUN is already harsh and unrelenting, starting to bake the roadway asphalt, making tinder of the scrub grass which passes for lawn in the Fort Bliss National Cemetery. I am forced to squint as I scan the row of bright white marble headstones until I find the one that says:

S L A
Marshall
Brig Gen
US Army
World War I & II
Jul 18 1900
Dec 17 1977

I am trying hard to remain the reporter as I stand at my grandfather's grave for the first time, twelve years after his funeral, that elaborate military ceremony attended by everyone in the family. Except me. Now, a raging controversy has brought me here, and so I start to fill my notebook with the details that sixteen years at the journalist's trade have taught me to gather. I write down the names of the two men buried beside my famous grandfather, note that the flags are hanging at half-staff in the windless air and that the forlorn sound of "Taps" is drifting forth from a distant bugler, amid a small group of mourners, the first funeral of the morning.

My notebook is filling quickly with the look and feel of this place. It is only after I have jotted down these things that I finally

3

allow myself to notice that my chest is tied in knots, my breathing is halting, and I seem to be shivering despite the heat. I am, I suddenly recognize, close to tears. I did not know what to expect when I finally came to my grandfather's grave, but I did not expect this, certainly not anything this intense after all the years. My head spins, my heart aches as memories of my grandfather come flooding back, those I still treasure, and those I have tried to forget.

I remember playing catch with him in his backyard in suburban Detroit and how this man we all called "Poppy" urged me to really "burn one in" and so I did, sending him a scorcher that broke his finger.

I remember descending into his basement office lair, the bookshelves overflowing, the lighting dim, the air cool, even during those muggy Midwest summers. He would be sitting hunched over his old Underwood, a cloud of cigar smoke encircling his head, as his two fingers produced what sounded like a burst of machine gun fire.

I remember tagging along when my grandfather went to the *Detroit News*, visiting the editorial page department where he worked, a hushed place with heavy wood paneling, leaded glass windows, bookshelves laden with weighty volumes, and where everyone was contemplating the serious issues of the day. But what I remember more was the roar of the presses in the bowels of the old building, starting slowly at first, then building to an imposing crescendo, and how soon there would be delivered to my grandfather's desk a copy of today's paper, smelling of fresh ink and urgency. To then see my grandfather's byline on the front page—"By S. L. A. Marshall, News Military Analyst"—seemed imbued with such magic that I soon resolved to pursue this career myself.

I remember, too, my grandfather giving the ROTC commissioning speech at the University of Virginia in 1969, the day after the twenty-fifth anniversary of D-Day, and how I was sitting in the crowd among those in freshly pressed uniforms who were about to become officers. My grandfather was speaking to hundreds of people gathered on the magnificent Lawn designed by Thomas Jefferson, but it seemed he was speaking just to me. For he was using the occasion in Charlottesville to sum up life's lessons only weeks before his sixty-ninth birthday.

"True decision-making," he said, "is the resolution of a dilemma, a leap into the dark where nothing is certain, but some ac-

S. L. A. Marshall, John Marshall, and S. L. A. Marshall, Jr., immediately following the author's commissioning ceremony for ROTC at University of Virginia, June 1969. Photograph by S. L. A. Marshall III.

tion is requisite. The gamble is there and unavoidable and one must go at it as a gambler. Moreover, when the worst trials come along, one may have to decide altogether in solitude. Facing life, or facing the unknown, a man must be prepared to risk. Remember that— always. You may come up a cropper now and then. But if you never risk, you never win."[1]

The awarding of commissions followed. Each new officer proceeded to the stage, where S. L. A. Marshall presented the commissioning certificate after the new officer offered a salute. I was wearing Army green that day, but with many conflicting feelings—honored that my grandfather had agreed to preside over the ceremony, but very much aware that I was not the gung-ho ROTC stalwart expected of S. L. A. Marshall's grandson.

I was only a middling student of what was called "military science," having joined ROTC during my first year of college to fulfill a family duty. But as the years of college passed, amid the tumult of the late 1960s and the war, I came to take more pride in what I saw as my creative side—English major, sports editor of the college daily, devotee of foreign films, Hemingway's prose, the Beatles' music. People I knew were shocked when they saw me in my Army uniform for Tuesday afternoon ROTC drills; I would respond with what I hoped was a shrug that conveyed this was not the real me.

But there I was on the stage, this newly commissioned second lieutenant in the Infantry, an Army branch assignment I had not sought, and I was just about to raise my right arm when my grandfather snapped, "Don't you dare salute me!" And then he enveloped me in a hearty bear hug, while expressions of surprise rippled through the crowd, followed by applause. Little did I know then that this public embrace was destined to become one of the last close moments the two of us would ever share.

Twenty years later, I look down at my grandfather's grave and wonder what he would think if he knew that I had come here on a research mission to discover whether S. L. A. Marshall, probably the nation's foremost military historian, was indeed "a fraud" and "a fabricator," as was now being alleged in national publications. Me a reporter on his trail trying to determine the truth about his life and work. Me of all people.

For I had done something my grandfather could not abide—I had taken a stand against the Army. I had finally come to a point where I could no longer uphold family tradition when faced with all-but-certain assignment to Vietnam. I had become convinced the war was wrong, for both moral and political reasons. That I would not go to Vietnam was something I had decided during my time in the Army. And that left me with just two options: I could try to win an honorable discharge from the Army as a conscientious objector, following the complex process in place then; or I could go to Canada or Sweden with my wife and try to create a new life there. Either course seemed sure to incur family wrath and rupture, with my grandfather and probably my father as well.

I had decided to seek discharge as a conscientious objector; I preferred taking a stand to taking flight. But my options were so limited that what I was doing did not seem courageous to me. Like so many men of my generation, I was trying to resolve the Hamlet dilemma presented by Vietnam—To be, or not to be, a part of the war? After much agonizing and months of study, I had completed a voluminous application for discharge as a C.O.

"My commitment to Unitarian Universalism is fixed and I can no longer deny the calling of my conscience," I wrote. "I must now submit this application—regardless of my family heritage or tradition. I can no longer hide my true beliefs beneath my uniform."

I had tried to explain this to my grandfather in a letter after my C.O. application was approved. I do not have a copy of that letter anymore, but I am certain it began with "Dear Poppy," as my letters to him always did. A letter from him came back soon afterward. It began: "Dear Mr. Marshall."

Even twenty years later, after all the times that I have read his letter, I take those two pages of paper into my hands and almost expect them to burst into flames, so incendiary is the language, so intense the emotions. It went well beyond the worst that I had imagined from him. I was staggered as I read:

"That the Army seemingly prefers to give you an honorable separation means nothing to this part of what was once your family, means nothing either that the Army will ship you back home free. You are not entitled to an honorable and you are simply playing the freeloader on the taxpayer. We know why you quit. It wasn't conscience. You simply chickened out. You didn't have the guts it takes. Vietnam or any point of danger was unacceptable to you. You may fool the Army but you cannot fool and fail your Family at the same time. No male among us has ever been like that and the women, too, thank heaven, are stronger. That means you don't belong. So go on the course that you have chosen for yourself, that of comfort and convenience, all sweetness, love and lollipops. I would not push the Army to change its course with you, nor would I counsel you to reconsider. Neither is worth doing. You will not be welcome here again and you are herewith constrained not to use our name as family in any connection. Truly, S. L. A. Marshall. Cate Marshall."

These words reverberate through my brain as I stand at my grandfather's grave. Our once-close relationship had become a casualty of the Vietnam War, never reported in any weekly body count, but a casualty of the war just the same. Our relationship might as well have been inscribed with the names of the dead on the Wall of the Vietnam Memorial in Washington. Because my grandfather and I were never reconciled. A few cautious letters passed between us, but no more. Which is why I did not attend his funeral. I figured I was not "welcome" there either.

What finally does bring me to my grandfather's grave is a national controversy early in 1989. Cate, his widow, had died only weeks before a front-page story had appeared in the *New York Times* under this headline—"Pivotal S. L. A. Marshall Book on Warfare Assailed as False."[2] Then came the article in *American Heritage* that had prompted the Times' piece, a ten-page lead story filled with accusations about Marshall's 1947 book, *Men Against Fire* and its surprising assertion—that only a few American infantrymen fired their weapons during combat in World War II. Marshall said that, on average, only 15 percent of infantrymen fired their weapons, and never more than 20 to 25 percent. He discovered this startling phenomenon, he wrote, "in the course of holding post-combat mass interviews with approximately four hundred infantry companies in the Central Pacific and European Theaters," what he termed a "systematic collection of the data."[3]

It was no such thing, contended Sarah Lawrence historian Fredric Smoler in his *American Heritage* article largely based on the research of two other men—Harold Leinbaugh, a World War II company commander and later an FBI agent who was incensed when he finally happened upon Marshall's assertion; and Roger Spiller, an Air Force enlisted man who became a civilian historian at the Army's Command and General Staff College at Fort Leavenworth, Kansas. The *American Heritage* article asserted there was no proof that Marshall did "company level interviews" during World War II and that his finding on firing came about because "Marshall made the whole thing up." This was, the article concluded, "a peculiar hoax."[4]

The magazine did not stop there, not in this accusatory age. Marshall's own background was riddled with similar deceits, according to *American Heritage*. He never received a battlefield commission in World War I, as he had long claimed, and he was "lying" when he said he had commanded troops in combat. Marshall, the article asserted, was a maker of myths.

And yet when the controversy first broke, I felt no urge to use my reporting skills to investigate the charges against my grandfather. My father and my younger brother reacted with far more outrage than I did—perhaps because they share his name. The two of them blistered the long-distance lines with invective and threats of lawsuits, even though I said the law makes it impossible to libel a dead person. They remained insistent, my brother playing on my sense of family loyalty when he urged, "You've got to look into this; you're the only one who can clear grampa's name." I was indeed the only family member who followed "Poppy" into writing, yet I had also been given a large framed portrait of the man, a truly remarkable likeness, and for years I had kept this portrait in a closet. S. L. A. Marshall's steely gaze was not something I cared to see staring down from any wall in my home. About the kindest way to describe how I felt about my grandfather was "ambivalent."

Days went by, with my brother's words echoing in my mind. I still had little interest in clearing the name of a man who excommunicated me from the family. But maybe there was another way to approach this, it slowly dawned on me. Maybe I could go after the "truth" about S. L. A. Marshall in much the same way I would go after any other news story, with careful research, thorough interviews, the concern for fairness that had guided me during my years on newspapers.

I did not know what I hoped to find. I had a hard time sorting that out. Would I feel heartened somehow if S. L. A. Marshall turned out to be far less than he had claimed? Or relieved if I discovered that the charges against him were dead wrong?

I did know this, though. I knew that if I found that S. L. A. Marshall was indeed a fraud, then that is what I would write. I had to. To be true to myself.

1

Detroit Years

I KNEW HIM, or I thought I knew him back then. My grandfather was famous, I certainly knew that, and that had a tremendous hold on me when I was a child. I was not just John Marshall, I was the grandson of S. L. A. Marshall and that made me more important, truly special, at least in my own mind. I did not go around bragging about my grandfather exactly, but I was never that hesitant about mentioning the connection to teachers especially, or others I wanted to impress.

A child's adulation is such a simple thing, so pure, so undemanding, even stronger than love in a way. I did not truly know my grandfather back then, nor did I need to. What little I knew was powerful enough. I knew he was a newspaperman, I knew he was a general, I knew he wrote books about wars, including *Pork Chop Hill*, which had been made into a movie starring Gregory Peck. And I knew my grandfather traveled all over the world to places I could scarcely imagine; he was always departing for somewhere like Korea, or Israel, or South Africa. And other famous people always met with him overseas, I remember hearing.

Often-told family tales further increased my grandfather's stature in my eyes. He was supposed to have played semi-pro baseball, supposed to have been interested once in a singing career, supposed to have survived numerous plane crashes and other perils. And he often appeared on television—what more could a kid ask of his hero?

Until I was twelve, we lived just a few miles from my grandfather's house in Birmingham, Michigan. We visited there often,

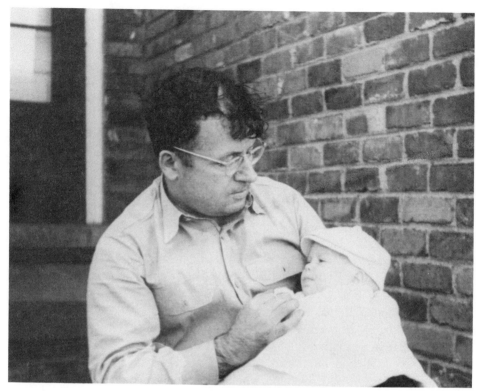

S. L. A. Marshall feeding infant John Marshall, 1947.

always on holidays, but also just to play in his big backyard, or maybe have Sunday dinner. Those 1950s' times seem so innocent now, so Ozzie and Harriet and so distant, especially after all the dislocations that came afterward.

Relatives in those days were not just people who sent cards at Christmas and maybe birthdays. They were part of our daily lives, they were our neighbors, they were our friends. Everyone on both sides of my family lived in the Birmingham area; my mother and her two sisters lived less than a mile apart. I remember playing for hours in my cousins' rooms, eating my gramma Povah's steak-and-kidney pie and feeling the crush of my grampa Marshall's bear hug every time we visited his house. To this day, I can still smell the cigar smoke that clung to his skin and his clothes, such a strange odor to a child, sour and sweet and dense.

The two families of Marshalls were particularly close. My grandfather was married to his third wife, Cate, who was much younger, and they had three girls about the same age as my brother, my sister and me. We were all great pals. My grandfather's young family made him seem less like a traditional grandfather to me. We were much closer than that. He was another father to me almost.

The two families of Marshalls even had our own private club back in those days. Our club was called the Phuzzant Buddies, a club that somehow came into being after my younger brother mispronounced "pheasants." We had special cloth patches made with our Phuzzant Buddy emblem, although we never got around to having them affixed to blazers, as we always said we would. And we had annual Phuzzant Buddy meetings convened around my grandfather's dining room table, very official meetings with minutes taken and actual agenda items discussed, most often who else in the world might possibly be worthy of Phuzzant Buddy membership. It was not an honor we casually dispensed.

We still had our Phuzzant Buddy meetings on Thanksgivings after we moved to Cleveland when I was in the sixth grade. I remember the trek back to grandfather's house, the crowded Country Squire station wagon speeding along the Ohio Turnpike, everyone in such a holiday mood, our anticipation growing about the times we would share again.

But the two hundred miles that now stood between us bred a new distance. Our family visits were far less frequent, and were sometimes strained from our trying to do too much; we wanted to reclaim the way things were, but they usually fell short. The past, it seemed, had passed.

My grandfather, who had been such a strong presence in my childhood, became instead a distant relation who sent presents on special occasions, including a check and a leather-bound Webster's dictionary when I graduated from high school in 1965. Along with it came a note that is still pasted inside the cover today:

"Dear Johnny, I do not think I can make it for your graduation.

Cate is still away and driving that far with the two gals by myself would just take too much out of me.

"I want you to know that I am proud of you. You have performed well in your scholastics, without ever letting your studies interfere with your education [a comment, it turned out, borrowed from Mark Twain]. Having fun as you go along is an important part of life, and so is keeping your sense of humor. You tend to be serious enough. Do not overdo it. The effect on others is unimportant. What counts is that you would finally bore yourself. That should be avoided like grim death. I maintain that a man should always be interesting to himself no matter how dull he seems to everyone else. And one can do that without ever really working at it.

"Work hard, but not too hard. Love well, but not desperately. Sleep sound, but keep one ear cocked for the alarm bell.

"I was going to buy you a piece of luggage; you will be traveling soon. Then I decided, what the hell, you should have some spending money and maybe you do not need any bags anyway. (PS: Try to keep them away from under your eyes.) As ever, SLAM (Poppy)."

I, the dutiful grandson, wrote back:

"Dear Poppy, As always, you were too generous in your gift to me. I can only offer my deepest thanks and say that I banked the money—though that certainly does not mean that it won't soon be spending money. By the way, your hunch about the luggage was correct; Mom and Dad gave me a tremendous American Tourister 1-suit. I greatly appreciated the advice you offer in the letter; in the long run, it will be far more valuable than the money. Thanks again for both. It would be great if our two families could get together soon. Your loving grandson, John."

A year later, I spent three months living at my grandfather's. He had landed me a summer job as a copy boy on the *Detroit News*. It was the lowliest position in the newsroom. It paid seventy dollars a week. It put me in heaven.

For years, people had been telling me that "you're going to be just like your grandfather" and I had beamed back, the special connection between us further cemented by each repetition of the phrase. People first started saying that when I developed a chunky physique and they saw the traces of my grandfather's prominent paunch. People continued saying that when I started to do well in English classes, particularly in writing. Those comments intensified when I became editor of my high school newspaper. The words had the ring of truth to me by then. My grandfather had gone from hero to role model for me. I was going to be a writer, too.

Then I was working on my grandfather's newspaper and living in my grandfather's house, the special connection between us acknowledged, at last, by him. I wish, though, I could remember more of that summer, what he said and what we did, places we went together, moments we shared, perhaps a ball game at Tiger Stadium, especially in light of what came later.

I do remember my grandfather was writing a Vietnam book in his basement office that summer, and how he would finally emerge upstairs around 6:00 P.M., exhausted but triumphant, a gimlet mixed by Cate soon raised in toast to another day's writing well done. I remember how he took an interest in what I was doing at the newspaper, solicited my observations on what was going on there, although he did keep his distance, not wanting to put undue pressure on me. I remember, too, how he treated me like one of his family, but also an adult, with few restrictions on when I could come or go, which I appreciated at nineteen. And I remember sitting in his book-lined study when he was gone and working on some of my own writing, pained love poems as I recall, although what I wrote mattered far less than the chance to sit in his place and imagine myself as a real writer, imagine myself as him.

When I left to go back to college at the end of the summer, I was flush with what seemed to have been built between us—a new and closer relationship, more mature, with a real affection and respect for each other that seemed sure to last. And that was reinforced the following spring when he sent *Battles in the Monsoon*, which he had inscribed: "To John Marshall goes this first copy of the new book—and Johnny, I hope you like it."

But college brought distance between us. I saw my grandfather only once or twice more before we were reunited on the stage in Charlottesville. By then, he was well-known as one of the country's staunchest defenders of American intervention in Vietnam, and one of the most outspoken critics of the press' performance there ("The most wretchedly reported war," he wrote in his much-noticed foreword to *Battles in the Monsoon.* "Never before have men and women in such numbers contributed so little to so many.")[1] S. L. A. Marshall had become The Unrepentant Hawk. My own views were starting to turn in the opposite direction, although I had no interest in debating such matters with him. I still hoped our relationship could avoid being poisoned by the war, as was happening across the generations in so many families.

My grandfather and I were reunited again at Fort Benning. He was the graduation speaker for my officer class at the Infantry School, doing a reprise of the role he had played at Virginia five months before. Again, the close connection between us was underscored in a public ceremony, the famous general and his grandson, now the Infantry lieutenant. In private, though, I found my grandfather distracted by other matters, not as interested in what I was doing in the Army as I had thought he would be. I remember being disappointed about that back then, but wonder now if my grandfather shared my sense of the growing differences between us, and how some things in those divisive days were better left unsaid.

Nineteen months later, little was left unsaid. My letter explaining my decision to become a conscientious objector was followed by my grandfather's letter disowning me and that was followed by years of silence, stony silence.

When my grandfather died six years later, no one in the family suggested I might attend his funeral in El Paso. So I remained in Oregon and sent an arrangement of red roses in my place, roses that my brother later reported had been displayed at the head of my grandfather's casket.

What I felt at the time was mostly regret, regret that no dramatic gesture across the gulf between us, no healing passage of time, nothing would ever bring about our reconciliation. And I suppose I felt some grief about my grandfather's passing. But the truth was—he had been dead for me for many years.

2

Setting out in September

MY COPIES OF MY GRANDFATHER'S OBITUARIES from national publications had long remained buried in a folder marked "SLAM." I seldom removed the folder from my file cabinet over the years; there seemed no point in dredging up such bad memories. But now, in the wake of the controversy about my grandfather's life and work, I retrieved the obituaries, searching for any hint of fraud, things that might be suspect.

There did not seem to be much, other than the notation he was "the youngest officer in the United States Army in World War I," the sort of sweeping claim that the controversy is calling into question. Otherwise, the obituaries were prominently displayed, lengthy and full of praise.

S. L. A. Marshall, who stood 5 feet five, was described by *Time* magazine as "a towering military historian who analyzed all the wars of modern America." It noted that he was "seldom far from the sound of gunfire," then continued, "Out of his experiences in the Korean War came his most esteemed books, *The River and the Gauntlet* and *Pork Chop Hill*. His writing was distinguished by narrative drive, a gritty attention to the details of combat and a plain-spoken sympathy for the men who suffered and triumphed on the front lines. He could not agree with people, he said, who thought that 'war is a game in which the soul of man no longer counts.'"[1]

Could this be the same man who was now being accused of "maligning American infantrymen with 'Men Against Fire?'" Could

16

this be the same man who was even being castigated by his harshest critic, Leinbaugh, for "knowing nothing about combat?"

The *Washington Post* used "noted military historian" to describe Marshall in its headline. "As a lieutenant colonel assigned to the Pacific in World War II," the *Post* said, "he developed the technique of doing battlefield history by assembling survivors soon after an encounter and interviewing the group about its operations. He used this method later with American troops in Europe, Korea and Vietnam, and with the Israeli army after the Sinai War of 1956." The Army's then-chief of military history was quoted next: "Marshall specialized in small unit type of action where he would talk to the people involved and elicit the details of what had happened. He was very good at putting it down in a vivid way, and he made people read things that professional historians might make dry as dust."[2]

The *New York Times'* obituary on Marshall started on the front page, that sign of a person's national importance. Marshall was described as "one of the nation's best-known military historians and a prominent figure on American and other war fronts for half a century." Again, his books were saluted for their "critical acclaim" and their "visceral" realism. A cited review of *The River and the Gauntlet* described it as "by far the finest book that has come out of the Korean War."

But the *Times* also said, "Though his detailed reporting of World War II and the Korean conflict won praise, similar efforts in five books on the war in Vietnam encountered some criticism from writers who said he had lost the larger meanings of the war in a concentration on the minutiae of it. Some critics, moreover, called him a hawk."[3]

Now, twelve years later, Marshall was being called much worse. "A liar." "A fraud." An instigator of a "peculiar hoax." I try to investigate these allegations while researching a three-part series about the Marshall controversy for the *Seattle Post-Intelligencer*, where I have worked for years as a columnist. I hear "genius" used to describe my grandfather by both friends and historians. I hear "charlatan" used to describe my grandfather by his critics. I hear very few descriptions in between.

The only way to sort this out, I finally conclude, is to take to the road around the United States. I must complete much more research, conduct face-to-face interviews with those involved in the controversy, as well as those who knew Marshall best—family members, fellow historians, compatriots, people like Gen. William C. Westmoreland and Mike Wallace, if they will see me.

Because I have begun to discover that my grandfather was a far more intriguing figure than I ever suspected. My opinion of him had been colored for years by our bitter break; I saw him as a harsh and unrelenting bantamweight bloated on his own sense of self-importance, with a distinct tendency to be vindictive, even cruel. But a different man was starting to emerge in my research, someone who still wore his flaws like a loud suit, but also a self-made man of the sort seldom seen anymore, someone who did not graduate from high school and still managed to create a historic life.

Writing for the first time about my grandfather and what had happened between us had also forced me to confront the pain of my estrangement from my family and my past. Too long, I had kept it a secret that I had been a conscientious objector. Too long, I had kept it a secret that I was disowned by my own family as a result. And I had let this fester, this wound to my soul. I am not alone in this predicament in late twentieth-century America. Many families are scattered across the country, going about our separate lives, isolated from loved ones at great cost that we may not acknowledge. As writer Norman Mailer has observed, "Very few of us know really where we have come from . . . . We have lost our past, we live in that airless no man's land of the perpetual present, and so suffer double as we strike into the future because we have no roots by which to protect ourselves forward, and judge our trip."[4]

My own journey had seemed so frightfully predictable at one time. I was Wally on "Leave It to Beaver," right down to the varsity jacket and burr-head flattop, the product of Republican parents in the suburbs and Midwestern public schools, president of the Junior Council on World Affairs, in no way a rebel. Then, I had gone to Virginia, a southern gentleman's school steeped in tradition, no caldron of student activism in the 1960s. Yet somehow I had forsaken my family tradition and refused to fight my country's war.

Was it only those tumultuous times, I wondered now. Was the split with my grandfather an inevitable result of Vietnam and the 1960s? Or was it because of his personality, and maybe my own? Is there a strange gene among us Marshall men ticking like a time bomb through our lives until it inevitably causes our adult relationships to self-destruct? Or could that painful rupture have been avoided, or lessened, or something? And wasn't it time to finally find answers, learn lessons from past mistakes, especially before they are repeated. By me. As a husband and father myself.

But driving one lap around America in search of such answers is no easy step taken with little forethought. I will have to take an unpaid leave of absence from my job and family savings will be drained at a frightening rate. Illnesses and emergencies will have to be dealt with long-distance. And there is no way to figure how long the trip may take, two months, three months, perhaps more.

Anne is the key to this trip. She is the one who will be left home with our two-year-old son, while also trying to start her own business in a new field after leaving TV news. Yet even in my own times of doubt about the journey, Anne keeps encouraging me to set out: "You've got to do it. If you don't, you'll always wish you had."

Her support surprises me, although it should not. There have been so many surprises in our life together, so many things so different from the way they were in my first marriage. I was married for thirteen years before and I was so sure that I never wanted children. I wanted my life to be devoted to my wife and the kind of life we created for ourselves. Freedom. Travel. A career. A nice house in a special part of the country. I wanted just us — until our divorce.

Two years later, I met Anne when we were both covering a weird story and we soon fell in love and it was such a consuming passion, all that I had longed to find but doubted I would ever share. I wanted to marry Anne and Anne wanted to marry me, but she was adamant on one point: She wanted to have children. Her first husband had said he wanted to have children, until after they were married, and she was not about to make the same mistake with me.

I trotted out all my best rationales for not having children, but Anne was unmoved. We would try to have children, she said, or we would not be married; it was that simple. So, after a time, I gave in. Anne was too special to lose.

We had gotten to know each other better before we tried to have children. We had traveled to memorable places, twice to Europe, once to Hawaii, once even to Tahiti. We had bought our first house. And then we tried to have children. And tried. And tried. We had tried for a year. Various doctor visits followed, various tests.

There was, finally, some medication Anne could take which might help. Within two weeks, she was pregnant. Nine months later, we were rushed into an operating room for an emergency Caesarian at 3:00 A.M., a nightmarish experience, but with a beautiful conclusion, our little boy.

We named our son Thatcher Scott Marshall. Thatcher is a family last name from my mother's side of the family. I wanted no first name or middle name with even a hint of Marshall. All our endless discussions of names had finally forced me to recognize the real reason I did not want children before was what had happened between the generations of Marshall men, and how I did not want any part of that as a parent.

But now I am a parent and I am amazed every day by what I might have missed, the discoveries, the tenderness. I cannot imagine my life without Thatcher, this amazing little bundle of love and life, the Big Guy, the T Man. He is another reason to undertake this trip. There will come a time when Thatcher will wonder about his famous great grandfather and I hope to be able to respond with some knowledge and maybe some insights. I do not want my son to be as cut off from his family past as I have been.

Thatcher has become an important part of my life. Anne is absolutely essential. And she is so steadfast that I had not anticipated seeing her crying, crying for one of the few times in the years I have known her, as I finally back my car out of the driveway at the start of my journey. She had always insisted we would make this trip work somehow, so I had given little thought to the moment of my departure. But now it is upon us and streams of tears are rolling down her cheeks and all her remarkable optimism seems drained not just from her face, but from her whole body. She points the camera at me; I force a smile, let go with a wave, a self-conscious gesture, silly-looking, dumb. I then drive away, my stomach churning.

The route is familiar, at least at first. The towering skyscrapers of downtown Seattle, this once-distant city now discovered with a vengeance. The Eastside suburbs with their gleaming office parks. The foothills of the Cascade Mountains up ahead on Interstate 90.

By late afternoon, I leave Washington behind, after dense forests of fir, high country cattle ranches, then orchards and vineyards, then barren desert plateaus, and finally the Columbia River, this vast inland sea. I catch Interstate 84 in Oregon, shadowing the route of the fabled Oregon Trail, the Interstate of its day stretching two thousand miles from Missouri, a seven-month trek, if travelers made good progress and managed to survive.

I pull off the Interstate and enter a rest area where the once-Wild West has been tamed with such signs as "Pets Allowed in Marked Area Only." I pause at the rest area's Oregon Trail display and soon find myself mesmerized by the words of an earlier traveler to these environs. James Nesmith had passed through here 146 years ago, and his words and those of other settlers paint a harrowing portrait of life, and sometimes death, on the Oregon Trail.

I feel a kinship with Nesmith. My mind has been filled with questions this first day of travel. What will I find by the end of my trip, will it be worth all the effort, and in what way? Nesmith had written similar thoughts about his own journey, but despairs about providing "any rational answer." I hope to do better than that, but who knows?

I stop for the night in La Grande, a college town of 11,354 in the Grande Ronde Valley, ringed by mountain ranges and jagged peaks. The sky is tall here, the air clear, so thoroughly West. I check into the Pony Soldier motel within sight of the Interstate and fight off the first pangs of loneliness after talking to Anne and Thatcher on the telephone.

The task ahead seems daunting now. The driving alone an immense challenge. I have put only 160 miles behind me today; ahead is one brief stop in Oregon, then 1,500 more miles on the highway until my first layover in Arizona, where I will spend time with John Westover, my grandfather's aide in World War II. I am counting on Westover to provide some crucial answers for me, but will he?

I take to pacing the motel room, trying to kill out such thoughts. Finally, I stand at the picture window and stare across the deserted motel courtyard to the tall Interstate signs looming above in the darkness. One sign says, "Texaco." One says, "Denny's." And another says, "Best Western."

Welcome, I think, to life on the road.

3

Liberating Paris

OREGON GIVES WAY TO IDAHO, Idaho to Utah, Utah to Arizona, the trip picking up definite momentum, 342 miles one day, 559 miles the next, 329 miles the day after that. The vastness of the West fills the windshield, all these cowboy movie panoramas of broad blue skies, brute mountains, red buttes, barren hills, scrub desert. The only sound often heard out here is the whoosh of traffic along the superhighway; otherwise, a profound silence lies across the land, broken only by sudden gusts of harsh wind. I pass through places which already look and smell of fall, with trees turned shades of gold and rust, peaks dusted with snow, this season's apples for sale at roadside stands. I pass through other places where summer still lingers, hot and insistent, these late September days.

Zion National Park is a natural cathedral encountered at the end of the five-hundred-mile day on the road, the evening sun striking rock formations of imposing shapes and impossible hues, bright reds, pale pinks, burnt oranges, producing feelings of reverence in places called Angels Landing and The Great White Throne. The Grand Canyon comes the next day in the first cloudy weather of the trip, the dull light turning the canyon's colors to muted tones of salmon and cement, the disappointed tourists in full vacation regalia.

The sun blazes down again by the time I reach Phoenix, cross Dead Man Wash, watch the temperature keep climbing to 106 degrees, hear a matter-of-fact voice on the radio point out that this is the 134th day of the year to top 100 in the Valley of the Sun. It is still over 100 in Tucson too, 120 miles to the south, and even the air conditioning cannot keep me from sweating when I am welcomed into their spacious condominium by John and Eloise Westover.

The Westovers are a genial couple, cordial and chatty, real salt-of-the-Midwest. John is six feet two, but appears taller, from his erect posture and the gray flattop that bristles atop his head. His facial features remind me of Lyndon Johnson, but without the basset hound overtones, and his manner is stentorian. Whether he's answering the telephone ("good afternoon, Westovers'") or engaging in conversation, his voice carries as if he were still delivering a history lecture at Western Illinois University. Eloise is tall and rail-thin, with an alert face and large glasses ringed by tightly curled red hair. She is a bubbly woman who tends to respond with a sprightly "ha-HA" at most anything even vaguely funny. She seems like she could have played a neighbor on "I Love Lucy."

I do not have to wait long to see evidence of my grandfather here. Westover admits "S. L. A. Marshall had a greater impact on my life than almost anyone" and a memento of their relationship is prominently displayed on what the Westovers jokingly refer to as "our bragging wall," a wall in the kitchen covered with framed photographs, citations, diplomas and awards, including Westover's Silver Star, won for valor in combat against the Nazis in North Africa, and a Bronze Star as well. Also included on the bragging wall is a letter which S. L. A. Marshall had written on Westover's behalf in 1972, a letter to the commander of U.S. Forces in Europe.

"Dear General Davison," the letter begins, "John Westover is on a quick trip to Europe, where he has been many times. To make a long story short, John was my personal assistant and companion in all of my experiences in ETO [European Theater of Operations in World War II], and as great a soldier as I have known. In his sphere, he is a man of unusual influence. I have urged him to detour and see you. His integrity and confidence are to be trusted absolutely. Your consideration will be appreciated. All best wishes, Slam Marshall."

I had read many similar letters in Marshall's correspondence files in the library of the University of Texas at El Paso, letters offering favors, pulling levers, proposing honors, little acts of kindness that softened my view of my grandfather. And Westover is soon telling me about what impact such letters had, how even though General Davison was away on the day when he visited, there was special treatment from those on the general's staff.

Westover emphasizes that this was not the first time he had experienced such a response because of his time with Marshall. Westover has given lectures on Marshall in places as distant as Chile and Pakistan, had been considered "an instant celebrity" at his last Army duty post at Fort Riley, and had been mentioned in twenty-five books, all because of his association with the man he still calls "the Colonel."

Westover readily acknowledges his debt to Marshall, but he makes no attempt to repay it with adulation. He has his criticisms, sometimes harsh criticisms, of S. L. A. Marshall. A year of shared foxholes and jeeps and occasional close scrapes gave Westover many glimpses of the flaws of the man, so many of them stemming from Marshall's resounding self-confidence and the way he confronted the world. As Westover says, "He was a cocky bastard; he never expressed any self-doubts."

Westover makes this comment as we sit across from each other in his living room. He is settled into his favorite lounge chair and I am on a couch ten feet away and the walls echo with Westover's recollections of my grandfather. I must have asked some question to set off this monologue, but that question has long since been lost, buried under an avalanche of reminiscence. A half hour passes, then an hour, then another hour, and still Westover keeps it up, as my mind grows numb. I dare not interrupt, I keep reminding myself, something important may come of this, something I must not miss. Only later do I discover that Westover has replayed his standard repertoire of Marshall memories, the well-traveled stuff of countless party chats, public speeches, published articles.

I hear how the first words which Westover ever heard about Marshall had come from one of his former professors at the University of Missouri, who had traded his cap and gown for a major's uniform and was working in the new Army military history section in the Pentagon. He warned Westover, then about to depart for the Continent: "There's a crazy man running around Europe with wide-open orders. His name is Marshall. He's no good—don't have anything to do with him!"

I hear how, three weeks later, Westover had not only encountered that "crazy man," he had somehow become his assistant, his jeep driver, his fellow toiler in the historical section of the European Theater, where Marshall was deputy chief. This prompted Westover to write Eloise: "Colonel Marshall and I are going on a roving job. I am not sure just what my part will be, but it's going to be work. The Colonel is a slave driver—I'm probably going to be a slave."

And I hear how Westover, under Marshall's tutelage, soon became a proficient practitioner of Marshall's pioneering historical research technique, what he liked to call "The Post-Combat Group Critique." Discovered by accident during his participation in campaigns in the South Pacific, this technique became Marshall's way of lifting "the fog of war" and revealing "the truth of battle." Marshall became convinced that military history should no longer be left to the hazy recollections of commanders many years after a war. Military history must be gathered while soldiers' memories are still fresh—what worked and what did not, all those gritty and sometimes grim details that time would soon obscure. And the best way to discover this, Marshall found, was to gather all of the surviving men of a unit, from privates to officers, and then have them piece together the details and chronology of what had happened. Everyone in the assembly was free to correct or contradict everyone else, regardless of rank, with the historian orchestrating the discussion, using his questions to keep things flowing. And time was absolutely crucial to the success of Marshall's technique; the group critique should take place within hours or days after a battle. That often required the historian to work near the front lines, which Marshall often did, contrary to *American Heritage*'s intimation that he usually remained at headquarters in the rear. "I came as close to being killed as a historian," emphasizes Westover, "as I did as an artillery forward observer."

Westover tells me how he was accustomed to doing historical research in library archives and was initially skeptical about Marshall's approach. But Westover soon came to see its worth, as the two of them conducted group critiques, sometimes together, sometimes thirty yards apart, with the survivors of the D-Day assaults on Utah and Omaha beaches. Their resulting reports often revealed tragic flaws in American operations but, as Westover reported home to Eloise, there were "no kickbacks on the veracity of even the smallest details." "The general [Maj. Gen. Charles H. Gearhardt, commander of the Twenty-ninth Division] has been so happy with our work that we've suddenly become important people around this headquarters," Westover wrote. "Everyone stands in awe of the Colonel." In later years, Westover came to believe that Marshall's group critique method had "revolutionized writing of military history. Because of it, battles are recorded more accurately and in greater detail, making histories that are written today more alive and accurate."

But Westover's favorite recollection of Marshall is that crazy time in the summer of 1944 when the two recorders of history suddenly became participants in history during the Liberation of Paris, source of so many legends, some even true, and many centering on the exploits of Ernest Hemingway. Marshall knew Hemingway, had even spent time at his home in Key West in 1936, and they would meet again on the road to Paris in a bombed-out cafe called Claire de Lune, where Hemingway would burst through the door and yell, "Marshall, for God's sake, have you got a drink?"

Or so S. L. A. Marshall wrote eighteen years later in an article called "How Papa Liberated Paris" published in, of all places, *American Heritage.* But Westover cautions me, "Some of what your grandfather relates there, I don't remember in the least. Slam's point of view was that his memory was infallible. At times, though, I think your grandfather's memory was not as accurate as he thought it was."

What Westover recounts about the Liberation of Paris becomes a telling lesson in the malleability of history, how history is shaped by the memories of those who witness it and the intentions of those who record it. For Marshall's magazine article, written soon after Hemingway's death, was clearly intended as a corrective to the legend of the Liberation of Paris, a way to replace Hemingway Myth with Marshall Truth. As Marshall wrote, "Many tall tales have been written about Force Hemingway. The real story is good enough. As a war writer, Hemingway spun fantastic romance out of common yarn."[1] But Westover's first reading of the *American Heritage* article convinced him that Marshall was making some myths of his own.

Before he wrote the article, Marshall had asked Westover if he would mind sharing his own recollections of the Liberation of Paris and Westover, ever the good soldier, had responded with an eight-thousand-word account gleaned from his letters to Eloise. Westover was a diligent writer of long letters home filled with detailed observa-

In this photograph taken by Ernest Hemingway, John Westover (*left*) and
S. L. A. Marshall are shown with their jeep during the drive toward Paris
along with the Spanish woman who accompanied them in the mad dash to
liberate the City of Light. Courtesy S. L. A. Marshall Military History Collection, University of Texas at El Paso.

tions, and Eloise saved more than a thousand letters from her new
husband by war's end. Westover still retains great faith in the accuracy of his letters, and that is why he was so surprised and shaken by
Marshall's "How Papa Liberated Paris."

The accounts of Marshall and Westover do share some similarities. Most of the places they mention seem to mesh, as do the
times when events took place. And the mood of the advance toward
Paris and inside the city itself seems the same in both accounts—a
chaotic mix of fear and euphoria. The jeep that carried Marshall and
Westover kept filling with gifts of flowers and champagne, while
kisses and embraces were being showered on the two Americans and
most of the other men in the advancing column, as if they were
cinema stars. "I came the closest to being drunk," recalls Westover of
that joyous time, "that I ever did in my life."

But the differences between the accounts of Westover and Marshall are far more striking. Carlos Baker, author of the definitive *Hemingway: A Life Story*, had read both accounts, along with that of Hemingway's driver. Baker wrote to Westover: "I've got your account, I've got Marshall's account. I've got the driver Pelkey's account. Are you sure you were in the same war?"

For it was not just in the minor details where the accounts differ, although there were plenty of those. Marshall and Westover do not agree on how many people were present at the legendary Liberation dinner they attended at the Ritz with Hemingway; do not agree on whether correspondent Ernie Pyle made it to Paris; do not even agree on the name of the Spanish woman who rode in their jeep for days during the advance. "Irene," says Westover. "Elena," says Marshall.

The recollections of Marshall and Westover really diverge when danger lurks. Westover recounts a hazardous encounter with a burning German ammunition truck, "a rather difficult obstacle for our party in the open jeep." He writes, "We would have to pass that exploding vehicle and cross a bridge. The tankers merely pulled their heads down into the turrets, but we had no such protection. We would have pulled off the road, but we were living an impossible escapade and were not willing to pull back. I dropped back and allowed a fifty-foot gap to develop between our jeep and the tank ahead. When there was no longer any chance that he would stop while we were alongside the blaze, I gunned the jeep and roared past. Instinctively, the Colonel, Irene, and I pulled our heads low, but there was no protection in that vehicle. Fortunately, there was no explosion as we passed and the searing heat was too brief to make any difference."

Westover's burning ammunition truck is, in Marshall's account, a burning ammunition dump, the length of a block. And Marshall recalls: "The stacked shells were already blowing sky-high, and even at a distance, the smoke, blast and flame seemed like an inferno. . . . Metal showered the roadway, and the heat was like a blast from molten slag. . . .

"I yelled: 'We can't make that run.'

"'We've got to,' Westover yelled back, 'or the tanks will crush us. They're not stopping for anything.'

"That's how it was. The jeep-borne people spliced into the tank column were held feet-to-the-fire by their own friends. That Mazeppa ride lasted not more than forty or fifty seconds by the clock, but the clock lied. There was no protection against either the flying metal or the infernal heat. . . .

"We pulled out of it whole-skinned. One shard had smashed through the hood of the jeep. Another had smacked the metal panel next to the jump seat, missing Elena's bottom by inches. The quarter-ton still perked. It was hellishly hot, and we were horribly thirsty."[2]

The Liberation of Paris appeared to have given Marshall his own case of Hemingway-itis, that well-known affliction characterized by an exaggerated sense of high drama and personal import. I had always thought that there were some similarities between Papa Hemingway and Poppy Marshall, two men born only 362 days apart at the turn of the century. Both seemed better to encounter on the page than in the family. I had talked to my grandfather about Hemingway on several occasions and found a begrudging admiration that often tipped toward antipathy. Because, I had long suspected, the two were too much alike and played the same game of magna persona. So when I read my grandfather's descriptions of Hemingway during the Liberation of Paris, I was struck by how he could also have been describing himself: "The excitement and danger of battle were his meat and drink, just as the unremitting obligation to carry on was his poison."[3]

I am disturbed by the excesses of my grandfather's account of the Liberation of Paris. So is Westover. His voice is pained when he says, "Did he have notes on that? Slam said, time and again, 'when I look at my notes.' But what was he referring to? I don't know if he kept a personal log."

"I don't know either," I say. "I hope I will manage to uncover some of his notebooks on this trip, although no one seems to know where they are."

Westover presses on, getting a second wind. Out come clipped articles, old scrapbooks, letters in a ring binder, combat reports bound in leather, and many black-and-white photographs. I see glimpses of my grandfather during World War II, at an age close to mine now, my grandfather obviously invigorated by all the challenges and the dangers. I see him sitting beside a foxhole, smoking a large cigar. I see him standing beside a jeep in the snow, bundled up in a bulky greatcoat, just after his promotion to full colonel, his helmet bearing a much-oversized eagle of the rank, painted there in jest by his men. And I see him conducting a group critique in Brest, down on all fours, a field map spread out in front of him, a pencil pinpointing some detail, all that taking place when, as Westover recalls, firing at the front was not far off. That evening would see one hundred rounds of artillery hit the outpost.

Finally, I excuse myself and retire to the study. I am exhausted, need to sleep, but cannot. My mind reels with questions and more questions to ask Westover and how to lead up to the big question that has brought me here. *American Heritage* had directed much of its ammunition against a central tenet of Marshall's *Men Against Fire*, his finding on firing. The *American Heritage* article cast grave doubt on whether he was pursuing the question of weapons firing during the war or had tracked such matters with, as he wrote, "a showing of hands and questioning as to the number of rounds used."

Westover had vehemently contradicted *American Heritage*'s assertions when I interviewed him over the telephone from Seattle. He stated flatly that he and Marshall had discussed firing problems during their time together—what seemed solid proof that Marshall was pursuing the matter. But now in Tucson, I must try to determine if Westover, blind-sided by the Marshall controversy, has taken to stretching the truth. To protect the reputation of his old boss.

4

Under Fire

THE SUN COMES UP hot and intense in Tucson and the Westovers are early risers, full of cheer and purpose. John has already dispatched some bills and letters by the time I return from a half-hour run. Eloise, a University of Missouri journalism graduate, is all set to perform the duties of a short-order cook. "Pancakes, eggs, toast—what can I make you?" she calls out when I take my first step into the kitchen.

"Toast and coffee would be great."

John Westover and I soon depart on the sixty-five-mile drive south to Fort Huachuca, the last of the Southwest frontier posts still in use, where we have an appointment with an Army historian interested in the Marshall controversy. Westover is at the wheel and I am in the passenger seat, this reprise of the role he played for my grandfather four decades ago.

I am asking questions about my grandfather, getting Westover to share his insights into the kind of person he was and the forces that shaped him, especially before I knew him. What I am coming to believe is that my grandfather struggled mightily to overcome his lack of height and his lack of education, so I try that thesis out with Westover, who towered over his boss and had a doctorate.

"Slam would not come out and say he was sensitive about being short, in so many words, but I felt it all along; height was a factor with him," Westover says. "And not only his height, or lack of height, but also his lack of formal education. It was very clear that he had a feeling that he needed to prove himself, although he was

31

actually somebody who least needed to do that. His striving to prove himself surely came from wanting to overcome the handicaps of not having height and not having an education . . . . If you've got a college education, you've got the credentials. But he didn't have those credentials, the credentials to command the respect he wanted. So he put up that front instead."

That front made quite an impression on people, including John Keegan, the esteemed British military historian, author of *The Face of Battle*. Keegan first encountered Marshall during a 1964 speech in England: "He chose to wear the dress uniform of a brigadier general. It sat very badly on his tiny, corpulent person. It went even worse with his manner, which was aggressive, hectoring and rude. He cheerfully insulted those who asked him what he thought were stupid questions. He exuded energy and vulgarity in about equal measure. But I did infallibly detect that he was someone apart and above any military historian I had met before. I subsequently came to believe, as I still do, that he was touched by genius."[1]

I move on to ask Westover about one of the more annoying points in the Marshall controversy—the assertion by some of his critics, Leinbaugh particularly, that Marshall had "never been under fire" or had "never been in combat." I think both contentions are probably wrong and are tangential anyway. The worth of Marshall's great volume of work is not going to be changed by whether he had fired a weapon in anger or dodged a bullet. Westover had been with Marshall when they went to interview combat units at the front, so I still feel compelled to ask about whether they were "under fire" and how Marshall had reacted then.

"The Colonel wasn't cautious; he took a business-like approach," Westover says. "Sometimes they would pull a unit right out of the line to talk to us, and this didn't bother him at all. He had tremendous concentration."

"But how did he act?" I continue. "Was he cocky in those situations, did he strut about?"

"He displayed not bravado—just a sense that this is what we have got to do. And we were under fire actively, particularly on that trip into Paris, in Brittany, in Brest, and at various division headquarters. He got down in his hole and snuggled in as close as anyone. He was not the type who stood there and said, 'They can't hit me.'

S. L. A. Marshall, kneeling in center, writing on map, during group critique in Brest, France, September 1944. Courtesy S. L. A. Marshall Military History Collection, University of Texas at El Paso.

He had none of that. He had a healthy respect for fire. Hemingway, on the other hand, was a show-off. Slam did what was necessary; there was none of that striding about."

We are on the approach to Fort Huachuca now, passing the traditional outskirts of a military post—instant apartment complexes, used car lots stocked with hot Camaros, pawn shops ready to buy or sell anything. Bruce Saunders is waiting for us on the sidewalk outside the U.S. Army Intelligence Center and School. Saunders, outfitted in a historian's wool tweed sportcoat despite the heat, escorts us to his basement office.

Westover's eyes are drawn to the green volumes of the Army's official history of World War II, this seventy-two-volume work which occupies six feet of shelf space. So many of these books are the result of the work done by Marshall, Westover, and their compatriots in Europe. The "Green Series" is their great gift to posterity—an unprecedented vein of research ore that continues to be mined by historians. There is pride in Westover's voice when he motions toward the "Green Series" and says, "Getting it while it's fresh—that was Slam's contribution."

"Military history teams went into Grenada on the third day of the invasion, using the same method that S. L. A. pioneered," adds Saunders, "although now they videotape after-action interviews . . . . Marshall convinced the Army that battle is a confusing business and the more you can learn from the past, the more it will help in the present. The Army is the most into this process of any of the services; the Army is really committed to this thing."

Westover and Saunders continue to chat. I find myself reflecting on how the "Green Series" and Army historians like Saunders are part of my grandfather's lingering legacy. Most of us die and leave behind little more than dust and memories; S. L. A. Marshall left behind far more. His life had such an impact that Saunders and Westover talk about him as if he were still alive today.

We adjourn for lunch, my first visit to an officers' club in two decades, yet just as I remember it—the ageless decor, the harried service, the monthly calendar of festivities still featuring surf 'n turf night.

The conversation at our table soon centers on the Marshall controversy. I ask Saunders if he attended the annual meeting of Army historians earlier in the year when one of his compatriots, then historian at Fort Benning, had presented his research paper on Marshall. It is a paper which, I have been told, went after Marshall with a blunderbuss.

"I heard Charlie White's paper on Marshall," replies Saunders, without elaboration.

"Well, what did you think of it?" I ask. "And what did the other historians think of it?"

"The guys I hang around with thought it was a terrible cheap shot, but it was not terribly unexpected from Charlie White; he fires first, thinks later," says Saunders.

"Then what are your own thoughts on the controversy? What is the effect on his reputation?"

"It is a tempest in a teapot which overlooks the worth of the man and his work. He had a major impact which is substantial."

Saunders pauses for a moment, then adds: "It's like the Queen Mary passing by and you spot a barnacle. It's small change. It missed the big picture."

Saunders' comment seems to hang in the air, at least to me. In the past months, I have read and heard so much criticism of S. L. A. Marshall, some of it highly personal, even savage, a chorus of angry voices that seemed to drown out any dispassionate assessment of the man's work. Now, Saunders manages to cut through that with phrases like "a barnacle on the Queen Mary." Whether many others share his estimation is something I must determine on my journey. For I cannot be satisfied listening only to those who scream loudest, players in the controversy with their own grudges and agendas, the kind of people relied upon by American Heritage. I want insight, not just invective, and will take the time to find it.

On the return trip to Tucson, I begin to ask Westover about his discussions with Marshall about firing problems, but he begs off and I do not press him further, knowing full well that I can ask those questions tomorrow.

In the evening, I treat the Westovers to dinner at El Corral, a Tucson steak house in the true Western tradition, a raucous place where seldom is heard that cholesterol word. We have a fine time. The Westovers spend much of the dinner reminiscing about their long life together, and treating me as if I am a longtime family friend.

The next morning, the mood at the kitchen table is entirely different, brisk, businesslike. I have a list of questions in front of me and Westover sits opposite, prepared for this interview, what our time together these past few days has been building toward, as we both seem to sense.

I take out copies of after-action interviews I discovered in El Paso on my brief research trip for the newspaper, accounts of units in action during D-Day which carry no notation of the interviewer. Westover immediately recognizes the first critique as his own. He is all-but-certain that the second critique was done by Marshall, a conclusion based on when it was conducted and how it is spaced ["'The

Colonel' had intense concentration, thought in complete thoughts and seldom made corrections, so he usually single-spaced."]

These critiques could be crucial to the Marshall controversy. Their narrative provides direct evidence that firing problems did hamper some D-Day units, a phenomenon noted by the interviewing Army historian, either Marshall or Westover. As one of these critiques recounts, "Some of the men froze on the beach, wretched with seasickness and fear, refusing to move. Most of the survivors toiled painfully to the foot of the hill where the enemy might well have found and destroyed them, since they had no fire power."

One of the critiques also contains the signatures of twenty-two men, soldiers of every rank from private to second lieutenant, probably as many men of Company M, 116th Infantry, as could be assembled three months after D-Day. "This is important," I say to Westover, "because *American Heritage* staked its credibility on the research of Roger Spiller, the Army historian at Fort Leavenworth. Yet the magazine quotes Spiller as saying, 'I just haven't found any suggestion that he [Marshall] did company-level interviews anywhere.'"[2]

"This is a company-level interview," Westover says triumphantly. "The signatures would have been used by Marshall to make sure he got the spelling of the names right. THIS IS ABSOLUTE PROOF THAT MARSHALL DID COMPANY-LEVEL INTERVIEWS."

A broad smile washes across Westover's face, with the recognition of this dent in the armor of Marshall's critics.

S. L. A. Marshall's own credibility in *Men Against Fire* came from his position first as deputy, then chief Army historian in Europe and his assertion that he conducted "approximately 400" group critiques of combat companies during World War II. Westover has doubts about the four-hundred-company figure—he believes that Marshall probably did one hundred critiques himself and read five hundred critiques of the historians under him—but Westover has absolutely no doubt that Marshall did conduct many such critiques.

American Heritage, on the other hand, takes Spiller's "not finding any suggestion" that Marshall did company-level interviews and then tries to build a case that Marshall's "systematic collection of data . . . appears to have been an invention." Since Spiller did not find company-level reports, the magazine's reasoning goes, there must not be any. Marshall must have made the whole thing up. This conclusion is a great leap beyond Spiller's research. Especially in light of these critiques that I found in El Paso.

"All *American Heritage* can say with any certainty," I tell Westover, "is that Spiller did not find company-level reports. That's it. And I have already found one such report myself and, more important, you know he did many more."

Westover is positively gleeful at my reasoning: "I'm with you 100 percent! I think *American Heritage* got the wrong man; it was not good scholarship. A word like 'hoax' is a loaded word, one you use when you're trying to pin something on someone. *American Heritage* has gone from being a publication for historians to being a profit-making operation. I've been disappointed in the magazine for six or seven years. It went from a history magazine to an issues magazine. It moved away from real scholarship."

"But I have a problem," I say.

"What's that?"

"Whether you and Marshall ever did discuss the failure of infantryman to fire their weapons in combat."

Westover's smile evaporates, as I recount how back in April he had told me that "hell we did discuss such matters," which is what I had written in my newspaper series. Then Spiller wrote me, saying Westover had told him just the opposite—he could not recall Marshall discussing his ratio-of-fire findings with him.

I hand over Spiller's letter and Westover seems to blanch noticeably, especially when he reads: "I don't mind that he [Westover] changed his story for his *American Heritage* rebuttal, and I won't speculate on his motives for doing so, but as I think I told you when you were here, had Westover said something different, my article would have been different."

Westover immediately seizes on the telephone interview as the cause of the problem. Spiller had called unannounced, and he had not been feeling well and there followed a long interview for which he had no time to prepare. Questions may have been misunderstood over the phone, Westover suggests, answers may have been misinterpreted.

But the real problem, I tell Westover, goes beyond the telephone interview. For Spiller later sent him a copy of his upcoming article on Marshall for a British military journal and specifically asked for his comments or corrections. And yet Westover, in his written response, did not protest these statements: "John Westover, usually in attendance during Marshall's sessions with the troops, does not recall Marshall EVER asking this question [about troops firing their weapons]. Nor does Westover recall Marshall ever talking about ratios of weapons usage in their many private conversations."[3]

Westover now counters, "The suggestion that I was sitting in during all of Marshall's interviews is ridiculous. That is a misstatement. Often I was a few hundred yards away doing my own interviews, sometimes I was a couple miles away."

"Then why didn't you tell Spiller that was a misstatement? And why didn't you tell him then that you and Marshall certainly had discussed firing problems. Your failure to correct him makes it appear you did change your story once the controversy broke."

"I'm perfectly willing to agree that I misled Spiller, but he may have misled me, too. I wouldn't rule out that Marshall and I talked about the Queen of Sheba. I can't give you specifics about what we were talking about, but we must have discussed firing problems. I'm not perfectly sure when, but that's looking back forty-five years. I can't say on such and such a day, we discussed this."

"Or," I add, "that you definitely discussed it at all."

"I can say that firing problems did not sound improbable to me. In my own combat experience in North Africa and Italy, a hell of a lot of people didn't fire their guns in order to avoid confronting the enemy. Slam clearly should have called his finding a 'generalization.' He tried to quantify something that you simply can't quantify. I know I talked about such broad things myself, but I doubt I would ever have come up with a specific percentage, as Slam did. I do remember, too, that after Men Against Fire came out, I said to Eloise, 'A lot of the ideas in this book are very familiar to me.' Now, you come here and you are asking me, 'Did you talk about this?' But I don't remember. I can't remember."

Every word out of Westover's mouth now seems to detonate doubts in my mind. So many doubts that I almost do not hear when Westover makes an important point: that Marshall would not have had to ask troops point-blank, "Did you fire your weapons?" There are much better ways to pursue that line of inquiry.

"A good interviewer doesn't come right out and ask someone, 'Are you bigoted?' or 'Do you brush your teeth?'" Westover says. "How many people will answer that kind of question truthfully? The answer is, of course, no one will. What I'm saying is that the worst thing is to ask a direct question. I may have told Spiller that Marshall didn't directly ask people if they fired their weapons, but he wouldn't have to. He would have been listening to what people were saying as their story progressed and he would have been thinking that through."

What Westover is saying only confirms what Marshall himself once wrote on the subject of interviewing: "I early learned that when trust is withheld, one proceeds to get it through indirection, instead as the American reporter usually does, head down and horns thrust upward. Even in a tight security matter, by a line of questioning that boxes the compass without touching the sensitive nerve while eliminating every other hypothesis, one may bet affirmation of that which merely started as conjecture."[4]

But as soon as Westover makes a trenchant point, he proceeds to say something troubling again. He keeps explaining himself over and over, as if he hopes the sheer weight of assembled verbiage will somehow produce the magic rationale that will dispel all doubt.

"Not recalling a specific conversation forty-five years ago doesn't mean such a conversation did not occur," he continues. "I feel caught in the middle here . . . . I don't know, I'm really concerned, I'm sort of shook up, John. I've been as honest and consistent as I know how to be. If I've been given different questions, I'm going to make different answers. But now my own validity comes into question.

"I've been a friend of Slam's, a driver, a booster, but I have never been two-faced. I have never been uncritical of him; I have tried to be as forthright as I could, and consistent. When I've said that Slam was 'an intuitive thinker,' I meant by that that he read so much, he talked to so many people, he had been mulling over this in his mind for months and years. That is what Men Against Fire was; it was a crystallization of his thoughts. If he didn't write his research down, that doesn't mean he wasn't right. It just means that it doesn't satisfy those who are used to working with documents—historians. Because in conventional history, you deal with documents.

"I was skeptical about Marshall—I had been told that he was no damn good—but Marshall has changed my life.

"And maybe some of the blame for this controversy does come back here, to me. But at what benefit to me? If Marshall ends up being bigger, it doesn't make me bigger. If he's a damn liar, it doesn't make me smaller. I've shone in his light, and gotten more attention from it, but I certainly did not base my career on it."

Westover's face is drawn now, his voice is raspy, his mood subdued. He seems spent after three hours of answering questions about Marshall's integrity and his own. There is silence across the table. We stare at each other. Then, suddenly, out of Westover's mouth comes a plaintive cry that echoes off the kitchen walls.

"Who's the guy," he shouts, "who's done any study that's better than Marshall's?"

5

Military Heritage

THE WIND BLASTS DOWN from the Mazatzal Mountains, tears over the treeless country of northern Arizona toward the land of the Navajo. This is not a wind which comes and goes in gusts; this is a relentless blow; it scours the ground and sends clouds of dust streaming across the highway. The wind slams into the side of the car and I squeeze the steering wheel so tight my knuckles start to ache, this buffeting a perfect reflection of my troubled mood after three days with the Westovers.

I am trying to understand how John Westover's "hell we did talk such matters" in a telephone interview has become "I don't remember, I can't remember" when we are together in the same room. I am trying to understand how one man answering one question can go from denial to equivocation to admission to regret to rationalization to apology. I am trying to understand whether that means he is lying, or telling the truth, or a mixture of both. And just what is "the truth?"

I used to think I was someone who was capable of finding "the truth" about people, or at least a decent insight into their character. That's what I prided myself on doing as a newspaper columnist. Give me an hour [as I have had] with Tom Wolfe, Gloria Steinem, Bernard Malamud, Judy Collins, Carl Bernstein, Geraldine Ferraro, Dave Winfield, or Joseph Campbell, and I would strip away the public façade and get at what was underneath, the real person. I knew the right questions to ask to discover this, I thought. I knew the

41

right way to ask them. I had, after all, been at this business for almost two decades. I was no naïve innocent.

But the time with the Westovers has shown me the shortcomings of this common journalistic conceit. I do not despair of my own abilities after the Westovers, but I am more wary. People have hazy memories, personal agendas, and their own opinions about whether S. L. A. Marshall should be saluted or damned. I am starting to see the wisdom of what my grandfather wrote in *The River and the Gauntlet*, his saga of the Eighth Army's tortured retreat in Korea: "The giving of praise or blame is always easy but the understanding of anything is difficult; it is a truth which applies to this story."[1]

Long hours on a deserted Interstate finally still my troubled thoughts. I pass the Continental Divide in the afternoon, arrive in Albuquerque in early evening just as a rainshower subsides and a few clouds part to the west and the city is bathed in brilliant orange light from the setting desert sun. Then, suddenly, a rainbow appears, its sweeping arc encircling the city and the mountains beyond, a moment for wonderment on the road.

The next day, I call upon Lucian K. Truscott III. His is a storied name in the Army. His father, Lucian K. Truscott, Jr., had risen to the rank of lieutenant general and had been the highly respected commander of the Fifth Army in Italy during World War II. S. L. A. Marshall had known him well from their days together in El Paso during the 1920s; they shared an interest in military matters, but also a love for the game of polo. Truscott's son, Lucian III, spent World War II as a cadet at West Point, then embarked on a career as an infantryman, commanding a combat company in Korea and combat battalion in Vietnam, one of few officers with such frontline experiences in both wars. He retired as a colonel. His son, Lucian IV, also graduated from West Point, but his disgust with Vietnam derailed his Army career soon after West Point; he broke with his family's military tradition by resigning his commission, a defiant act of anger and protest. Lucian IV, my contemporary, later went on to write popular novels about the Army, including *Dress Gray* which became a TV miniseries.

The Marshalls are not the Truscotts—their military tradition runs far deeper and is truly illustrious. Still, I am struck by similarities between our families, the experiences of the three generations of men and the wars they confronted, and how the eldest cast a long shadow over the men who came later. But there is one great difference between our families, as I had found out from Lucian IV during an evening spent together in Seattle. He had told me how—despite his father's distaste for what he had done during Vietnam, his very public stand against the war and the Army—their family had hung together. No final edicts were laid down and later regretted, no bonds were broken, no love turned to hate. And now I hope to discover how that happened.

I find Lucian K. Truscott III curled up underneath his 22-foot Winnebago, performing some maintenance. He springs to his feet and greets me warmly, then leads me inside their spacious condominium where picture windows overlook a vast expanse of golf course. We take seats in the living room, the handsome appointments in stark contrast to Truscott's garage attire. And in stark contrast, it turns out, to the man himself.

Truscott is a tough-talking hard-charger, a short, wiry, well-muscled man in his late sixties, with his silver hair worn in Caesar cut, a rather bulbous nose and searing eyes. His personality is pepper and sandpaper. His speech is frequently punctuated with "goddamn!" I have no trouble imagining Truscott barking out commands to men in combat. Indeed, it seems like what he should be doing today, rather than puttering around with a Winnebago.

We start talking about my grandfather. Truscott had met him twice around 1950, once at Fort Benning, once in Japan. Their encounters had been brief, but Truscott recalls, "I was impressed with Marshall because he had written *Men Against Fire*. Everybody in the Army had read *Men Against Fire*."

Truscott had much direct experience with the actions in Korea that became the basis for *The River and the Gauntlet*. He had been the aide to the assistant commander of the Second Division and they had been all over the field. "We saw all the units," Truscott says. "I was damned familiar with everything that went on."

So I proceed to ask him about the accuracy of *The River and the Gauntlet*. Marshall considered this his "most thoroughly researched work," but I had heard grave reservations raised about its accuracy. I had exchanged letters with Clay Blair, the author of three massive Army books in the last ten years, including *The Forgotten War*, a nine-hundred-page history of the Korean conflict. Blair had never met Marshall, but had often used his work as source material, something he had come to do with, as he put it, "a sense of unease." That developed because he had "found Marshall to be inexplicably sloppy about names and identifications—to a degree that would not be tolerated even by newspapers. *The River and the Gauntlet* was especially notorious in that respect."

But Truscott, who had been there, recalls having a different reaction to *The River and the Gauntlet* soon after its publication in 1952. "I had personal involvement and all of us who did were absolutely amazed by all the detail he got into that book," Truscott says. "And how accurate it was."

I hear much the same endorsement of Marshall's reporting from Col. Lewis Millett, who won the congressional Medal of Honor for a bayonet charge he led in Korea. Marshall had recommended Millett for the medal after conducting a group critique of his company. Millett told me that he was "amazed" by the accuracy of the account that Marshall was able to construct, including details of his own actions in combat that he himself could scarcely recall.

My conversation with Truscott turns from Korea to Vietnam. I have no idea what he thinks about Vietnam, but he certainly does not leave me wondering for long.

"I was in Vietnam in 1966–67, before the drug problem hit, and so much about the war that disturbed the country," he begins. "My G.I.s wore their helmets, their flak jackets, and there were none of those things like you see in the movies. When I told somebody to do it, we were in the Army and we were fighting a war—when I said to do something, goddammit, they did it. That's why *Platoon* disgusted me. If the Army ever got that bad, if what it depicted did happen in Army units, I would be outraged. There's no way that would have happened in the battalion I commanded."

I ask Truscott what he thinks about the war now and how it was fought. I am well aware there is a revisionist Vietnam theory these days, a belief that if the military had just had its hands untied in Vietnam, then everything would have worked out great. I find that simplistic, at best, and dangerous, at worst, a fantasy for those who will not admit the war was lost for a hell of a lot more reasons than sheer firepower. I do not say this to Truscott. I am here to listen to his opinions, which he readily provides.

"I really thought we were right in Vietnam at the time," Truscott says. "I thought we were fighting against this communist ogre who was going to spread all over the world. We had to draw the line somewhere."

"Could we have won in Vietnam?" I ask.

"There's no doubt that the war in Vietnam could have been won, but at a horrible cost of life to the Vietnamese. That would have involved using atomic weapons against the North. And we should have gone into Laos—that we didn't was disgraceful, because the Communists just continued using Laos. We should have gone into Laos, into Cambodia, should have cut off their damn supplies and then fought the Vietnamese on a more or less equal basis."

None of what Truscott says is any great surprise. His opinions are about what I would expect from someone whose career was the Infantry. He argues strategy, not politics, not morality. I press on to more personal matters, treading lightly.

"I wonder, if you don't mind me asking, what was your initial reaction when your son started to run into trouble with the Army? And what did you think about those who were opposing the war?"

"I could see how people got turned off by Vietnam. This war was in a faraway foreign land and it kept continuing when there was the unsettled atmosphere in the country, caused by the young people in the 1960s. Lucian, back then, was a real radical. I know what it is like to have a kid be a goddamned radical in the forefront of what was going on. And my daughter Susan wasn't far behind.

"Son Lucian—he even went after mandatory chapel at West Point. He decided it wasn't right, that it was combining church and state. He and some classmates decided to fight it and see if they could get it eliminated. There had been a twenty-five cent deduction taken out of the pay of West Point cadets for chapel; it had been going on for generations. Well, in 1972, the U.S. Supreme Court decided, 9–0, that mandatory chapel should be eliminated at all the service academies. That's the little dent that Lucian made in the history of the 1960s. And he never knew where I stood on mandatory chapel. But I think he did a hell of a great thing—To HAVE

THE GUTS TO SAY SOMETHING IS WRONG AND THEN WORK TO CHANGE IT!"

"But if your children were so radical," I inject, "with views that were so different from your own, why didn't that split your family, as happened in my family and so many others?"

"We stood behind them, it didn't matter what they did," Truscott emphasizes. "These were our kids, for better or worse, and, by God, we'll stick together as a family."

"Did you actually come out and say that? This is something I want to understand now, especially since I have a son of my own. I wonder why it is that some families managed to stay together in the 1960s, despite their differences over Vietnam, and some families did not."

Truscott replies, "The only time we verbalized it was when we had a knock-down drag-out with one of our kids and then I said to my wife, 'Damn, I want to tell you something. That's our kid. For better or worse. There's no way we are going to do anything but stick together.'"

"Do you now see some lesson in that for other families?"

"Those kids were such knotheads, or so it seemed to us, when they were twenty. Well now they're forty—and both sides are goddamned glad that neither of us said, 'I can't put up with you anymore. Get out of my life.'"

"But didn't you feel Lucian was taking a stand against you?" I ask. "And against what you had devoted your life to—serving in the Army?"

"In no way did I feel that he was rebelling against what I had spent my life on. Nor did I feel he was rebelling against me. Look. I have the greatest admiration for what young people did during those times in the 1960s. When I saw those Chinese students in Tianenmen Square, I thought what they are doing is just what the kids in this country were doing in the 1960s. How can you have anything but respect for them? I mean, that guy standing by himself in front of a tank in China, that absolute classic photograph. Well, a lot of the radicals in the 1960s had the same guts. Especially when people in my generation had spent their entire lives doing exactly what they were told to do, always following orders, not varying from that."

I leave soon after that, feeling stunned as Truscott accompanies me to the door. He pauses to show me his military library, including several books written by S. L. A. Marshall.

"I'm sorry," Truscott says, "that I haven't been able to tell you more about your grandfather."

"No, don't worry about that. What you've told me has been very helpful."

Very helpful indeed. Before meeting Lucian K. Truscott III, I assumed that what happened between my grandfather and me during Vietnam was a reflection of "the military mind," its rigid insistence on discipline and doing things this way or else. But Truscott, this hard-core combat vet, has shown me that those in the military do not always treat family members as troops.

That my grandfather disowned me may not be indicative of anything more than his own state of mind. What he did may have been the desperate act of an embittered old man striking out against someone he loved who left him deeply hurt.

6

El Paso Roots

BACK ON THE INTERSTATE, next stop: El Paso. My mind flashes back to my visit there six months ago. El Paso is the place where my grandfather grew up, attended high school, became a family man, then left until he returned to retire. He had visited most of the world by then, walked the streets of Paris, Tokyo, Jerusalem, Johannesburg, Saigon, and New York, but he could not shake El Paso's hold on his soul. El Paso, he emphasized, was "the only city I ever loved."

Maybe I would have loved the El Paso my grandfather remembered so fondly, that rough-and-tumble frontier town where the Wild West lingered and possibilities road the breeze. But I find it difficult to love the El Paso of today, where Texas and the Rockies end in barren hills, discount cowboy boot outlets, burrito dens, a monstrous metal smelter, an Army post named Fort Bliss, and a meandering canal of muddy water called the Rio Grande. Just across the river is Juarez, Mexico, teeming with a million people, more than double the number in El Paso, and hauntingly poor, almost a Third World outpost, the main reason why El Paso has some of the foulest air of any city in the United States.

My first research trip to El Paso had passed in grueling routine, long days locked in a library, long nights in a town where I seemed to be going weird. Dinner one evening was six greasy pieces of fast-food chicken, accompanied only by beer. Another night, I sat amidst the hooting hordes in a sleazy club where nude dancers were grinding away on the patrons' laps; I saw my image reflected in a smoky mirror, this stranger with a vacant look on his face.

48

El Paso was part of the reason for my behavior, this town where I knew no one, and so different from Seattle. But the pressures of library work may have been more responsible for the way I was acting. I was new to the peculiar tortures of archival research, which, I soon learned, combines tiresome page-turning and nagging eyestrain with a guilty fascination that comes from reading someone's most private thoughts. And no matter how exhausted a researcher is, the archival materials beckon with their siren song suggesting that it may be only a few more pages until paydirt—some wondrous document certain to shed new light on history.

I knew little of this when I first took the elevator to the top floor of the mammoth new library at the University of Texas at El Paso. I passed under brass letters which proclaim "S. L. A. Marshall Military History Collection" and entered a room as quiet as a tomb. I scanned shiny wood floors, long library tables, bookcases made of teak, an oriental carpet, four easy chairs covered with leather, plus a few photos and mementos I immediately recognized. Gathered here were the five thousand volumes which my grandfather collected in his life-long love affair with books, one of his traits that I do share.

There was much more than just my grandfather's books. Stored out of public view, open only to library personnel, were other materials related to S. L. A. Marshall, all collected in gray cardboard boxes that consume more than seventy feet of shelf space. There were papers (both official and personal), scrapbooks, correspondence, photographs, certificates, transcripts, passports, contracts, newspaper clippings, radio and TV commentaries, plus all the assorted flotsam and jetsam of a confirmed pack rat who lived nearly eight decades and threw out almost nothing. Not even his 1927 membership card to the Cloudcroft, New Mexico, golf course ("Highest In The World, 9,000 Feet Above The Sea").

This great mass of material had only been broken down into the most general of categories ("Military Orders," "Financial Records," "Mementos"), so I had to rely on the guide duty of Thomas F. Burdett, a retired Army sergeant who serves as the half-time curator of the Marshall collection. Burdett turned out to be a cordial, but perennially harried chap with faintly British airs, the clipped mustache, the tweedy sportcoats, the formal manners, the distinct tendency to hoist his pants so high that his belt seemed to encircle his chest.

Burdett still wore his standard-issue service shoes, those black "low quarters" that remind veterans of great labors in search of a spit shine. Throughout my first visit to the library, Burdett kept trudging back to the storage shelves, then returned minutes later with more leavings of my grandfather's life now delivered by library cart.

I started with S. L. A. Marshall's autobiography, *Bringing up the Rear*, a title that seemed highly ironic in light of the questions being raised about his combat experience. The version published in 1979, two years after his death, had been edited by his wife, Cate, who "helped smooth the book into shape," or so it said on the book jacket. But what was published included less than half of the 325,000 words Marshall had written. And what he had subtitled "Some Papers About My Experiences at Home and Abroad in War But More So In Peace" had been transformed by Cate's chainsaw editing into something that became instead "Famous Folk I Have Known, Mostly Soldiers." Which may be why Cate had decreed that the unedited manuscript was not to be read until after her death.

Since Cate had recently died, I was the first library researcher to plow through the 771 pages of legal-size paper. My great hope of finding something that no one else had was tempered with wariness. I knew how suspect autobiography can be, especially when written so late in life, a time more for justification than dispassion, this last chance to apply some flattering cosmetic to what one did and why.

I worked through the memoirs at the pace of a snail on Qua-ludes, comparing the published version with the unedited manu-script, making notes on the differences between the two, page after page after page. The first day passed with so little progress that I started to view the memoirs as a tar baby, threatening to consume all of my efforts and energy in El Paso, even if I worked nine straight hours at the library every day without even stopping for lunch, as I soon decided that I must.

The first night was the worst. I walked out of the library in the evening, filled with apprehension about the task ahead and feeling as though I had not slept in a week. Then I returned to my room in a deserted motel and my father was on the phone from St. Louis, wanting a complete report on all that I had already learned about his father, offering suggestions about what I must look for next and who I must interview, a call that lasts for an hour. And then as soon as I got off the phone, a mammoth thunderstorm raked the area with lightning and torrential rain. I stood on the balcony and watched the deluge pour down on the lawn where automatic sprinklers were still going full blast. And I wondered if this was some portent of how this was all going to go, with me on the trail of my grandfather, confronting his past and my shortcomings, amid great storms and strangeness.

Things improved slightly in the days ahead. The research remained a grind, but one with a certain rhythm, and it grudgingly gave way to something that approximated progress. Soon, I was reading about my grandfather enlisting in the Army, at age seventeen, to fight in what he still describes as "The Great War," a phrase that always causes me to shudder. For the war's aftereffect was, as Hemingway wrote in *A Farewell to Arms*, that "abstract words such as glory, honor, courage, or hallow were obscene beside the concrete names of villages, the numbers of roads, the names of rivers, the numbers of regiments and the dates."[1]

The *American Heritage* article had questioned many of Marshall's long-standing assertions about his World War I service—that he had won a battlefield commission, that he ended the war as the youngest lieutenant in the Army; that he and his unit had seen combat in some of the war's bloodiest campaigns. Trying to check on these matters ran me smack into a roadblock of my grandfather's making, a statement that gave rise to my own doubts about whether he had done what he claimed.

For this man—who made a career out of recording what happened to soldiers in battle—seemed to suffer from amnesia when trying to recall what he had experienced when he first went to war. In his published memoirs, he writes: "Though I participated in the Soissons, St. Mihiel and Meuse-Argonne campaigns, except for certain graphic incidents that stayed in my brain, I cannot write factually of either my unit's part or my personal role. Any attempted reconstruction would be brick without straw."[2] In his unedited manuscript, this passage continues: "The only reporting of my personal experiences was in letters home, long since fed to the furnace. No extracts therefrom are to be found in newspaper morgues. That is why this part of my narrative is almost wholly impressionistic and fragmentary."

This facile explanation had the false ring of dissembling. So I asked Burdett if he remembered reading any of my grandfather's letters home from World War I and off he marched to the storage room. He returned with letters I soon unfolded in my hands with utmost care, letters home from a young doughboy written in tiny handwriting on onion skin, some of it emblazoned with: "On Active Service with the American Expeditionary Force."

I found myself fascinated with the writer of these letters, so modest, so earnest, so purposeful. He seemed so different from the man I remember. The lad in these letters writes to his father about his postwar plans and how "it all depends on the terrain, and upon what you and mother think. I do intend, however, to finish my education if possible and to make something of myself." And he writes to his mother: "Most men when they came overseas left behind a sweetheart or a wife. But, mother, I want to say that I left someone back home that was infinitely closer to me than any sweetheart or wife could ever have been and though I left you behind, sweet, yet I felt you were ever with me. It is because of that fact that I have kept to the straight and narrow ever since I have been in France. I have tried to be the kind of boy that I know you and father wanted me to be and I think that I have succeeded."

What this teenage soldier writes home about combat is in character with these circumspect letters. There are passing references to being "under bombardment," mingled with expressions of pride in his unit. But if he has indeed seen "the worst" of war, as he writes at one point, he either does not want the censors to remove such descriptions or he does not want his parents to share his experience. As World War I historian Paul Fussell has observed, "The refusal of the men to say anything in their letters home indicates how pervasive the style of British Phlegm became. The censorship on the line doubtless imposed inhibitions, but this hardly accounts for the unique style of almost formulaic understatement. . . . what possible good could result from telling the truth?"[3]

A letter to Marshall's father, written two weeks after the Armistice, tells of his division moving to the front toward the end of July and how it was never withdrawn from the front "for more than just a few days." And he also writes: "I have been up to the Alsace front near Belfort, was at St. Jean on the Toul front, north-east of Thiacourt, in the St. Mihiel drive and at the Argonne just a few days. I was gassed, slightly, at St. Mihiel and in the hospital for a few days. It was phosgene that got me and while I was sick as the devil for a few days, it left no permanent effect on my lungs. Consequently, I am entitled to a wound stripe, tho I have never worn one."

Amidst all this chatty commentary, one of my grandfather's statements suddenly screamed off the page at me. He is writing to his father about his current assignment at the Officer Candidate School at La Valbonne and he concludes: "Now that the war is over, it's very doubtful whether any of us will be commissioned."

Sixteen words. One sentence. Probably written with no forethought, and so inconsequential at the time. Yet seventy years later, these words convict S. L. A. Marshall of the kind of lie that his critics and *American Heritage* are alleging. For his published memoirs included the account he had so often related, about how he had ended the war as a lieutenant in the Infantry, the honored recipient of a battlefield commission presumably in recognition of his bravery. But this letter home confirmed he was still a sergeant at war's end.

I felt outrage at this discovery, mingled with sadness. And then my mind filled with questions. I wondered when S. L. A. Marshall first figured he could get away with this fraud. Did he think he was so famous by that time that no one would dare question his claim? Did he feel relief when he told this war story in some speech and no one in the audience accused him of being a liar? Did he have any lingering fears in 1956 when the book jacket of *Pork Chop Hill* described him as having been the youngest Army lieutenant in World War I? Or had he been telling his false story so long that he had come to believe it himself?

I moved on to investigate the assertion of Marshall's critics that his unit in World War I—the 315th Engineers of the Ninetieth Division—was "involved in road work and building delousing stations." These engineers were rearguard soldiers involved in safe tasks far from the horrors of the front, it was implied. But I found the official history of the Ninetieth Division tells a much different story—of the Engineers sometimes being thrust into the fighting along with the Infantry and often being under fire while performing their crucial road work. This led to the 315th Engineers suffering thirteen killed and fifty-six wounded in the St. Mihiel campaign, thirteen killed and eighty-five wounded in the Meuse-Argonne campaign, not massive casualties, but certainly not the result of cushy duty in the rear.

American Heritage had used the slight of the Engineers' work to build a case that Marshall himself had never been in combat during World War I, alleging that his first experience with battle was another of his sham inventions. I found this hard to refute, at least at first. World War I record keeping seemed spotty at best. But the history of the Ninetieth Division does make the following mention of Marshall's own Company A during September operations: "As the opening up of lines of communication were recognized to be the matter of primary importance, detachments of engineering troops went forward with the infantry. One platoon of Company A, under Lieutenant P. M. Nicolett, and one platoon of Company C, commanded by Lieutenant R. A. Minter, accompanied the assaulting wave. The platoons were prepared to remove obstructions; but as the infantry chose to hurdle the wire, the platoons fought, filled trenches, cleared some wire and brought up ammunition."[4]

I did not know whether Marshall had been with Nicolett. But within a month after St. Mihiel, Marshall was sent to take an examination for West Point, an honor accorded few of the troops in his unit, and he was later sent to the officer candidate school. So Marshall was no Private Sad Sack lost in the Company A ranks; he was a teenage sergeant whose leadership abilities had quickly won notice. A sergeant of this caliber might well have been chosen among the twenty-five men on Nicolett's frontline mission.

Another dangerous mission under Nicolett took place several days later. This operation received a brief mention in *A History of the 90th Division*: "An enemy ammunition dump two miles in advance of the infantry was blown up by a party of infantry and engineers under Lieutenant Nicolett, of Company A."[5] Marshall's participation in that mission seemed to be confirmed by his brother who said the doughboy's "salient memory concerned a small ammunition dump left dangerously close to American lines after a shift of positions." Charles Burton Marshall had made this observation in a letter to military historian John Keegan twelve years before his brother's war record was called into question. Burt Marshall described his brother's recollections of being sent out to destroy the ammunition dump that was reportedly unguarded: "A dozen made their way out furtively and on arrival were dismayed to find the dump guarded by a detail of equally dismayed Germans. The two sides . . . blazed away at close range. Nobody was hit. Suddenly, the Germans took off at a trot. The Americans, all but overcome by fright, did their work and tremblingly crawled home."

I was worried that the incident was another of Marshall's fabrications concocted many years after the war. But Burt Marshall said otherwise over the telephone: "That was something he told me about the time he came home from the war in 1919, when I was about eleven. It impressed me; I was a kid fascinated with my brother's war experiences. And I have a very clear recollection of him recounting that back then; that was definitely 1919 recollection." Which, to me, was more evidence of some combat experience.

In the library, I also found my grandfather's World War I scrapbook, compiled after his return to El Paso. The scrapbook's pages were faded to a dirty khaki color and emitted a musty odor reminiscent of an attic; an old black shoelace has been pressed into service to keep the scrapbook from falling apart. I paged through this fragile offering with reverence, carefully examining its many faded photographs, postcards, and newspaper clippings.

There was a piece of waxed fabric, olive green in color, which my grandfather writes is "a piece of the wing of a Gerry plane shot down in our lines at St. Mihiel near Thiacourt on the 14th of September. Fell about 6,000 feet."

There is a pocket-sized menu from a post-Armistice banquet at Le Mans, the dinner tables set out on a footbridge over the Huisne River, the bounty including "radishes, fruit cocktail, roast young chicken, early June peas with sage dressing, breaded veal cutlets, candied yams, creamed asparagus, brown gravy, strawberry shortcake, ice cream, candy, nuts, coffee, cigarettes." Dinner was followed by dancing on the footbridge, memories of war seven months before put aside for the night. My grandfather's date for this enchanted evening was Yvonne Danizart, "a French girl from Monoco." It was, he recalls, "the best time I had while in France."

So eagerly did I devour the scrapbook's treasures that I missed the inscription on the inside cover. I only noticed it later, going through the scrapbook once again, my eyes straining to decipher my

S. L. A. Marshall as lieutenant in France after the World War I Armistice, 1919. Courtesy S. L. A. Marshall Military History Collection, University of Texas at El Paso.

grandfather's tiny handwriting that says: "To my true 'Buddy' & fellow sergeant Charly Jones, this little book is dedicated. Charly and I shared one another's woes and 'bully beef' for a year and a half and he generally gave me most of the beef even though it was inedible. If one of us went on a raid, the other went along just for company. At the front I found him the most reliable sergeant in my platoon and when he crumpled up with three machine gun bullets in his head during the Argonne offensive, near Bantheville, he was about five yards from me and we were going forward."

I gasped when I finished this inscription, then read it again to make sure I had not made some mistake. Words and phrases leapt off the page—"going forward," "three machine gun bullets in his head," "crumpled up," "five yards from me." This inscription had eluded other researchers, but my excitement was tempered by the tragedy described, a harrowing image of battlefield death. I turned to the division history, seeking confirmation of this incident, and found it in the final casualty accounting: "Killed, sergeants. William C. Jones, Co. A., 315th Engineers, Killed Nov. 8th."

The scrapbook inscription might not be what historians consider "independent evidence" proving that S. L. A. Marshall saw combat action in World War I. But it was good enough for me. Soldiers may lie about many of their experiences in war, as my grandfather sometimes did, shading the truth here or there, recasting various incidents with the sound of guns. But soldiers do not lie about the deaths of their best buddies. That would betray a fallen comrade. They would not do that. Period.

And then it all suddenly started to fall into place for me, how the trauma of his best friend's death must have led to my grandfather's troubles adjusting to life after the war, what Vietnam has taught us to recognize as "post-traumatic stress disorder" (PTSD), a war's aftershocks in the mind. It did not take much for me to imagine my grandfather awakening in the middle of the night in El Paso, his bedclothes soaked with sweat, another attempt at sleep haunted by that real nightmare of Charly Jones being hit in the head, going down and dying there beside him, and just three days before the Armistice would quiet the guns at long last. If Charly could have made it just three more days, my grandfather must have thought, seventy-two hours for God's sake—was that too much to ask?

S. L. A. Marshall came home from the war, full of such pride and purpose. He had left El Paso as a seventeen-year-old boy and returned as a nineteen-year-old man, wearing the Sam Browne belt and the jaunty airs that marked him as an Army officer. He had every intent of conquering his old world, just as he had his new world in France. "To make something of himself" was what he had promised to his father.

But all he seemed to be able to make of himself was a failure. Even half a century later, the hurt of those years had not lost its sting. S. L. A. Marshall was not a man easily given to introspection—in fact, he was downright wary of it, as if it were unmanly somehow and might lead to trouble. But his years of failure after the war caused even him to ponder self-doubts. "The next several years are fuzzed up in my recollections," he wrote in his memoirs, "because not remembering them makes me more comfortable."

He had taken a try at the Texas College of Mines, doing well in sports, but finding little satisfaction in studies. Years later, he would always claim to have earned not a single college credit—to underscore the irony of being later named the outstanding alumnus of what became the University of Texas at El Paso. But in the university's library, in the special collections' room that bears his name, I discovered this was another of Marshall's personal fairy tales. For I held his college transcript in my hands and it showed that he earned twelve college credits in his only semester of higher education: A in English 1, B in Geology 1, C in Economics, D in Chemistry 901.

And it was not being knocked unconscious in a college basketball game which suddenly convinced him to quit school, as he recounts in his memoirs. It was, his brother has written, the after-effects of a severely broken shoulder in a college football game and the lingering respiratory problems from that gas in France. Plus a malaise of the soul he could not shake. "He seemed," Burt Marshall remembers, "spiritually unsettled."

There followed, in short succession, a rush into marriage; a new son born just a year later (Sam, Jr., my father); various attempts at trying to discover a career, from the brick-making trade where his father had advanced to plant superintendent, to selling coal, to selling paper, all these attempts by the young husband and father destined for failure. All that Sam Marshall could do with any success was, it seemed, accumulate debts. They kept piling up until they totaled three-thousand dollars, a sizable sum, especially then.

Exactly four years after the end of the war, the former doughboy stood watching the Armistice Day parade in El Paso, his spirits glum, his prospects slim. "I was still adrift," he remembered, "and at war with myself for being such a fool." Where he happened to be standing to watch the parade proved to be his redemption, or so his story went. He walked right into the *El Paso Herald,* presented himself to the editor, asked for a job, and was hired. A surprising succession of scoops soon followed, some by dumb luck, some by his gritty determination to work fourteen to eighteen hours a day to get ahead. Not even his self-taught two-finger typing style deterred this cub reporter's progress. He had soon earned the nickname of "The Extra Kid." He had the knack for newspapering.

There were times during my research in El Paso when what I found made me wish I could ask my grandfather hard questions, try to pin him down, make him address the differences between what he wrote and what actually happened, admit his distortions, fess up. But there were other times when I felt my objective journalist's guise slipping away, replaced by feelings of familial pride. My grandfather's turn into journalism, after all of his postwar travails, was one of those moments. I wished I could have shaken his hand, I wished I could have been transported to the cluttered newsroom of the *El Paso Herald* in 1923 where—amid the clatter of typewriters, the stink of cheap cigars, and the chatter of rough-hewn men—I could have watched my grandfather stride forth into the career that the two of us would later share.

I tried to approximate that experience, as best I could, two days later when I set out on a family pilgrimage to visit all of the places in El Paso that I could connect with my grandfather. It was Easter Sunday, a perfect spring day. I traveled from the banks of the Rio Grande, where a young Mexican girl was being baptized in the muddy water before an excited crowd of onlookers, to the base of the Franklin Mountains, where prosperous El Pasoans poured out of church services and piled into their well-polished station wagons.

I visited the solid working-class homes where my grandfather once lived, including the one where I could easily imagine the postman trudging up the steps and knocking on the door because he had

John Marshall at his grandfather's grave, Fort Bliss National Cemetery, El Paso, March 1989. Courtesy *Seattle Post-Intelligencer.*

another letter from "young Sam in France." I visited the imposing El Paso High School, which was finished while my grandfather was still serving overseas; the downtown site of the *Herald* where his first written words saw print; the closed and crumbling brick plant where his father had contributed thirty-five years of toil; and the parched cemetery where his parents, Caleb and Alice Marshall, are buried side-by-side within sight of the Interstate and the freight-car tracks.

There was much backtracking on my pilgrimage. Streets unexpectedly dead-ended, addresses did tricks, new buildings intruded on the landscape. I was often forced to pull over and consult the map. But the map provided no guidance to the effect that all these stops had on me, how I was struck with new respect, even awe, at how my grandfather had gone from these modest beginnings in this nowhere border town to a place of national and international prominence. He could easily have stayed here, I kept thinking. He could have lived in El Paso. But he drove himself on from here, far from here, relentlessly. He did make something of himself.

The last stop on my pilgrimage was my grandfather's grave. And I was moved to do something I had not done on my first visit there a week earlier. This time I did not carry a notebook, and some of my ambivalence was left behind, too. So I bent down and knelt at my grandfather's grave, my head bowed, my eyes misty. And, after a time, I placed a bouquet of Easter flowers beside my grandfather's headstone, a small family peace offering, many years late.

7

Research Partners

OW I AM SPEEDING through downtown El Paso again on my way
to the airport, only this time I do not have a plane to catch. I am
heading to meet a plane and pick up someone and my mind is
filled with a prickly uncertainty. Because that someone knew S. L. A.
Marshall far better than I ever did. That someone is my father.

He is coming here to help me with my research in the library.
At least that is what is supposed to happen. And that is what I hope
will happen. But I have doubts, grave doubts.

For one thing, my father seems to have become absolutely obsessed with this Marshall controversy. Retired now, with few demands, he has turned the defense of his father into a new full-time
job. He counterattacks with letters and telephone calls. He is demanding an accounting—or better, a mea culpa—from those who
have committed grievous sins against his father, those responsible for
what he has taken to calling "the slanderous travesty."

His resolve to smite the enemy has resulted in a laborious analysis of the 6,400–word article in American Heritage, a complete tab-
ulation of words anti-Slam and pro-Slam, the bitter fruits of his findings presented to the magazine's editors in letters that are minutely
detailed and acutely contentious. My father has also fired off some
high-explosive rounds at Col. David H. Hackworth, Marshall's assistant during one of his Vietnam trips, his new Westover before Hackworth's bitter split with the Army. Hackworth, who likes to be
called "America's most decorated living soldier," had devoted a
chapter of his best-selling autobiography, About Face, to the savaging

of S. L. A. Marshall, even including his failure in bed with a Saigon prostitute. "General have many things in head but nothing in dick,"[1] the prostitute reported later, according to Hackworth. "All I can say," my father had written Hackworth, "is that you are an absolute ingrate. You know that, in his entire association with you, Slam had no interest but enhancing your associations, persona, and career. Yet, you write and spit on him. Shameful!"

I may share some of my father's outrage, but I do not share his approach. Maybe I cannot be objective after all in this controversy, maybe I would rather help defend my grandfather. But I can be fair, I can be scrupulous about seeking facts, can avoid trading in half-truths and innuendoes, as Marshall's critics have done. So, as I near my rendezvous with my father, I am wary about his vitriol coloring my attitude, tainting my research.

And one other matter is adding to my apprehension now—my relationship with my father. We are not close. We are, in many ways, strangers to one another. The number of days we have spent together since my father drove me off to college in 1965 do not total a month. This prompts some regret for us, but mainly relief.

Because there were so many times of storm and stress and slammed doors, these drag-out arguments fueled by some strange fires within us, disputes over matters great or small with so many bitter words we would rather have back. There were arguments over my passing by a penny on the sidewalk, over the Alabama girl I was so sure I would marry when I was seventeen; over the F that I received in freshman biology at Virginia ("why don't you just quit college now," my father snapped); over something said on a street corner in Vail, Colorado; over the decision of my first wife and I not to have children; and over the Army and Vietnam, so many of the worst arguments over the Army and Vietnam.

I may not have discussed Vietnam with my grandfather, but I did discuss it with my father, ad nauseam. I seemed to suffer from an insatiable urge to play student provocateur with my father, to confront him with my great insights into America gained in college, mostly with his money. I still have one of his letters from those antagonistic 1960s' days, a response to one of mine where I expressed my disappointment in my Infantry assignment and also enclosed, for his study I guess, an *Atlantic Monthly* article on the military-industrial complex. My father pressed his pen to paper with enough pressure to puncture concrete, so broad is the lettering, so dark the imprint. The essence of his sentiments was: Our country, right or wrong, or get the hell out.

My father wrote, "As I see it, you're in the Army, or practically so—and an officer, leader, and gentleman at that—get used to it, and for once in your life think positively. Put those kookie peacenik ideas out of your mind—they don't fit a uniform. Make up your mind to do what you have to do, but do it with some style, class and elan; not as a cowardly dragon who judges his own sense of history and morality transcends national judgment and personal obligation."

Five months after that letter, I came home from college for the last time in my Mustang, not thinking or not caring about how the car's back window displayed an American flag decal turned upside down, that symbol of distress, a small sign of protest that became a red cape in front of my raging father. The battle royale ensued, with more heels dug in, more shouts hurled about, more doors slammed. Another family fifteen rounder ending in a draw, with two losers.

My father did not write back in anger when I wrote him about my discharge as a conscientious objector, although I am sure he shared the sentiments of his father. My father did not write back at all. For months. A year passed before I started attending graduate school a hundred miles from his home in St. Louis and we reestablished contact, very cautious contact.

Brief notes and clipped newspaper columns became our favored means of communication after that. But for years, I could not shake my 1960s' notions about my father and how his was the bad example I vowed to avoid—this pursuer of the hollow American Dream, this organization man who did whatever the company wanted, uprooted his family, left them alone at home for long stretches while he was on the road, only to have the company turn traitor (ignoring his hard charge from traveling salesman to sales executive), his marriage finally a casualty too, and family tragedy to follow.

It was sixteen years before my father, my brother, my sister and I were all together again after my mother's funeral. Sixteen years since her suicide. And that brief weekend reunion in San Antonio, a time of kidding and conversation, had only begun to heal the scars that still remained from her death.

My father tried, I had to grant him that. It cannot be easy growing up in the shadow of a famous father and sharing his name. And it cannot be easy living alone in your late sixties, after years of an off-and-on relationship with your second wife, and with none of your own three children any closer than seven hundred miles away, a son in Seattle, another son in Charlotte, a daughter in Belton, Texas. We Marshalls are scarcely the only American family like that these days—we may even be typical—although I doubt that provides much solace for my father in a small apartment crowded with so many nice things once displayed in spacious family homes. Maybe this causes my father no grief or regret, although that seems unlikely. He has a sentimental streak.

My father does seem to have mellowed in his old age and that has done much to temper my views of him, as has my recognition that my own life is not free of mistakes either. The passing years have banked a lot of our fire and ire.

The birth of our son had brought out the best in my father. He had only come to visit Thatcher once, a stay that seemed much too short for such an occasion. "I am not that comfortable around little babies," my father had apologized. But he had left behind gifts that had touched me deeply. An heirloom cradle that he had somehow managed to construct at his kitchen table and a mammoth scrapbook that he had spent countless hours compiling, the story of our family and my life told in old photos, report cards, and other mementos that I thought were lost forever.

"This is my best effort at passing the torch to the newest—and first—little Marshall of his generation," my father had inscribed in the scrapbook. "The only kid to carry on for a proud, humble and variously successful Marshall clan. A clan that respects and treasures family highly, even if detached."

Now, my father is walking out the airport gate and I am thinking how much better he looks than I remember, quite the jaunty traveler, with his bulging leather case in one hand and a sleek Canon typewriter in the other, his blue blazer worn with polo shirt, khaki pants, and Gucci loafers, and as warm a smile as I can recall.

"Good to see you, guy," my father says.

"Good to see you, Dad," I say, as we embrace briefly.

First moments together are always awkward for us. Our barometers still kick in, scanning for any storm warnings. And the older I get, the more I look at my father and wonder if I am seeing myself twenty-six years from now. That is usually only a semi-frightening thought. For many years, my father had looked resplendently boyish, ten or fifteen years younger than his real age, with his skin smooth and taut, his green eyes so clear, his black hair combed back from that distinctive widow's peak and held in place with Wildroot, at least at one time, a smell I still can recall. My father was always handsome, almost film star handsome, in ways I would never approach. Old age has brought fullness and redness and lines to my father's face, but he still has far more hair than I do (which is not fair) and the gray has only lately started to appear. I see some of his father's jowls starting to drop from my father's cheeks, much to his chagrin, but no hint of that pointed Roman nose that was my grandfather's most prominent facial feature. All three of us share a Marshall paunch, our least favorite form of family inheritance.

Soon, my father and I are settled into a motel room, with a baseball playoff on television, and our conversation takes off at a gallop through many hours and many subjects: What the film *Field of Dreams* means to men. Whether writing talent can be inherited. Whether annual physicals are necessary. What various relations and ex-relations are doing these days. Why anchovies are the crucial ingredient of pizza. And the Marshall controversy—its origins, course, and status now—and what we hope to accomplish in El Paso.

We both focus on discovering the smoking Slam notebook from World War II, complete with quotations and computations on how many men fired their weapons in this battle and that. But we do not hold out much hope for that. Our more realistic goal is "whatever we can turn up in a week."

I intend to focus my attention to my grandfather's correspondence now to add depth to the portrait I have compiled of him thus far. I want to know more of what he was thinking at the time, instead of having things recalled decades later for his memoirs. And I want to know what other people thought of him when he was alive, whether critic or admirer. All these private thoughts in unpublished materials should reveal much about the man and his work.

But I am still bedeviled by his experience in World War I, what my grandfather referred to as "my university." For I have received a letter that questioned one of the central findings of my newspaper series, Marshall's scrapbook inscription about Charly Jones. Charles White, the Army historian discounted by his compatriot at Fort Huachuca, had written me that there was no way Marshall could have been "going forward" with Charly Jones when he was hit. Marshall was attending officer candidate school at La Valbonne by then, White insisted; Marshall was nowhere near the front. My heart plummeted. What I had put forth as proof of Marshall's combat experience in World War I now looked to be another fairy tale, a very early and very damaging fairy tale, if White were right.

But was he? White, who had recently transferred to Germany, had also asserted that Marshall "went so far as to impersonate a general officer for nearly five years before he was promoted to brigadier general in the Army Reserve in 1957." I know that is untrue. Marshall had been promoted to brigadier general five years before in the Michigan State Troops, a special section of the Michigan National Guard. That may not have made him a general in the Army, but he was not impersonating a general either. White's assertions, though, still remain a burr on my brain.

My father and I leave the Holiday Inn early, full of anticipation, even excitement, on the first morning of our joint research mission. We travel a few miles on the freeway in what passes for rush hour in El Paso, then exit and head up the hill to the university. The University of Texas at El Paso sits on a butte to the west of the city, its broad avenues, big buildings, and well-tended tennis courts standing in stark contrast to the ramshackle shacks and unpaved pathways of Juarez easily seen from the campus.

I introduce my father to Burdett, appropriate pleasantries are exchanged, and Burdett brings forth the first library cart filled with those gray boxes I know so well. My father and I are seated at a library table and we start making our way through file folders— which makes me smile at the thought of my grandfather happening upon this scene, his son and grandson doing research on him here.

I am working through his incoming correspondence, my father is working through his military records. "It makes me feel like I'm rummaging through someone's drawers," my father remarks. The work is slow, tedious, tiring; the morning's anticipation is soon buried under an avalanche of paper producing nothing new or important. I start to feel the same despair I felt on my first day here before. My morning's work does not even get me through all of the letters written to Marshall by people whose last names begin with A.

My father and I break for a brief lunch in a student cafeteria, many speaking Spanish. Our main topic of luncheon discussion is our frustration, which only seems to increase it.

My afternoon is consumed by reading more letters received throughout my grandfather's life, with many people expressing their thanks, including Lt. Gen. Lucian K. Truscott, Jr. He writes to Marshall in 1945: "I have thought of you so many times during this war. I appreciated the historical studies which the *Infantry Journal* sent to me as the result of your visit to the Pacific. I found them most useful." And Maxwell Taylor, then a major general serving as commandant at West Point, writes Marshall in 1947 with thanks for an advance copy of *Men Against Fire:* "You have again produced a book of real military value, stressing as it does the human factor in warfare."

These are not startling to me. Then I finally come across a letter thanking Marshall for his "truly wonderful offer to entrust your field notebooks and other papers to the US Army Military History Research Collection" at Carlisle Barracks, Pennsylvannia. Those elusive field notebooks, whose presence haunts my research. I know some Marshall materials are at Carlisle, but have been told they are of little importance. Still, I plan to visit Carlisle and maybe this letter will help unearth something previously overlooked.

I show the letter to my father, saying, "That's the best thing I've found all day."

"That's good," he replies.

But it's not good, and we know it. It is almost nothing to show for a day's work by two researchers, as our behavior demonstrates back at the motel. A couple of drinks uncorks all the day's disappointment and we erupt in full whine, like two wolves baying at the moon, and with about as much effect.

I bemoan the great mass of the Marshall collection. My father bemoans that it is not catalogued and computerized. I bemoan my difficulties in pinning down my grandfather's World War I record. My father bemoans the "misfeasance of *American Heritage.*" I bemoan my son's problems adapting to my absence, which Anne has related on the phone earlier today. My father bemoans what S. L. A. Marshall mementos are not out on display in the Marshall collection. I bemoan my father's smoking.

"I am depressed," I declare with great finality, as if that were not already as plain as Wonder Bread.

The next morning's research at the library yields more of value in one hour than the entire day before. Research is like this, I am finding, unpredictable but cyclic somehow, hours of monotony followed by a few minutes of elation.

"Look at this," I say to my father. I hand him a General Accounting Office form that denies Marshall's request for additional compensation for his World War I service, a denial sent to him in 1923, five years after the Armistice.

"I guess that shows how badly he needed money then," says my father, looking over his reading glasses. "He was just starting out at the *Herald* and he already had family responsibilities. I was two at the time."

"No," I reply, "there's much more to this paper than that."

I point out how the request for extra compensation is for the period while Marshall was, as the form reports, "in training for a commission from Oct. 23, 1918, to Jan. 18, 1919."

"So?"

"That means he could not have been with Charly Jones when he was killed."

"Oh."

We fall silent.

Marshall's attempt to reap perhaps four-hundred dollars more from the Army now seems to prove he was not present at his best buddy's death. There is a chance that the date is fabricated on this form—that Marshall had not really reported to officer training on October 23, 1918—but I doubt it. He would have known that the Army was going to check the date with its records, so why endanger his request with some falsehood. No, this pay form must reflect when he actually left his unit. I am so relieved to make this discovery that I pause scarcely at all to reflect on what it says about the scrapbook inscription, Marshall's first recasting of his World War I service, the first lie.

I press on with his correspondence. The letters I find most fascinating are the personal ones. These letters are the measure of my grandfather at various points in his life. I watch him, as a teenager, writing love notes and love poems to his mother, words of such lush emotion that they seem to require violin accompaniment.

"Will you believe, sweet, that I think of you always, that you are near me no matter what I'm doing," wrote this nineteen-year-old from France. "You are so near, I see you in the clouds and trees, your voice I hear—the whispering breeze reminds me, and the song of birds, that you are near. Always, Mother dear, your ever loving son, Sam."

I watch him, in his early fifties, writing chatty letters to a man whose wife he will soon steal away for his own. And I watch with horrified fascination, as this sorry soap opera starts to unfold, their first meeting as a threesome in Japan, the subsequent visits by Cate and her young daughter with my grandfather in the States, and his often-stated interest in all of their welfare ("Please write me whenever you get time," he tells the husband, "and if there is any way in which I can serve you, just name it.") How could anyone be surprised when this charade turns incredibly ugly, with stormy encounters, angry threats, lawyers on the doorstep, court battles, too. Yet my grandfather seems to acknowledge no responsibility. He writes to a friend, "For some reason, I can not reach the time when heavy problems do not beset me." And I am left thinking how easy it is to perceive the inevitability of actions in someone else's life, assess blame, feel knowing and wise.

My grandfather is certainly beset with "heavy problems" at this time. For the bitter imbroglio with his third wife's former husband follows soon after the death of his second wife, Ives. She had succumbed after an eighteen-year battle with multiple sclerosis, this stunning woman, wheelchair-bound, an invalid. "Ives was," my father says, "the best woman I ever met."

I have often looked at the photograph of Ives standing beside Ernest Hemingway on the deck of his fishing boat off Key West in 1936, the two of them smiling as my grandfather clicks the camera— Hemingway burly and tousled in the sea breeze, a rakish grin on his weathered face; Ives statuesque and elegant, even in her loose-fitting fishing clothes, a woman who could easily be a model, her hair cropped close in the stylish way of that time, and accenting a face that is so pretty and fresh. Just about when her illness first struck. I attempt to recall Ives from when I used to visit her as a child, but I cannot make out her face. All I can see is the large wall in their home covered with weights and pulleys and bars, what I remember as great things for child's play, this place where Ives battled her disease with an exhausting regimen of forced exercises.

Reading the few surviving letters between Ives and my grand-father during World War II is to witness a love story with epic over-tones, two people in love during what should have been the prime of their marriage, yet at the mercy of much beyond their control, the war, her illness, the miles between them. I am touched by their willingness to make grave personal sacrifices as so many did back when war had, for the last time perhaps, the fervor of a crusade.

All my grandfather had done in the past two decades seems to prepare him for the moment when world war comes again. He had chosen military matters as his area of expertise, had read and studied the field with diligence, building his military library to several hun-dred volumes from the copy of John Masefield's *Gallipoli,* which he purchased for $1.50 in El Paso upon his return from France. He had reported on wars, too, as a newspaper correspondent in Mexico and in Spain, and had written two prophetic books when war first en-gulfed Europe. *Blitzkrieg* and *Armies on Wheels* had brought him his first national notice. And by that time, he had begun his correspon-dence with Maj. Gen. J. F. C. Fuller, the respected British military historian and strategist, who would become Marshall's "mentor," dozens of letters on warfare between the two exchanged over more than two decades. Marshall even served as Fuller's unpaid literary agent in the United States because he believed Fuller's writings "have great value for Americans who are interested in military policy."

Marshall is a man poised for this war, with much to contribute and perhaps much to gain. Yet he is also a man torn between duty to his country and duty to his wife, a conflict heightened by his ambi-tion and pride in his work, just beginning to bear the respect he covets. He writes of his anguish to Ives just before he would volun-teer for service and reenter the Army as a major. "Dear Sweetie

Pants Pie," he begins. "I have given you so much turbulence when you are deserving of a tranquil life. Too, when ever the time has come that I have calculated there would be a turning back to more peaceful ways, always I have done badly, and gone in the other direction. Of this I have not been unmindful. There were so many things which I should have done for you, and have not done. So many things that I have said I would do some day, and now seem farther than ever in the distance. I feel that I have been a very bad husband. This time, however, I do not want you to believe that there is thoughtlessness in what I am doing or that I seek ought for myself.

"Ives, as God is my witness, I know that I would be much, much happier in Detroit, with the two of us just pegging on together, and sometimes I almost curse the day that I began doing the things which seemed to have qualified me for this strange undertaking. I am not like Charles or Spike, rushing off to war, responding to the excitement of it, wanting a change in pace. Hell no, I can't be like that, and I want you to believe that I can't. You have always been so very dear to me and I have loved you far too much for mean ambition to become a competitor of the things which I would do in your interest. Believe that of me.

"But I would not love you half as well as I do if I did not feel that you love me because I am a man who believes in things other than himself, and puts honor above his own desire. I cannot see how I can say other than I have, and be willing to serve my country if it wants me, instead of asking it to serve me. My heart may tell me one thing, but today there are so many other voices."

Their words of love later continue across the Atlantic. Ives' only surviving message is a short telegram without any punctuation, words that seem to sum up her attitude despite her travails: "EVERYTHING FINE HERE CHIN UP REMEMBER THEY CANNOT DOWN A MARSHALL I LOVE YOU IVES." One of Slam's own letters from the time, which opens with "My Darling Rumpelstiltskin," goes on to conclude: "Honey Baby, I wish I could gather you in my arms right now and take about 1000 kisses—like a prospector—from wherever I could re-stake my claim. I miss you terribly. . . . A year spent apart is a year lost to us, and we will never get it back. I have your love and I think about it and that is the only thing that keeps me afloat."

Portrait of S. L. A. Marshall in World War II khaki uniform, with inscription to Ives Marshall dated December 15, 1943. Courtesy S. L. A. Marshall Military History Collection, University of Texas at El Paso.

John Westover had told me about how devoted my grandfather was to Ives and how devastated he was to learn that Ives would no longer be able to write her own letters because of advancing paralysis. That lightning bolt of bad news from home is reminiscent of another shock my grandfather received during his first service in France. He heard then about the death of his younger sister, Mildred, struck down by the 1918 influenza epidemic that swept the country and claimed five times as many American lives as the war.

Westover had strong memories of my grandfather's reaction to the bad news about Ives' paralysis: "That was Christmas time in 1944 and Slam had gone out to the movie, *Dark Victory*, which was about a woman dying slowly. His chin was below the deck then, he was downright morose, very discouraged. He would talk at length about Ives, the places they had been, the things they had done, and what a horrible disease multiple sclerosis is. It was very clear that he loved that woman. Ives occupied his thoughts so much that he would feel the need to get out of the office and go into the field, to get his mind occupied with other things."

After the war, Ives' condition continues to deteriorate, while Slam's influence with the Army continues to grow. *Men Against Fire* is published, and his work becomes so highly regarded that he is returned to active duty forty-seven times in four years, all these times away from Ives. He admits guilt about his many absences and what they do to "this strong, yet frail individual giving me the confidence to keep going."

Few people know what my grandfather is enduring then, the heartache caused by Ives' worsening condition, how so many hours off from the newspaper are spent doing free-lance writing to raise the six thousand dollars a year required for Ives' care. One person who does is W. S. "Doc" Gilmore, Marshall's editor at the *Detroit News*, his newspaper mentor, and friend. At the time of Ives' death in 1953, Gilmore writes, "My Dear Sam: I can say to you now what I have said to others many times: That a man never lived who carried a heavy burden so bravely, so courageously, so uncomplainingly as you. You had more trouble than 10 men usually have in a lifetime, but no one would have known it from you. You have many admirable qualities which men like to see in men, but none is to be remembered more than this great courage."

Ives' death prompts an outpouring of condolence letters followed by "thank you" letters from my grandfather. His letters reveal a person stripped naked, his public façade cast aside, his pain transparent, intense. As he writes:

"When such a thing as this happens, one simply continues to regret that it wasn't more perfect and that one didn't try nearly hard enough. After many years of such an experience, all perspective becomes pretty greatly foreshortened and most of life seems pretty meaningless. That is about the situation. While I have a consciousness that suddenly pressure has been lifted, at the same time there is also the total loss of that around which my life and activity had been organized. I feel it will be a few days yet before I can begin again to think normally and see things in their natural light."

That same day, he writes another letter which, in one paragraph, captures the trials he and Ives endured during their years together, their desperate loneliness, the rejection too often directed at those with handicaps and their families.

"I will tell you now that nothing so endeared you to me as your sweetness to Ives when we were last in New York," my grandfather writes to Gen. Lyman Munson. "That day when you filled her room with flowers she remarked that it was the kindest thing that anyone had ever done for her in years. And when several nights later you had us to dinner, she told me going home that she had met new friends whom she would treasure through her lifetime and indeed she did. During the last few years of her illness it was surprising how old friends fell away from her. We lived to know what it meant to be virtually ostracized from society simply because my partner was an invalid. I believe that out of the last five years there were not twenty times that we were asked to go anywhere and it was not because we hesitated to accept. So we had to figure out places to go by ourselves. I tell you this because I want you always to remember that what you did out of the goodness of your heart was a milestone in her life."

I am nearly crying when I finish reading this passage. I am overcome by its poignant glimpse of that hotel room, the door being opened for the first time, flowers everywhere and Ives' great surprise, a squeal of delight followed by a tender hug in her wheelchair perhaps, and maybe some shared tears.

I am startled when a rustle of paper across the table suddenly reminds me I am sitting in a library and so is my father.

"Were you at Ives' funeral?" I blurt out.

"Of course I was there," he replies. "I did everything then, took care of all of the arrangements. I even bought the casket."

"Was that because Poppy couldn't do it himself?"

"Right. He was really out of it then, totally lost because of his grief over Ives."

8

Uncharted Territory

THE PROBLEM AT NIGHT is letting go. Spending so many hours at the library reading so many documents produces a strange state of exhaustion and delirium. My father and I are so caught up in the fever of the hunt that we return to the motel room and, like a couple of punch-drunk fighters in the late rounds, we still keep at it, long after we should have quit.

We replay the day's discoveries, weigh their significance, analyze where we are, ask questions and more questions, questions that seem to need immediate answers, not tomorrow, right now. My father is even more caught up in this than I am. He keeps asking me if I have checked this or I have checked that. And when did so-and-so occur? And where did that happen? And who said that first? I reply I am sure it is in my research materials somewhere, I could probably find it in a few minutes. Which I keep hoping is indeed true. Worst of all, my father keeps trying to get me to play editor of *American Heritage*, provide the magazine's rationale, why they published what they published and why now? As if I had some clue.

My eyes glaze over from the continuing rehash of these questions and I tell myself I should ask my father to stop. But I hesitate, fearing he may misread that as a lack of diligence on my part, when I am supposed to be the one who is the professional at this. So I stay up until midnight, combing through all the research material I have collected, while my father goes to bed before me and dreams of more library papers, fitful sleep indeed.

What keeps us going at the library are the moments of shared laughter over what we sometimes find. Every few hours, I seem to happen upon another letter with my grandfather's favorite all-purpose phrase. "Your good news [or 'your words of praise' or 'your welcome letter' or 'your kind thought']," my grandfather writes, "hit me like a good cocktail on an empty stomach." Which always produces another laugh for my father and me.

Another time, I pass him a black-and-white photograph of an earnest lad in a khaki uniform, standing in front of an old clapboard barracks, posed with that mixture of pride and discomfort that a starched set of khakis produces. This classic Army shot could have been taken at any post at any time in the last four decades.

"Is that you at camp?" my father asks.

"No," I reply, "that's YOU at camp."

Then, my smiling father returns to another file folder with the intriguing label "Miscellaneous" and I submerge myself in more papers, filed year-by-year. I am slowly progressing through my grandfather's life and wondering if all lives have the same unmistakable symmetry, with his fifties such a sharp peak. This is a man on the march. With each passing year, his reputation seems to grow, his correspondence widen. His counsel is repeatedly sought by the Army and what he says seems to have a significant impact.

In 1951, Marshall's efforts for the Army in Korea prompts Lt. Gen. Raymond S. McLain, the comptroller of the Army, to include this rave in Marshall's official service file: "These papers and other work which Colonel Marshall has contributed through various services on duty with the Army has marked him as a man of profound and accurate observations, meticulous in detail. It is hard to imagine the great influence which he has contributed towards our military thinking. He is a man of great stature, in my opinion, and is very definitely General officer material."

Men Against Fire may prompt controversy forty-two years after its publication. But when it first appears, it prompts mostly favorable reviews and spurs the Army to research and to action. Within months of *Men Against Fire*'s publication, Col. Branner P. Purdue, who is the chief of the Troop Training Division for Army Ground Forces in the United States, writes to Marshall: "Your 'Men Against Fire' becomes more of a challenge, the more we study it. It being a challenge, and a valid, legitimate challenge at that, we are trying to overcome faults of training—and of battle actions—which you so graphically pointed out. In my opinion, the most damaging of these faults is the unwillingness of the majority of riflemen to shoot." Adds Purdue later: "We are taking steps to change our infantry doctrine."

Later in the 1950s, one such change includes a new, more realistic course in rifle training (called Trainfire) which is clearly aimed at correcting the firing problems Marshall had first pointed out. Trainfire supplements standard marksmanship training, firing at bull's-eye targets, with a new kind of course that includes pop-up silhouettes of men to simulate battlefield conditions. The Army pamphlet on Trainfire describes its origin: "In 1954, under supervision of the United States Continental Army Command, a group of infantry experts began to develop a course in rifle marksmanship instruction that would prepare the soldier to use his rifle effectively in combat. The group was also instructed to evaluate the then current method of instruction and recommend better means of integrating rifle marksmanship instruction throughout the basic training program. . . . In their study of these problems, the experts analyzed battle reports and other written accounts. They talked at length with hundreds of combat-wise infantrymen of all grades and wrote down their individual stories about specific conditions of battle having to do with problems of finding and firing at the enemy. These official accounts and personal stories were carefully studied at the Infantry School and other Army agencies."[1]

The message here is clear. The Army considered firing problems a serious matter; ordered thorough, independent studies conducted on the subject; concluded there was indeed a problem requiring corrective steps. Marshall's current critics can continue to assert that firing problems in World War II were a myth of his own making. They can huff and puff all they want, but they cannot blow away this document. It stands as a strong rebuke to their allegation.

For although Marshall's name is not mentioned in this Department of the Army pamphlet, the imprint of his thinking is unmistakable. As is pointed out in the handwritten message on the first page of the library's copy. "Note," Marshall writes, "that this DA pamphlet confirms my WWII findings."

My father has discovered this pamphlet and reads it aloud with the smile that comes from familial pride in the accomplishment of a loved one. And it makes me think about how sad it was that my grandfather's own father had not lived to see his son in the 1950s. Caleb Marshall had come so close, dying late in 1949 at age seventy-five. He had retired just a couple months earlier from his general superintendent's job at the brick plant after thirty-five years there, and he was then on his way to England to visit the brother he had not seen in fifty-three years. Caleb Marshall was stricken on a train in Illinois, an entire suitcase filled with presents he would never get to deliver. Sam had rushed to his bedside from Detroit, arriving in time to embrace his gravely ill father and hear him say, "Well, son, I know this is the end of the line." And then they had been together in the hospital those last few days.

"What his two sons owed to this man is beyond power of earthly expression," my grandfather had written in the unedited manuscript for his memoirs. "Though he received no formal education beyond the third grade in elementary school, he possessed more wisdom, a deeper concern for the rights of man and a greater feeling for the language than anyone either of us ever knew. These may have been his lesser gifts to us. Duty ever commanded him and he was incapable of doing anything that might dishonor his name and those he loved. We had always before us his example of fortitude, of how to take the bumps and lumps without discouragement and of accepting risk gladly as a rightful part of male life."

At the time of his father's death, Marshall had been writing *The Armed Forces Officer,* a guidebook that would serve officers in the Army, Navy, Air Force, and Marines for more than three decades. But only the third revised edition in 1975 credited Marshall's authorship. I am finding that *The Armed Forces Officer* is the kind of project that Marshall frequently undertakes for the service—projects often with no credit and with little or no pay. His countless speeches at Army schools are part of this contribution to the Army he loved. So is his uncredited inscription on the massive memorial at the Bastogne battlefield in Belgium, four thousand stirring words carved in stone in giant letters. Many of these efforts have been long since forgotten, especially now in the rush to damn the man.

But *The Armed Forces Officer* was still having a strong impact after Vietnam. Gen. Fred C. Weyand, Army chief of staff, writes to Marshall in 1975 that he had been "looking for just the right words to impress on the officer corps the importance of values, ethics and ideals." His search had ended, the Army's leader said, with rediscovery of *The Armed Forces Officer*. Weyand then had copies of the first two chapters of the book ("The Meaning of Your Commission," "Forming Military Ideals") distributed to all the generals in the Army.

Marshall follows *The Armed Forces Officer* with two of his best-known works—*The River and the Gauntlet* in 1952 and *Pork Chop Hill* in 1956. Both of these Korean War sagas are written from Marshall's own interviews at the front during two separate trips to the war zone, an estimated 800,000 words in notes for *The River and the Gauntlet*, 50,000 words for *Pork Chop Hill*.

There are some marvelous ironies to the story of Pork Chop Hill. What happens becomes a telling example of the power of the popular media to transform memory and alter history. For Pork Chop Hill had escaped notice in America until Marshall's book years later. And the book itself remained in obscurity ("a commercial failure," Marshall admits), perhaps because publication came so long after that bitter stalemate.

But that all changes dramatically in 1959 when Gregory Peck stars in a film version of *Pork Chop Hill* (for which Marshall apparently received $2,500). The obscure fight of Pork Chop Hill is suddenly elevated to legendary status by the much-praised film by Oscar-winning director Lewis Milestone (*All Quiet on the Western Front*). The film even becomes one of Peck's favorites from his long and illustrious career. "We made a realistic war film, without sentimentality, without Mom's apple pie, without letters from Sally in the old hometown," Peck has said of *Pork Chop Hill*. "I like it because of the extreme, tragic irony."[2] And the film also turns *Pork Chop Hill* into Marshall's best-known book. This story of a little battle that he alone deemed worthy of coverage.

Still, Pork Chop Hill does have all the elements of war that Marshall found so fascinating. Here is where we part company. I have never been to war and am thankful I have not. Yet my grandfather kept going back to war almost until he was seventy. Granted, he was an observer most of the time, not a participant, and it was his chosen profession. But as I come to know my grandfather better, I am still amazed that anyone would want to devote so much of a life to death, the study of what is, after all, killing on a mass scale. I cannot fathom anyone wanting to lay claim to having seen "more of war than any man in modern times," as one of his book jackets says of S. L. A. Marshall. That that man happens to be my own grand-father is profoundly disturbing to me.

Pork Chop Hill, though, does provide an insight into what kept drawing him back to battle for so many decades. A movie publicist's simple question—"What did Pork Chop Hill mean to you?"—prompts a lengthy meditation.

"The Hill itself was worthless for any tactical point of view," Marshall writes. "Its retention could not help the American position. The troops knew this; they knew that they were being ordered to recover and hold ground, at a high cost in American lives, which probably would be surrendered later because it lacked true defensive value and was a fire trap for people who held it. Yet over two days and two nights, two battalions of relatively green and youthful G.I.s were put into this blood bath, and the courage with which they fought was not less absolute than if they had been called to defend the line at the Potomac. They did this for the sake of U.S. 'policy' and because they were led by unseasoned but eager and valiant lieu-tenants who believed in obeying orders when given in the name of the United States. . . .

"It is a big parade of tired Americans going into fire, taking the worst that comes, doing it with that willing protestingness which is typical of our fighters, helping one another, seeing in their leaders that uplifting something which they had always vaguely sought in the face of their country, and still never quite understanding why."

It is now Saturday noon and special collections soon closes for the rest of the weekend. My father and I pack up our things, the piles of Xerox copies, the legal pads filled with scribbles, the leather valises packed to overflowing, all this paraphernalia that identifies us as mounters of a serious research expedition. We take a seat outside the library while my father smokes a cigarette. It is hot in the sun, more like summer than fall, and we are warmed too by our first sense of accomplishment. And that is enhanced by elation at being liberated from the library, for a day and a half at least.

But I am exhausted, dead tired from what we are trying to accomplish here, while also trying to avoid any flare-ups with my father. Back at the motel, I tell him that I want to lie down for a few minutes. I wake up three hours later. There follows a debate about what to do this Saturday night. My father is drawn to visiting Juarez, a rite he remembers from years past. I do not have any great enthusiasm for the idea. Maybe we could have a quiet dinner in El Paso, I finally suggest. My father reluctantly agrees.

We settle on a restaurant that I discovered during my first trip in El Paso, a place with surprising food considering its location in a fading motor inn alongside a freeway.

"Oh, so this is where the geriatric set eats," my father says as we take our seats. I feel myself clinch, then glance around the room.

"I guess so," I reply.

But my father's vodka is well-iced and my glass of wine is fine and pretty soon we start to talk about things we have never discussed before, as if we had been waiting for years for this very night in this very place. Which maybe we have.

Looking into our famous forebear's past somehow provides a license to discuss our own pasts with little held back. We talk of women we have loved at one time, and sometimes none too wisely. I tell my father about two women I might have married if sudden illness had not intruded at just the wrong moment, appendicitis in one case, cancer in the other, and what a difficult time I had dealing with the loss, especially the one who said her cancer had reappeared a few days after our engagement.

"We never even got to tell her children we were engaged," I say. "I spent many nights after that sitting on my porch and staring out at Puget Sound, waiting for the water to tell me, I guess, why this had happened to me."

"I didn't know about that," my father says.

"I never told you."

I venture for the first time into something that has begun to intrigue me after all this research on my grandfather's military past. I keep thinking how my father, who had always been so gung ho about my doing my Army duties and even serving in Vietnam, had somehow spent his entire Army Air Corps' career during World War II serving in the United States. I begin tentatively, uncertain where this may lead.

"I know you volunteered to serve in World War II, even making the papers as one of the first students from the University of Michigan to sign up on the day after Pearl Harbor," I say. "So I guess I have been wondering how someone with all that patriotic fervor did not end up fighting overseas."

"You can't understand what it was like when we were attacked by Japan," my father says, "unless you were there then."

My father proceeds to tell me about his flying days, about his progress as a pilot serving first at Randolph Field near San Antonio, then Pine Bluff, Arkansas, then Laredo, where he played a crucial part in setting up a training school for aerial gunners. He also talks about being married to my mother and living together there, all these stories that I have never heard before, stories I have never bothered to solicit.

"I guess I concluded that it was more important for me to help save our pilots' lives with good training than it was for me to be ending the lives of some Germans or Japanese overseas," my father explains. "And I guess, in the back of my mind, I always remembered your grandfather's advice that one should never volunteer for anything in the Army; you should just let it run its course."

I am surprised by what my father says. His approach to the war may make perfect sense, but it just does not sound like him, or at least the man I thought I knew. There is no denying he must have done a good job in the States during this war, even graduating from the U.S. Army Command and General Staff College at Fort Leavenworth, something his father never did. But my father was not the hard-core military guy I had long imagined. And that is not the only startling revelation to me in this conversation. There was also not, my father relates, what I always considered to be a military tradition in the Marshall family.

"There was no such thing," my father states flatly. "Slam's parents and grandparents were probably pacifists."

"So," I chime in, "I guess I was carrying on the real Marshall family tradition by being a C.O."

Which prompts my father to emit a mild chuckle, a triumph of sorts for us, compared to what would have happened if I had made that wisecrack two decades ago.

We do talk some of Vietnam and how the war, so different from the other American wars, had come along at the worst possible time for S. L. A. Marshall, so late in life when he was least likely to trouble with the war's complexities. War by then was war to him, a test of will and guts, more fodder for his slam-bang prose.

"Poppy was not what he had once been during Vietnam," my father says. "He was so set in his ways by then, with some failed perceptions, and he was beset by infirmities, although he certainly did his best to suppress them."

And the two of us speculate on the influence of his third wife, Cate. There is plenty here for far more qualified analysts of psychology. Cate was twenty-three years younger than her husband, two years younger than my father, and taller than both of them. She was "one tough broad," in the description of those days, a vigilant protector of the Slam flame. She may have loved Slam and their girls dearly, but there was about her, my father and I agree, a certain nasty streak. She had no aversion to settling scores.

I had seen that in her editing of my grandfather's memoirs. She had eliminated all but one reference to my grandfather's brother, whose Harvard and Washington ways she could not abide. And she had made sure that there was absolutely no reference to my father in the book, since the two men had also had a falling out, even though my grandfather had described him as "my dear son, Sambo" on at least two occasions in his original manuscript.

I have long wondered about Cate's role in the letter disowning me. She had been, after all, a cosigner. And I had discovered in the library that Cate, a Navy veteran, had actually written the dedication to S. L. A. Marshall's 1968 Vietnam book, *West to Cambodia*. The dedication shares the tone and emotions of that damning letter to me. "To all the good and gallant guys who fought for this country," the dedication goes, "and the back of my hand to the punks, professors and preachers who ran around ranting that they were careless killers of women and children in a no-good war."[3]

When I had heard that Cate had only a few more months to live because of cancer, I considered asking her who actually wrote the letter to me. It had had such an impact on my life. But I decided

S. L. A. Marshall riding in jeep as Grand Marshal of the 1974 Veterans Day parade in El Paso, with Cate Marshall, his third wife, seated in back of jeep. Courtesy S. L. A. Marshall Military History Collection, University of Texas at El Paso.

it would be selfish to force her to reopen old wounds. She had enough worries. I sent her a card instead with a warm note and a picture of our son.

The restaurant is almost empty now. Hours have passed. Our dinners have long since been cleared away and my father and I have downed several drinks. And even before we get up from the table, I am amazed by the course of our discussion, this venture into uncharted territory. I keep thinking how many years it has taken us to get to this point, a father and son actually talking "man-to-man," and me not reverting to the defensive fifteen-year-old, that maddening role I have played too often with my father. This week is the longest time we have spent together as adults and even if we never clear S. L. A. Marshall's name, we are doing something in El Paso that means more to us.

We stand in the motel room, a little shaky, locked in an embrace that lingers.

"I can't tell you how much this has meant to me," my father says, tearfully. "I'm proud to have you as my son."

"I'm proud to have you as my father," I reply, words I have never spoken before, words that surprise me.

There are rainstorms the next morning. Huge black thunderheads roll out of Mexico, sweep across the barren hills with flashes of lightning and torrential rain, a curtain of water falling on the landscape in some places and, twenty feet away, not a drop. By noontime, the skies have cleared and puddles on the pavement are the only reminder of the storm.

We set out then on a journey around El Paso, much like my Easter pilgrimage, with me playing tour guide this time around this city where my father was born and spent his earliest years. We stop at the city overlook in the Franklin Mountains and my father reads every bronze historical marker, perhaps trying to connect with this city so far in his past.

We stop at a lime green bungalow whose address I had found in the library, what may be the first house my father lived in as a baby, and I take a picture of him in front of this house, although he has no recollection of it. Up on Porter Street, though, the memories come back, as the car idles in front of two solid brick houses where his grandparents lived and his aunt.

"I would collect tarantulas here, scorpions, vinegarroons, too," my father says. "They were called vinegarroons because, if you stepped on them, they smelled just like vinegar. All those creatures could be found here; there were only a couple of houses in this neighborhood then. This was way out in the country; there was nothing between here and Fort Bliss."

In the distance, in the direction of Fort Bliss, a slow freight train makes its way, spurring another memory.

"I used to count freight cars as they passed on those tracks," my father says. "One time I counted 167 freight cars, 167. I know that must sound like I had a pretty exciting childhood, spending my time counting freight cars as they went by, but I can assure you that was a big deal then."

We move on after a time. We pass the huge Army hospital where my grandfather's life had slipped away for too many months after a series of debilitating strokes, his wife and daughters mounting a bedside vigil and seldom with any sense that he recognized them. Such a sad end to such a vigorous life.

My father and I head up Robert Wilson Boulevard, pass the Hock-N-Go and turn right into the cemetery, my father's first visit here since the funeral. I am not sure what to expect here with my father. Even I have felt a power surge of emotions at the grave.

We get out of the car and my father starts to pace, circling around the grave, but keeping his distance. He comes back and asks whether I agree the headstone should say more about S. L. A. Marshall's accomplishments.

"It's too austere," my father emphasizes. "There's no mention of the decorations he won, the books he wrote, or his service in Korea or Vietnam."

"I guess that hadn't occurred to me."

We fall silent for a time.

I finally ask my father if he would like his picture taken by the grave. He says he would. But he has no smile for the camera. There is an attempt at a smile, but it comes across as a grimace, my father's brow contorted, his shoulders slumped forward, his glasses clenched in one hand, his other hand buried in his pocket.

Then my father takes off on a hike by himself, reading headstones as he goes, crossing over the long straight driveway and heading back on the other side of the cemetery. When he returns, I put my arms around him, only this is not the hug of the night before. This is a desperate clutch together, our attempt to ward off pain, regret, loss.

We say nothing—our emotions are too strong to speak. We get back in the car and drive away, my father finally breaking the silence.

"That would not be a bad place to be buried," he says.

I do not answer. I do not know what to say. I have visited this cemetery twice before and I have always been filled with thoughts of the past. My father comes to the cemetery and confronts thoughts of the future, his own future, how little time he may have left.

We pass the rest of the afternoon in Juarez, amid the throngs in Sunday best, a festival taking place on the plaza outside the old cathedral, young Indians from the mountains dancing to loud drumbeats, smoky booths offering native foods. The side trip ends with icy Carta Blancas in a deserted bar with a baseball game on television, a chance to recover from the cemetery, our brush with mortality.

We are back at the library early Monday morning. Our pace quickens with the knowledge we now have three days left in El Paso.

I am getting a much different picture of my grandfather from his correspondence than I did on my first trip. Then, I had mainly sought letters to and from famous names, chiefs of staff, presidents, writers. And I had gained an impression of my grandfather as a tireless hustler, sending off complimentary copies of his books to anyone of rank, requesting copies of autographed photographs for his study, these little rituals of the insider's game.

This second trip, I read more correspondence with people who do not have famous names, people with little likelihood of advancing S. L. A. Marshall's career. I see him reaching out, warm-hearted, offering congratulations to soldiers who win medals, recommending many others for medals, sending condolences to widows whose husbands' brave deeds he had discovered in combat interviews.

I mention this to my father and he says simply, "That was characteristic of the man."

But it seems to change in the 1960s. His correspondence drops off, at least what's left at the library, and letters often have a mean edge. What made him seem such a character at one time, his peppery personality, turns harsher, transforming him into a caustic old man. Critics are not answered, they are counter-attacked; lawsuits are threatened and sometimes filed. Longtime business contacts are shattered, so many years of work together left in wreckage as S. L. A. Marshall storms off. He had written once that "to contend strongly, to agree warmly, to disagree fairly and to accept reversal without bitterness—these are the important things, the hallmarks of character." Now what he does contradicts that.

This is more the man I remember and it is painful watching his descent from the heights he had scaled in the 1950s, who he seemed to be then. I search for some explanation for this change in his behavior, beyond the advance of age. What I keep zeroing in on is his heart attack.

My grandfather was stricken while visiting New York in 1960. It was a rude shock to a man who had always prided himself on his capacity for hard labor and long hours. He was still hurt by how that heart attack changed his life more than a decade later. "I decided to pick up where I had left off," he wrote in his unedited memoirs. "But some things could never be quite the same again. Hard physical exercise, be it work or play, was now in my past."

He goes on to recount an event after another lecture at Fort Benning, when he assumed his health was returning to normal. He and Cate were on their way to his retirement ceremony in Washington, that much-anticipated celebration, when their plane was caught in a violent electrical storm. It hurled the aircraft about and he later remembered, "I disintegrated into a whining, crying child. Cate was disgusted with me, and from that moment I gave up being astonished at myself. So shocking was the experience that I read it as a warning that I dare not draw back lest I go soft all the way."

His press-on resolve may seem admirable, may even aid his recovery, but there is a pathos about it. His reference to "lest I go soft all the way" sounds borrowed from Hemingway, or at least a Hemingway character, so resoundingly macho. But it is characteristic of Marshall. I am struck by this statement's similarity to what he had written right after Ives' death: "I feel it will be a few days yet before I can begin again to think normally and see things in their natural light." A few days after almost two decades of dealing with Ives' illness. A few days—the thought makes me shudder. As does his reaction to the incident on the plane. His fears of showing any weakness seem destined to set him up for the bitterest frustration when the frailties of old age inevitably arrive. And it will be a trap of his own making, born of his bravado, source of much of his success but also a serious character flaw.

Marshall's retirement ceremony in Washington remains one of the high points of his life, perhaps the peak. He is still too weak from his heart attack to stand during the festivities that August day. But there is no mistaking his great delight at all the top brass gathered to pay their respects, including Gen. Lyman Lemnitzer, Army chief of staff. A reception is held in the office of Secretary of the Army Wilbur Brucker, a formal luncheon follows, then the awarding of the Army's highest medal for a civilian, the Decoration for Distinguished Civilian Service. And the ceremony concludes at Fort Myer, Marshall seated as the First Battle Group of the Third Infantry Regiment passes in review, and a battery of howitzers sends an eleven-gun salute thundering across the parade ground.

"No working newspaperman had ever been so honored by the military," *Newsweek* wrote. "But Marshall known as Slam to his friends was a special case. For during the past forty-three years he had been the Army's No. 1 admirer (I'm biased, I love the Army)—and its most articulate critic. As one general put it: 'Slam has had more effect on Army tactics and training methods than any other man outside the Army.'"[4]

The *Newsweek* feature continues for a page filled with praise, one measure of his reputation then, and such a contrast with what is being said in the controversy today. What strikes me most when I read the Newsweek article is its conclusion, a final quote from S. L. A. Marshall, one that now seems too revealing, even foreboding, considering what is to come.

"I don't want to be misunderstood. I never qualify with 'maybes,' 'buts,' and 'on-the-other-hands,'" Marshall emphasizes. "I'd rather be proved wrong than vague."[5]

I grow tired of plowing through library paper. I ask my father to share some of his insights into his father and he recalls: "A very overtly loving, very affectionate man, full of hugs and kisses; he was a touching kind of man, an embracing kind of man; he had a warmth and tenderness that just lived with him all the time . . . . Right now, there is so much talk about how cocky he was, how overbearing he was, how crude he was, how many negative qualities he had. But as a son, I really didn't see any of those things, and not so much because I loved him as because he had a really genuine modesty and tenderness around his family. I never heard him yell, never heard him cuss, he had all the qualities ascribed to gentility . . . . I never saw any downside at all until late in his life."

My father's recollection reminds me how little I know about their relationship. Such family matters did not matter much to me until I had a child myself and reached middle age. Now I try to make up for lost time. I ask my father about the impact his parents' divorce had upon him at a young age and he insists that "the reality of it didn't hit me in any way." What he recalls, though, does seem painful: "It was very quiet, there were no big scenes, all of a sudden he just didn't come home one day." I ask my father about the impact of sharing his father's famous name and he replies: "That name did me a great service everywhere I went. It seemed to carry a certain badge of integrity, intelligence, and it served me well. And my father was very active in supporting me; he would travel across the country to speak to groups or individuals that I thought were important or could help my career. He would travel to St. Louis just to attend a dinner party if he thought it would be helpful to me."

And finally I ask my father about the impact his father's career had on his own choice of career, since he had not stayed in the military, which he seemed to enjoy, and he had not gone into writing, which he also seemed to enjoy. He had instead become a salesman. My father says: "You never have regrets about things you didn't do. And, besides, I don't think I'm that good a writer. I'm a fair craftsman of the English language, with a fair vocabulary, some flair. But I am not an original thinking writer; I couldn't have written any of the books here, I don't think that way. And I never really wanted to stay in the military; I enjoyed it while I was there, but enough was enough."

My father pauses for a moment, reflecting on his career, then adds, "I thought I was going to conquer some world, but I didn't know what that was . . . . I guess I still don't."

We go out to a celebration dinner on our next-to-last night in El Paso. It is my father's treat, and what a treat it is. We are eating in the Paso Del Norte Hotel, the city's landmark gathering place since 1912, host to anybody of any importance who passed through El Paso, and recently restored to its former elegance by Westin. The waiters are clad in dusty peach uniforms, the china sparkles in subdued light, the table linen is crisp with starch and the menu is laden with entrees pushing past twenty dollars, rack of lamb, breast of duck, even fresh salmon. This is a world apart from where we have spent our time in El Paso. We feel as though we have hopped a plane to a city on the coast.

We are having this dinner tonight because the library is open late tomorrow and we plan to put in a full ten hours, the hard final

Ruth Marshall, S. L. A. Marshall, Jr., and S. L. A. Marshall strike a jaunty pose as a young family in El Paso, about 1926.

push. But we are already flush with accomplishment. When we left the library this afternoon, there were two library carts filled with thirty six boxes that we have reviewed. No smoking notebooks have appeared, but we have found quite a few rounds of ammunition that could be fired in Marshall's defense, things other researchers have overlooked or never bothered to examine.

"So let's please not rehash the *American Heritage* thing again tonight," I say to my father. And he seems to agree.

But the discussion takes a strange turn even before our food arrives when my father says to me, "You know what you did with the Army—your C.O.—was right. But it was stupid."

"What?"

"It was stupid because there was almost no chance that you would be killed in Vietnam," he says. "And it was stupid because of all the family hurt that was sure to ensue."

My face is suddenly aflame and I feel the old defensiveness flaring up, the old anger.

"Would you rather be having dinner here with me tonight," I snap, "or be reading my name on the Wall in Washington?"

My father seems startled, speechless.

I proceed to recount how I had indeed tried to avoid the family hurt as best I could, attempting to use connections to land a job as a NATO general's aide in Turkey, a job that I was told could not be arranged; so I went ahead with my C.O., only to have that aide's job finally come through months after I had already been discharged. And I also tell my father how I had turned down an American newspaper reporter in Germany who had wanted to interview me about my C.O. because he had heard who my grandfather was. I emphasize to my father that I never made my C.O. stand public as long as my grandfather was still alive.

These appear to be possibilities that my father had never considered but they do not put the brakes on his criticism.

He tells me how angry and bewildered he was when he received my letter explaining that I was getting out of the Army as a C.O., something he has never discussed with me before. He was so upset that he called Gen. William Westmoreland himself, then Army chief of staff, asking what in the world was going on. And then the call had come back from Washington the next day from some Pentagon general informing my father that I had met all the requirements for such a discharge, that I had even submitted one of the best C.O. applications the Army had ever received, although there was some question whether my discharge orders had been issued yet and holding things up might still be possible. But my father remembers saying something to the effect that "No, it's his life, he's got to live it." And my father relates how he wanted nothing more to do with me— ever—but Sally Jacobs, his second wife, had finally been able to dissuade him with much the same argument I had heard from Lucian Truscott III: "This is your son, this is your family; you just can't do that." Which ultimately led, my father says, to an explosive argument with his own father over his disowning me and a terrible break between the two of them, too.

I just sit there as my father says all this, letting him unload the old hurt, surprised by what he is saying, and not absolutely sure that I believe all of it, but no matter. I do not argue, I do not dispute, I just listen, and maybe that is crucial.

For things simmer down later as they never would have in the old days. And we sit in the Dome Room after dinner, the entire ceiling this vast expanse of Tiffany glass, the great mahogany bar in the center of the room, this place that my grandfather must have come many times from the *El Paso Herald* across the street.

And the history of this place washes over us, and the beauty of it, too. We sip our cognac and trade hushed talk, knowing in our hearts that we have been through too much together in El Paso to go back to the sad way things once were between us, that time of battle lines when we forgot there is such a thing as forgiveness.

9

Across Texas

THE LAST GLIMPSE OF MY FATHER in El Paso is outside our motel. He has taken a picture of me standing beside the car, then we share a few parting words and I pull out of the parking lot, relieved in some ways but more sad than I could ever have anticipated, as my father becomes a figure disappearing in the rearview mirror.

I head down the hill, make a couple of turns, then speed onto the Interstate, back on the road again. This is one of those rare mornings when the road means all of those things that it is supposed to mean in road movies, road songs, road myth. The road today is liberation from routine, the road is progress counted out in miles, the road is lunch in someplace different and nighttime in who-knows-where and the getting there filled with the promise of unseen vistas, unknown people, a clean slate of a day.

My father has forewarned me that I will be passing through the "Nowhere of Texas," a part of the state that seems as though it will never end, 238 miles east from El Paso just to get to Fort Stockton (population 8,688) with its six-foot statue of a roadrunner. Still, I am euphoric to be back on the road. The early part of the day is all desert mesas and shadowy mountains, so reminiscent of Arizona, but suddenly a sign tells me that I have entered the central time zone, one of those tricks played by the vastness of the Lone Star State. The middle of the day is rocky low hills with the occasional gnarled tree defiantly clinging to life, an area that looks like pictures I have seen of Africa, except for the rusting hulks of oil well machinery, ghostly reminders of black gold gone bust.

96

By late afternoon, I leave the Interstate, heading east on U.S. Highway 290, its undulating two-lane blacktop taking me through the rolling tree-covered landscape of the Texas Hill Country, a tranquil and welcoming ground. The light softens, the wind calms, the air cools, an expectant stillness descends at sunset and night starts to come on. I end the day's drive in Fredericksburg, a historic small town of handsome limestone houses constructed by German settlers, rocking chairs set out on front porches, roofs made of tin.

I carry Texas BBQ with me from Fredericksburg the next day, the spicy aromas swirling inside the car on the short jaunt to the LBJ Ranch. I savor this picnic lunch at a great stone table sheltered from the sun by an old oak grove. Then I walk around the Lyndon Baines Johnson state and national historic site and receive a telling lesson in how presidents, even once-reviled presidents, are recast as heroes. I find this process intriguing because S. L. A. Marshall is having just the opposite happen to him. And yet Johnson biographer Robert Caro has recently been revealing that LBJ had concocted his World War II combat record and had stolen his first election to the U.S. Senate.

There is no hint of any such questionable business at this shrine to the thirty-sixth president. Nor is there any hint of the LBJ whom I remember from my days as a college student, this president who managed to play both buffoon and villain, picking up puppies by their ears, pulling up his shirt to reveal his surgery scar, sending more and more men my age off to Southeast Asia to fight and often to die while insisting, "We seek no wider war."

Vietnam is not remembered at this national historic site. Vietnam is given the total tape-erase here, out of sight and hopefully forgotten. The only hint that there might have been a war on when LBJ was president are two history books in the gift shop, lost amid shelves overflowing with LBJ cookbooks, Lady Bird wildflower volumes, and audio tapes that include "President Johnson Remembers: Dogs Have Always Been My Friends." The new, improved LBJ depicted here is a kind of presidential Will Rogers, a folksy sage of the Perdernales, yet undeniably a celebrity, host at the ranch to the likes of Gregory Peck and Billy Graham. A bronze statue of LBJ stands at the end of a nature trail, this likeness so approachable and so lifelike, except that this LBJ is eight feet tall, reinforcing the image of a man who towers over mere mortals.

I later pass through rush hour in Austin, drive sixty miles north to where my sister lives near Fort Hood. Shannon is ten years younger, an eight-year-old when I went off to college, and a stranger to me ever since. She seems of a different generation, untouched by the events of the 1960s that were such a crucible for me. What she was marked by is Marshall family life after I had gone off to Charlottesville—my father's subsequent transfer from Cleveland to St. Louis, the disintegration of our parents' marriage, our mother's subsequent breakdown and suicide, and the scattering of family members that followed.

Shannon grew up in this maelstrom, and her life afterward seems to me to have been an unbroken chain of misfortunes, chronic illness, economic hardship, single parenthood, all the hardest blows at the worst times. Now, she has multiple sclerosis, which turns a walk across the room into a test of her will. Shannon battles on, supported by her rock-ribbed Christian faith, membership in a small church, hours of Bible study and prayer, a large portrait of Jesus dominating the living room of her mobile home. I do not pretend to know how our beliefs have developed so differently, or how this life of continuing crisis has come to ensnare my little sister with the striking face, the bright eyes, the warm smile. What I do know is that Shannon's travails produce a swirl of emotions in me, empathy, inadequacy, sadness. I feel fortunate for having been the first born in our family, when love still filled the house; but also guilt about remaining apart once the troubles and the pain began to erupt.

"All I remember about you," my sister is reminding me, "is that you were gone."

It is after midnight now and we are seated on metal folding chairs on the wooden stoop outside Shannon's mobile home. The day's one-hundred-degree heat has finally started to dissipate; a light breeze drifts down the treeless hill from the domed expo center. We are drinking some wine. Every now and then, a vehicle enters the trailer park and we are caught in the glare of the headlights.

"When did it all begin to go wrong?" Shannon asks.

"I don't know," I reply. "Maybe after we moved to Cleveland. There did not seem to be the same sort of problems before that."

"You mean there was a time when our family life was normal?"

We have indeed grown up in different families with the same cast of characters, but playing out a different sort of family drama, maybe not from comedy to tragedy, but close. So Shannon and I fill in memory blanks for each other, telling about "what it was like when I was growing up," serving as best we can as family historians of that time the other does not recall. We seek lessons in this exercise, forewarnings of trouble. We voice a determination to do better with our own children—a difficult goal to achieve at times, we admit, but definitely there. Our conversation forges a new bond in the hot Texas night, sister and brother, both parents now.

In the morning, we talk of Poppy and Cate. Shannon has many fond memories and says she found them supportive and helpful. I listen to what Shannon says, not mentioning my grave doubts about the role they played in convincing her to enlist in the Army. She appears to have been a victim of the traditional notion that putting someone with problems into the military will, in some way, "straighten them out." In Shannon's case, just the opposite occurred. Her problems intensified, leading to a disability discharge, and there were even worse problems after that, with Veterans Administration Hospitals seldom providing any cure, especially in initial attempts.

Shannon brings forth a small memento that Cate had given her after Poppy's death. It is a leather-bound copy of the *Rubaiyat of Omar Khayyam*, printed in England and now stiff with age. Inside the cover is a drawing of a pennant that bears the letters for El Paso High School, plus the signatures of six classmates there, the last one being "Samuel L.A. Marshall."

This inscription provides another rebuke for *American Heritage* and its flawed research. For the magazine had made an issue of Marshall's adoption of the middle name of Atwood, citing it as another of the man's calculated ploys. The *Omar Khayyam* shows instead that "Slam" was a high-school boy's invention, a trivial matter, except during this controversy.

Shannon and I are discussing this on what has not been one of her better mornings. She is not feeling well, as usual. And the neighbors' dog has chewed up her Sunday paper, scattering newsprint around the area, although the neighbors are not asking to use her phone as they often do, these people who consider cable television to be an essential utility in their trailer, but not a telephone.

"I don't know how you deal with all this stuff," I say, as I prepare to leave. "It would drive me crazy."

"I guess I'm used to it," Shannon replies. "And my faith is a great help too."

"That may be so, but I still admire the way you handle all this, the frustrations, the disappointments. And I admire the life you've made here for you and Sean. He's a great young guy, who obviously loves his mother very much. I know it certainly can't be easy, but I think you've done one heck of a job as a parent. I am impressed, very impressed."

"Thanks," Shannon says. "That means a lot to me."

The drive to Houston is only two hundred miles but seems to take a long time, the landscape now southern not western, flattened out, domesticated, no longer a place for cowboy boots, instead forests with a defined edge, some farms, small towns. I drive by churches with parking lots overflowing, some Baptist churches with black congregations, little children walking carefully in their Sunday clothes, roadside portrait of the innocence of youth.

In Houston, I am meeting with Frank Vandiver, historian, writer, former president of Texas A. & M. University, and acquaintance of S. L. A. Marshall. I have questions about his view of Marshall, the value of his work, and especially its accuracy. I am troubled by the comments of Clay Blair, a one-time *Time-Life* journalist, whose assessment had prompted one of my questions to Lucian Truscott III. I have corresponded with Blair, who never met S. L. A. Marshall but has definite opinions of his work. "I have frequently drawn on Marshall's work for my own books, and am most grateful that his work exists," Blair wrote. "But, I believe, all his books have to be used with care. The ones I have used lack the precision and accuracy expected of and required for good military history. This is not to say that any are intentionally or unintentionally fraudulent (as are so many military histories) or that he faked in any way, but rather that they are on the whole somewhat sloppy."

I had recalled Blair's comment during my research in El Paso and had found two letters of Marshall's that seemed to speak directly to his complaint. Both letters were written at the time of *The River and the Gauntlet* (1953) when Marshall was informed of an error in the book that Blair had said is "notorious" for its mistakes.

Marshall wrote in one letter: "Some months ago I had to consider the problem whether I wanted to write a perfect book or was more interested in getting this work out at a time when it would attract public attention. I then decided that I would have to compromise and I am sure that the decision was a correct one. Had I slowed up publication by even three months to give exhaustive attention to detail of which I was not completely certain, then the book would have been published after the truce and would have landed with a dull thud. That's just the way things go."

In the other letter, Marshall wrote: "As La Guardia used to say, 'When I make a mistake, it's a beaut.' I also made another artillery bobble in describing the movement by which the 17th got back across the river. The odd part of it is that when I was writing that part, it didn't seem to me that it was hanging together properly and yet, going back over it, I couldn't figure out where I had gone wrong. Fortunately, I don't sweat out these things very long after they have happened as I became aware a long time ago that it is simply impossible to do a story of battle without making some errors. So long as the balance is about ninety percent to the good, that's as much as anyone who has my limits can expect to score."

I find Marshall's candor refreshing, his admission of mistakes so different from *American Heritage*'s stonewalling when I had tried to get the editors to correct errors. Yet I am a journalist, not a historian, and maybe Marshall's goal of 90 percent accuracy will seem grossly inadequate to Frank Vandiver, as I am about to discover.

I meet Vandiver at Tony's, a Houston institution where he and his wife are having dinner with their daughter to celebrate her birthday. This is indeed a tony restaurant, with dark paneling and plush wallpaper, a place that seems less air-conditioned than class-conditioned, the natural habitat of Houston's moneyed elite.

I follow Vandiver into the bar and find I am in the presence of a man of great exuberance. Vandiver may wear an impeccably tailored suit, but he comes across as James Whitmore playing Truman in *Give 'em Hell, Harry*, some of those same Whitmore features, the shock of hair, the aging country boy features, the bluntness of a mule skinner. One does not interview Vandiver, the ritual thrust and parry. I present a hint of a question and Vandiver lets 'er rip.

"I met Marshall once and he always struck me as sort of a model," Vandiver says. "There was Douglas Southall Freeman doing his history of Robert E. Lee and there was Slam Marshall doing his history of World War II. I encountered him in the Office of Strategic Services, I think, and he was telling me how important it was for historians to go with the troops and get into that experience. They should land with the first wave, he told me, and it seemed idiocy to me at first. Then, I saw it was the only way. To me, Slam Marshall was a model of how contemporary military history ought to be done."

"But there have been questions raised about the accuracy of his work," I inject. "And I found a letter where Marshall says he works fast and figures that if he gets 90 percent of what he's writing right, then he figures he's doing a good job. As a historian, do you find that 90 percent figure shocking?"

"If it was but 50 percent, he was way ahead of the game," Vandiver replies. "The fact that Marshall says he was not 100 percent right shows he understood the situation, and how difficult it was. I am a historian of the Civil War, and of General Pershing, and I think the important thing—what I look for—is what was a historian's attitude toward history. Is it a cowboy-Indian rah-rah affair? Not with Slam Marshall. With him, it was a serious business. And he was pretty damn good."

"Then what was your reaction to the article on him in *American Heritage?*" I ask.

"It pissed me off," Vandiver snaps. "To me, it was nitpicking."

"I've had it described to me as 'character assassination.'"

"I'm glad somebody was honest."

"But there still remains the matter of Marshall stretching the truth about his own war service," I add, "puffing up his own experiences."

"It is quite understandable that he would reminisce that way," Vandiver says. "One thing you have to realize is how historians talk about actions of others versus their own. When I'm talking of others, I try to be damn careful. When I talk about myself, I want to inflate the story."

I leave the next morning for New Orleans, after making one stop on my way out of Houston. I search through a nondescript neighborhood on the fringe of downtown until I find the Mark Rothko Chapel. Inside this simple building, an octagon of tan brick, are fourteen huge canvasses by the abstract expressionist, all created for this space. These austere canvasses are a somber tour across the dark end of the palette, subtle shadings of maroons and purples and charcoals, verging toward black but still illuminated by hope. Rothko's own spiritual struggle is written in these paintings, completed a few years before he ended his life. I stand alone inside this contemplative place, then pause outside beside Barnett Newman's *Broken Obelisk,* a monument of shattered promise dedicated to the memory of Dr. Martin Luther King, Jr.

I return to the road with reluctance, the freeway now a jarring clamor. I make my way across eighty miles of Texas until I cross the Sabine River and enter Louisiana. The highway rides stilts above eddies of murky water and the vegetation is lush and menacing. Road signs soon recite poetry: Chloe, Evangeline, Lafayette. A truck stop lures travelers with tigers in a cage.

A storm has just passed when I finally reach New Orleans in the evening. I exit the Interstate on the edge of the city and the streets are still slick with rainwater, the night air as dense as a steam bath. I open the car windows and think I can smell the sweet perfume of magnolias, mixed with the pungent odors of the Mississippi.

The street lights are dim, only a hint of what they are in most places, and that makes the teeming activity on the sidewalks seem even more frantic, almost foreign. Many streets offer no clue to their names, as if this were insider knowledge.

I am relieved to have college friends here, Bobby and Alex Miles, both New Orleans natives. They welcome me with a traditional dinner of red beans and rice. There is much at the Miles' that reminds me of our place back in Seattle, the older home in an older section of town, the wood floors, throw rugs, art crowding the walls, a packed bookcase taking up one wall of the living room. The talk at dinner is of college days, old friends, what has happened to everyone in the passing years.

I am given the keys to the condominium of Bobby's parents, a vast space with a view of the Mississippi. I pour a glass of wine to celebrate my good fortune, then turn on the television and San Francisco is in flames, San Francisco is in ruin from a monster earthquake. I cannot pull myself away from the ghastly images of this place of many fond memories, where I spent one glorious August on a fellowship at Berkeley, where I took Anne on a surprise weekend to celebrate the first anniversary of our engagement.

My depression grows with each new report, collapsing freeways, severed bridges, people buried alive. I call Anne late at night, fumbling for words about the earthquake threat to Seattle, and how precarious this makes our lives seem.

"I know," she says. "I've been thinking the same thing."

Over the next few days, I turn the floor of the condominium into a sea of paper, spreading out all the research materials I have gathered. I go through hundreds of pages, note questions about my grandfather that remain to be answered, other people I need to see.

Foremost among them is Gen. William C. Westmoreland. I have questions for him about what he thought of my grandfather, and what the two of them discussed during his visits to Vietnam. Col. David Hackworth has raised an important question about Marshall's work in Vietnam, something only Westmoreland can answer. Yet I have sent him two packets of materials, along with a request for a brief appointment, and have received no response. So I decide to call Westmoreland from New Orleans, although I would rather not since it is easy to say "no" to a stranger on the telephone. My reticence is heightened by wondering whether what my father told me in El Paso is true—that Westmoreland had ordered an examination of my impending discharge from the Army as a conscientious objector.

I call anyway. I really have no choice. In a week, I expect to be in South Carolina, where Westmoreland lives.

I make one call, then another, and suddenly I am talking to Westmoreland, his voice icy, his mood impatient. And it is apparent that the general has not read the material I sent and has only slight acquaintance with the Marshall controversy. I try to provide an instant summary, and who I am, but I have spoken only a few sentences when Westmoreland interrupts.

"Weren't you a draft resister who went to Canada?"

"No," I reply, startled. "I was a conscientious objector who received an honorable discharge from the Army."

There is silence on the line. My mind searches for something to add, then I say, "You know, under the process set forth in regulations."

Silence again.

"Well," the general finally says, "would you still be a conscientious objector today?"

"I don't know. Nobody has asked me that recently."

I can feel the chance to interview Westmoreland slipping away with every word that comes out of my mouth. And I do not like what I am saying, all in hopes of gaining access to Westmoreland.

The general will not let the matter drop: "Do you still believe those same things you did back then?"

"I probably do believe many of the same things."

More silence.

"If the U.S. declared war on Russia tomorrow," Westmoreland asks, "would you fight?"

"I'm too old!" I snap in frustration. "And what I want to talk to you about is not what I did, but what my grandfather did during Vietnam. That's why I need your help."

This, thankfully, turns the conversation away from me and toward my grandfather. I trot out every possible rationale I can for Westmoreland to meet with me—the Hackworth charges only he can answer, how little of his time I need. Westmoreland seems swayed, but not much.

"I'll call you when I get to Charleston," I finally say.

"Oh all right," Westmoreland responds.

10

Return to Victory Drive

THIS IS NO PLACE I ever wanted to revisit. When I last left Fort Benning, Georgia, it was with an immense sense of relief. I hated this place, this "Home of the Infantry." I counted the days until I could say farewell forever to Fort Benning.

But now I am back in the morning rush-hour traffic heading up Victory Drive in Columbus, past the pawn shops, the topless dance clubs, the well-worn motel rooms that have served thousands of soldiers. And then I pass a giant billboard with an American flag and the words: "Love It or Leave It!"

This is beyond déjà vu. This is altogether too strange. Here I am again in the tenth month of the ninth year of a decade, and I am in another two-door blue car entering Fort Benning, and I am filled with uncertainty about just what this experience will entail. My unease only intensifies when I park the car and Airborne troops are marching toward the parachute towers, shouting cadence with various chants, while loudspeakers atop Infantry Hall blare martial music.

And I recall what it had been like to come to Fort Benning in 1969, how foreign and forbidding this Army world had been, my first step on the treadmill that seemed to lead inevitably to Vietnam. "The Infantry School provided a rude awakening from the vagaries of ROTC," I had written in my conscientious objector application. "And I started to have growing doubts as to whether I could allow myself to function as an Infantry officer. Something seemed wrong to me, a chord inside me had been struck.

"I objected to all the emphasis on more efficient ways to kill—

106

an instructor holding up two water buckets and pointing out what a better job of tearing the metal apart an M-16 [rifle] round does than an M-14 round. I disliked handling weapons. I found the aggressiveness required for hand-to-hand combat training totally foreign to my character. The long parade fields of hundreds, maybe a thousand, soldiers in synchronized bayonet training, yelling 'Kill, Kill!' at the top of their lungs—this I just could not accept. And when a classroom battlefield-situation problem emphasized that if a man started fleeing to the rear, it would be my duty as platoon leader to shoot him (with the hope that he would only be wounded) in order not to jeopardize the mission, this I knew I could not do. Whatever the mission, I could not see myself acting as a life-and-death decider and shooting one of my own men."

Now, I am back in a classroom in the mammoth Infantry Hall again, amid a crowd of freshly minted second lieutenants, and I feel as though I have never left. The lecture hall looks unchanged, with broad risers stepping down to the stage, six lieutenants seated around each table covered with pale green linoleum, cinderblock walls painted the color of urine, faded blue drapes surrounding the stage and that perennial star of the Army educational system—the screen for the overhead projector.

This is a class in leadership being taught to the Army's newest junior leaders, with the instruction provided by Maj. Harry Christiansen, a thirty-seven-year-old officer who has been teaching at the Infantry School for two years. Each table of lieutenants has been grappling to "define what a group is, in the military." Their responses have been jotted on a blackboard by Christiansen until that magic moment when he plops a slide into the overhead projector and the Army's own definition appears on the screen, displayed there long enough for some lieutenants to copy it down in their notebooks.

I am trying to fight off drooping eyelids, but not these eighty-four lieutenants. Part of their responsiveness is the result of Christiansen's teaching style, hard-charging and tough-talking ("kick some ass" is a favorite phrase). And the lean-and-mean major also happens to be that most feared form of lecturer, The Roamer, who moves about the hall with the threat that he may call on any student at any moment. Still, these lieutenants do seem resolutely enthusiastic, raising their hands at the slightest prompting, greeting each reference to the Army's hard-core Ranger training or combat itself with that now-popular expression of Army gung ho, a low growl that goes, "HOOOOOO—AAA!!!!!!!"

What a difference it makes when there is no war on, I think to myself. To these lieutenants, recent combat is the 1983 invasion of Grenada, a short little strike against a tiny nation where the outcome was money-back guaranteed. To the lieutenants in my class, recent combat was last night's TV news, the graphic behind Walter Cronkite tallying the weekly body count. We lieutenants knew that, six months after Benning, we could be leading a platoon of troops in Vietnam. That likelihood shadowed us wherever we went, from calisthenics in the crisp Georgia dawn to midnight thoughts on the pillow.

The Army even played on these thoughts, using Vietnam as a gambit. "Voluntary indefinite status" was dangled in front of us, with the promise that volunteering for an extra year of service (a three-year commitment) guaranteed the choice of a specialized school after Benning and also choice of an initial tour someplace before Vietnam. "Voluntary indefinite status" seemed about as "voluntary" as signing something with an AK-47 rifle pointed at one's head. But it was "indefinite" in the same way the war was, a calculated gamble that this new "Vietnamization" of the war might work, thus reducing the need for more American Infantry lieutenants in the meat grinder.

This was not any heroic way to approach the service of the country, I recognized when I opted to go "vol indef." But the time for heroism in Vietnam was past. The first American troops were being withdrawn from the war when I arrived at Benning and those still being sent were part of a holding action that would ultimately waste another twenty thousand American lives in pursuit of that obscene pretense called "Peace with Honor."

We lieutenants could not know that back then. But we knew the rush was still on to produce more Infantry lieutenants for Vietnam. And so we had only nine weeks to go from college students to leaders of combat troops, nine short weeks. These 1989 lieutenants instead have sixteen weeks of training at Benning. What a terrible irony—better-prepared Infantry officers being turned out when there is no war. How many fewer names might be on the Wall in Washington if Infantry lieutenants had had sixteen weeks of training during Vietnam.

A break in class is soon called. Most of the lieutenants file out of the lecture hall for coffee and doughnuts, but one comes over to me and asks why I am visiting an Infantry officer class. He is John Hart, a twenty-three-year-old lieutenant with a distinctly bookish demeanor. Hart, by the longest of long shots, turns out to be a fellow graduate of the University of Virginia's ROTC program. We chat about our times in Charlottesville and at Benning, and Hart tells me that he is the son of a career Infantry officer, the brother of a West Pointer, and he himself is a Distinguished Military Graduate of Virginia ROTC. But the life of an Infantry officer has not proved to be of Hart's liking, despite all his years of modeling himself on officers like his father. So Hart has availed himself of an option never available to the lieutenants in my class; he has decided to spend eight years instead in the National Guard.

"What was the reaction of your family?" I ask. "What did they do when you told them you were going into the National Guard instead of the Regular Army?"

"There was a sense of surprise, but my family was supportive of my decision to go into the National Guard. The Army and I are just not that well suited together."

I think back to my own class at Benning and how many of us might have loved to have had some option because "the Army and I are just not that well suited together." There was no chance of that when the war was on. Which leads me to ask Hart about what he and his classmates know about Vietnam, ancient history for these young officers.

"We have all read books on Vietnam, books like *Platoon Leader*, and we have seen the movies," Hart says. "The crazy thing about Vietnam was that it went on so long and was so different. People do talk about it. My personal feeling—and I have a liberal girlfriend who wonders why there is not a monument in Washington to those who went to Canada—my personal feeling is there were so many elements to that war that a lot of people were deceived into thinking they knew what it was about and what was happening. There was the Infantry perspective, the foreign affairs perspective, the liberal arts perspective. There were lots of perspectives on that war."

"There sure were," I agree.

Class resumes, with Major Christiansen back on the group dy-namics beat, explaining how people always fit into such roles as "information giver," "information seeker" and "harmonizer." The lec-ture finally turns toward something concrete when Christiansen mentions Lt. William Calley and promises an upcoming class will address "what Calley didn't do and what he should have done in the My Lai massacre."

Again, I am startled by how things have changed in this Army today. The story of the My Lai massacre had broken in a blaze of headlines when my class was at Benning and Lt. Calley himself was staying here in the Bachelor Officers' Quarters, which caused the post to be invaded by an army of reporters and photographers. Calley and My Lai were all that anybody at Benning was talking about those days, especially after the photographs were published showing the carnage at that village, and all the result of what was supposed to have been an American military operation. We lieutenants went to our classes, many of them taught by veterans of Vietnam, and we were hungry to hear some explanation of how such a horror could have happened, what dark forces might have been at work on these infantrymen, things we might not know about yet. Instead, our instruc-tors talked little about My Lai and about all they said was they had never heard of any such thing happening while they were in Vietnam, not even a whisper. It just could not happen, they assured us.

Now, Lt. Calley and My Lai are part of the curriculum at the Infantry School and I am disappointed that I will miss the discussion. For I would really like to hear how My Lai is explained, whether the Army now contends, as General Westmoreland does in his auto-biography, that the blame for the massacre rests on all those college students with draft deferments who forced the Army to deploy losers like Calley as officers. Or would the Army somehow acknowledge, as I would assert, that tragedies like My Lai were the inevitable result of a war where battlefield triumphs were measured by the number of people killed, victory through body count.

I leave the classroom and walk down the long central corridor to where my graduation from the Infantry School took place, the vast auditorium named in honor of General George Catlett Marshall, that legendary American leader who had once sent me an inscribed

phtograph of himself, at the request of my grandfather. Lights illumi-
nate the stage, and my thoughts drift back to the ceremony when my
grandfather had served as the main speaker, just as he had during my
Virginia commissioning. I cannot remember what he said at Benning, although I recall it was similar to his speech at Virginia, but I
do remember visiting him the night before in his spacious guest quarters. I watched him being interviewed by a TV correspondent, then
we chatted afterward. I was mainly complaining about this martinet
major who was enforcing a mustache regulation that limited facial
hair to no wider than one-sixteenth of an inch, or so he insisted.

Such a mustache was about three hairs wide and I was locked in
a stupid test of wills with the major. He threatened I would not
graduate if I did not chop my mustache down to size, even if my
grandfather was delivering the graduation speech. This was my first
clash with a by-the-book military asshole and I was incensed.

My grandfather listened patiently, allowing as how he had
known a few officers of this stripe and they were not something to
emulate. But he made it clear that it was my decision on what course
to follow. He would not get involved, my grandfather said.

I shaved off my mustache the next morning. I had taken my
challenge as far as I could, and I did not want to embarrass my
grandfather. So I joined the graduates of the Infantry School, a lieutenant with a clean-shaven lip who had supposedly been taught
something about following regulations. What I had learned was a
different lesson—how small minds can be obsessed with small
matters.

This afternoon sees me back out in the Fort Benning "boonies,"
these forests of pine that I once knew so well. I hear the familiar
whoosh of the wind through the tops of these trees and the sound of
gunfire in the distance. I feel the warmth of the southern sun on my
neck. And I recall how fresh these forests smell after a rain shower,
how frosty they get on a November morning, how dark they are at
4:00 A.M. when light seems as though it will never return. Days and
nights in these Georgia woods taught me many things.

Now, a new group of Infantry lieutenants is about to learn.
They sit sprawled on the ground, their faces covered with camouflage
grease, packs at their sides and black M-16 rifles, their last hot meal
almost finished.

Maj. Dennis Boucher tells me, "This is their first week-long field exercise, with their first full-blown opposing force. It is a Latin American scenario, a low-intensity conflict. They'll be moving on patrol through the night and sticking close to their patrol bases in the daytime."

Boucher will oversee this exercise, while Capt. Don Dietz will stay with this platoon of lieutenants, teaching and critiquing. These two officers are a Mutt-and-Jeff odd couple—Boucher, tall and thin, a studious-looking Clark Kent type, and Dietz, short and scrappy, a hard-muscled, hard-mannered captain who looks as though he stepped off a recruiting poster.

This group of lieutenants is three-quarters of the way through Benning, much further along than the lieutenants I have watched in class this morning. The difference shows. These lieutenants have replaced "HOOOOOO—AAA" with a quiet-spoken purposefulness, tinged with sardonic humor about the lieutenant's lot ("We've got a nineteen-second life span," quips one. "That's why we're getting paid so much," adds another, referring to their monthly salary of $1,789). These lieutenants also display a cohesiveness from weeks spent together, the friendships formed, and the growing self-confidence about mastering the challenges of Benning.

But that does not come easy, as the start of the exercise shows. They are practicing the most basic sort of infantry maneuver, a road crossing, in which security is set out on the flanks and the men sprint across the road in pairs. But proper distances are hard to maintain, the men bunch up. And when they cross the road, they are no quieter than a pack of Cub Scouts.

"Before we move out tonight, it's the big time," barks Dietz. "You've got to get things taped up, get into the silent mode."

Back and forth, the lieutenants go across the road, each crossing some improvement, but the lieutenants still much too easy a target. A harsh critique by Dietz follows, then he peppers the group with questions that seem to come from some Army version of Trivial Pursuit, esoteric stuff like "What is the Soviet theory on parallel indirect fire, hub to hub?" The lieutenants answer his questions with ease.

Dietz then calls on one lieutenant who must deliver a twenty-minute class on reconnaissance patrolling. The lieutenant steps up and lectures without hesitation. Again, I find I am impressed with these lieutenants' preparedness, such a marked contrast from my own class, where many merely went through the motions. I am moved to ask Major Boucher how these lieutenants compare with his own class at the Infantry School.

"They're better than we were, I hate to admit," Boucher says. "They're more articulate, better read, they knew more when they got here than we did. The Army did a better job before they arrived at Benning, whether they're from the two-thirds of this class who went through ROTC, or the one-third who went through West Point."

A break gives me a chance to talk with some of the lieutenants. I tell them that I went through this course "way back in 1969" and how I am now traveling around the country trying to find out what I can about my grandfather, S. L. A. Marshall. Two lieutenants immediately say that they have read Men Against Fire. Then I ask the lieutenants what has drawn them to the Army, and especially the Infantry, and they all talk about how much responsibility they will have as young officers and what challenges, so different from civilian life after college.

And I ask the lieutenants about Vietnam, what they know about the war, how they analyze what happened to American forces there, why the war was lost.

Robert Balcavage, a twenty-four-year-old West Pointer, is the first to speak: "I've probably read thirty books on Vietnam, and each has something different. And I talk to guys who've been to Vietnam whenever I can; they're a source of good knowledge. The thing I hear is people feel that the Army's hands were tied in Vietnam."

"What they teach us, more than the grand defeat," adds Jim Boehl, "is that social factors—and maybe rightly so—led to bringing the Army back before its mission was accomplished."

"We're obviously a generation away from Vietnam now, so we can examine what happened," adds Brian Coppersmith. "And it's clear that we screwed up in Vietnam. It was a bad undertaking."

Joseph Bolton concurs: "It was a micro-managed war, with LBJ practically acting as a field commander, making decisions about operations a world away. That almost destroyed the Army. And there were political constraints. And the Tet Offensive led to a retreat that destroyed morale in the Army, led many to drugs. We never should have gotten involved in Vietnam, if we had played our cards right."

"But," I inject, "Do you guys think you could do any better in a situation like Vietnam? Could you avoid the same mistakes?

"I do wonder about that," replies Coppersmith. "Not a lot has changed, although we're a better Army now."

"The Army was not given a clear mission in Vietnam," says Bolton, a twenty-five-year-old West Pointer.

"But, in a sad way," continues Coppersmith. "Vietnam was the best thing that could have happened to this country. Because of Vietnam, we have not gotten embroiled in any more petty regional actions. But if the same decision were made on Central America, there is not a lot to be done to make it a different situation."

Many of the lieutenants nod in agreement. Bolton supplies a coda to the discussion, a lieutenant's sort of coda: "I'd just do my job."

I think about these lieutenants a great deal during dinner. I did not know what I would find at Fort Benning, or what I would feel. But I did not anticipate being so impressed with the lieutenants going through the Infantry School. After I became a conscientious objector, I viewed the military with suspicion and even derision for years, much as many people in the country did then. I listened to the military's growing chorus of excuses about Vietnam, all their bullshit about how the war could have been won if only the civilians had not gotten in the way, even though civilian control of the military has always been a tenet of American government. And I listened to the crowing from the military about successes in Libya and Grenada, as if these triumphs against two-bit powers were any redemption for the debacle in Vietnam. I did not buy it. I had been in the military. I knew the military traditions of buck-passing and ass-covering.

But I also had not spent much time with people in the armed forces in the passing years. I was content to cast my scorn on the military from afar, that easy stance. Visiting the lieutenants at Benning is causing me to reexamine my own position on the military, just as General Westmoreland's surprise question has made me ponder whether I am still a conscientious objector. I have thought about that over the last few days. The last two decades have provided nothing to convince me of the value of violence among nations. Wars after Vietnam seemed no better, no matter the combatants or the cause. War is still humanity's worst failing. I remain a conscientious objector, I have concluded, and probably always will be.

But how should I view the military and those who choose to wear its uniforms? As fools? As dupes? As the enemy? I am starting to think not. Their way is not my way, but that does not mean some stigma should be attached to either set of beliefs. I have felt respect for these lieutenants at Benning, their dedication, their reasoned approach to their work. If there are to be armies, then these are the kind of young leaders that armies should have.

This could be the basis for a new perspective on my grandfather's work as well, it begins to dawn on me. Maybe this is how I can reconcile myself to what he did with his life, all his efforts to bring about a better Army, the books, the articles, the speeches, the missions to those combat zones, a lifetime devoted to war.

Because the lieutenants are also reminding me of how I came to terms with something I had done at Benning, what I once saw as "my role in the war." After graduation, I had stayed at Benning on temporary duty and, at my suggestion, wrote an evaluation of the Infantry Officer Basic Course. I had produced a twenty-six-page report, much of it critical. I found particular fault with how little time we lieutenants spent in tactical exercises in the field (just six days in nine weeks), how poorly we were evaluated (90 percent of our grade came from multiple-choice tests), and how few of us in a class of two hundred officers had a chance to perform in demanding leadership positions.

"It is entirely possible," I wrote, "for a graduate of IOBC to face his first platoon of troops, never having stood out in front of a platoon before in his life. Incredible as this statement may sound, unfortunately, it is all too true. Probably two out of three members of my IOBC company never had a leadership position above squad leader in the duration of the course."

Before setting out nineteen specific recommendations to improve the course, I also emphasized: "IOBC should act to weed out those officers who should not be entrusted with the lives of a platoon of men, those officers who would do far better for themselves and the Army if they were not in a combat branch. As composed now, the IOBC grading system does no such thing; rather, it passes the buck to stateside units or units in Vietnam and allows them to make this regrettable discovery. There are probably at least ten such lieuten-ants in every IOBC class and it seems a crime that they and the Army should be made to suffer an error in branch selection until it is possibly too late."

I felt pride when I received letters about my evaluation from two of the top officers at Fort Benning. I had written the evaluation for the Leadership Department; its director, Col. John Hoefling, wrote, "I can assure you necessary changes will be made. Colonel Car-ley, our director of instruction, has given it his personal attention and General Berry will see it. I have already made the changes you sug-gested in Leadership." The letter from Brig. Gen. Sidney B. Berry, the assistant commandant, included: "You made a number of excellent points. Your comments on platoon evaluators and Vietnam instruction were particularly thought-provoking. Your ideas should favorably influ-ence the Infantry Officer Basic Course program of instruction."

I wrote a shorter version of my evaluation for *Infantry* magazine. And when that article was published—in an issue that also con-tained articles by both my grandfather and by Hackworth—there was an editor's note explaining that some "quick fixes" to IOBC had been made because of my evaluation.

This was heady stuff for a twenty-two-year-old second lieuten-ant just starting out in the Army. But by the time I was a first lieu-tenant, I was having second thoughts. Then I was in the period of study and self-evaluation for my C.O. application and I wondered if my evaluation at Benning and the changes it wrought had helped unleash more efficient killers in Vietnam. Really. Becoming a C.O. was such an intense, inward process that I pondered matters which now seem unreal.

What I finally decided about my IOBC evaluation was that it had probably helped save lives, not end them. Better-trained lieuten-ants were likely to be more cautious lieutenants. Such officers would make sure their men's lives were not squandered in John Wayne combat theatrics, or through bumbling on the battlefield, both ghastly sins. This is, it now occurs to me, what my grandfather also worked to accomplish on a far grander scale.

My grandfather is my main focus the next morning as I make several stops before leaving Fort Benning. I want to find out what impact the Marshall controversy has had at this citadel of the Infantry, this place that one local guidebook describes as "the world's most influential military center." Here is where Marshall's work often received the most serious consideration and here is where the controversy may have most tarnished his reputation.

I meet with Albert Garland, a brusque retired lieutenant colonel who is the editor of *Infantry* magazine. Garland, I have been told, is a Marshall critic and almost the first words out of his mouth after our handshake are "I am not a Marshall man." But Garland's dispute with Marshall seems based not so much on criticism of his work as on professional jealousy. "I always thought 'who the hell is this guy, Marshall?'" Garland snaps. "They always rolled out the red carpet for him at Benning. It was like he was Jesus Christ with the goddamned Gospel— that's the way the Army reacted to your grandfather."

"Why do you think that was?"

"He was kind to the Army, kind to the hierarchy," Garland replies. "I do not remember him writing anything derogatory. For some reason, he was kind to the Army when the Army needed friends. He did a noble service for the Army that way. But I just flat resented him—this is a guy who I thought was telling me how to run my own company. As a peon, I could never understand Slam's influence. I was against Slam from the beginning."

"But what are your thoughts about this controversy and especially the criticism of *Men Against Fire?*"

"Slam extrapolated a few conversations into an overall picture, which is why I do not accept him from a historical perspective," says Garland. "Whether he was right or wrong about what he wrote about firing problems—I won't argue. I don't think you can prove it or disprove it. But I'm not about to play with it. I just flat don't know."

"Do many other officers share your views?"

"We critics of Marshall were in the minority when he was alive and we still are. Most senior officers are still Slam supporters. My camp is the minority camp."

I also meet with Lt. Col. Russell Eno, who is head of the communicative skills department at Fort Benning, a position akin to chairman of the humanities department. Eno oversees the teaching of English and military history to all students in the Infantry School, courses for sergeants through captains. His slight build and wire-rimmed glasses give him the look of a small-town accountant, despite the Combat Infantryman's Badge on his uniform earned during his tour as an advisor to the Vietnamese Army. Chamber music plays softly while Eno and I talk in his office, the place crowded with pictures and mementos from Germany, reflecting his academic roots as a German major.

Eno wastes no time in emphasizing that S. L. A. Marshall's work continues to be read and discussed at the Infantry School. He brings out a report written by a captain on the Battle of the Bulge where Marshall's work is cited prominently. He also pulls out a slide for classroom use with a quote of Marshall's: "Battles are won through the ability of men to express concrete ideas in unmistakable language. All administration is carried forward along the chain of command by the power of men to make their thoughts articulate and available to others."

I ask Eno if the controversy has led to a reconsideration of Marshall's work at Fort Benning.

"We don't distrust everything Slam has written," he says. "Nor, for that matter, do we accept it at face value. Nobody will destroy his reputation because of this controversy. All soldiers and officers still need to go ahead and read Slam's books. If people say his books are bogus because of this, they will miss important points. He always had expertise."

"Then you really do not see his reputation slipping?"

"I think S. L. A. Marshall's work has sufficient merit to be around here for a long time. Is it all 100 percent accurate? Who knows. But it is meaningful. S. L. A. Marshall was held in very, very high esteem here. It's healthy, I think, for him to be seen as a human being. But the pendulum has unquestionably swung to the other side. Now, it's probably coming back again."

I make one last stop at the Infantry School. I walk into the library on the main floor of Infantry Hall. I go to the card catalog, where, to my utter surprise, I find a card listing my own article in *Infantry*. Then, I move on to what I am seeking here, the cards with S. L. A. Marshall's name, sixty-four cards in all, from *Ambush* through *World War I, The American Heritage History of,* books, articles, critiques, commentaries, even a poem on infantrymen.

I go to the stacks where many of S. L. A. Marshall's books are kept in multiple copies. And I head upstairs where separate bookshelves contain the "U.S. Army Infantry School Recommended

S. L. A. Marshall talking with three officers in Vietnam, 1966. Courtesy S. L. A. Marshall Military History Collection, University of Texas at El Paso.

Reading List." I find S. L. A. Marshall's *Night Drop* on these shelves, *Pork Chop Hill*, *The Soldier's Load*, *The River and the Gauntlet* and his suddenly-controversial *Men Against Fire*, forty-four well-worn copies of *Men Against Fire*, more copies of *Men Against Fire* than any other book on the recommended reading shelves.

I have what I need here by now. I walk out of the library, out of the Infantry School one last time, past the mammoth statue of the combat leader out front, his right arm motioning his men forward, his mouth frozen in the Infantry motto of "Follow Me!" And as I leave, I think back to one of the other things that Eno had said, his words echoing in my ears: "If S. L. A. Marshall's work were not being used here, there would not be so many copies of his books in our library. If there was any backlash against him at the Infantry School based on the controversy, those books would be gone."

11

A Protégé's Allegations

OR THREE STATES the landscape has been unchanged. There
have been pine forests, rolling hills, red dirt, car dealerships
owned by guys with first names like Bubba. Billboards have carried messages with conservative fervor ("In case of nuclear attack,
the ban on school prayer will be lifted" or "A Lawman, Plain and
Simple, Joe Price for Sheriff"). This is the Old South, comfortable,
slow-paced, poor. And then Atlanta's brash skyline appears in the
distance, like some apparition from another world.

Atlanta reminds me of Seattle and I feel a twinge of homesickness as its skyscrapers fill the windshield. Both cities are the same
size and share the same preeminence in their region. They are the
magnet cities of the Southeast and the Northwest, these opposite
corners of the country, both the big success, cities trying to sell
themselves as "world class." So newcomers flood into Atlanta and
Seattle, people searching for new starts in the next great place, their
arrival transforming the city they had sought, with more traffic,
higher prices, suburbs stretching far into the countryside, and something inevitably lost.

I hurry through Atlanta, late for my appointment. I cruise past
where I am supposed to turn, then have to backtrack until I find a
once-posh residential neighborhood now invaded by corporate complexes of mirrored glass. I head up the steep driveway, past the
stately old oaks, to the sprawling brick house where reside the aging
retired general and his wife. Their black maid shows me into the
television room at the back of the house where they sit. I bend down

120

to shake the frail hand of Maj. Gen. Joseph Harper, do the same with his wife, Maria, then take a seat and pull out my questions, although I already sense that they will be of no use.

They had been such good friends with my grandfather, the Harpers had told me over the phone. They had been house guests in each other's homes, exchanged calls and letters, including one I had discovered in El Paso, a 1955 letter from my grandfather who had written Harper: "Your visit to our home was a refreshing delight to the entire family. Among all our national VIPs, you have the most highly developed talent for behaving like a normal human being. This is the quality in you which makes your many friends cherish you so warmly."

Now, General Harper, is repaying the favor, saying, "I considered Sam Marshall one of my best friends; he was just the finest guy. I admire him tremendously. I never heard any criticism of him."

My attempts to probe beyond platitudes prove fruitless. I hear a few war stories and much detail about the Harper's serious health problems. For the first time, I am face-to-face with what I had always feared this trip might become—encounters with elderly people trying to dredge up recollections of Sam Marshall from failing memories.

But the Harpers, both eighty-eight, are cheery hosts and animated talkers who seem excited by this visit of their old friend's grandson. So I play the listener for an hour, and offer thanks when General Harper spends many minutes scrawling an inscription in the history of the regiment he commanded in World War II, a glider Infantry regiment of the fabled 101st Airborne Division.

The book is called *Sky Riders,* and it contains many photographs of then-Colonel Harper and his men during some of the war's most brutal fighting, including a heroic defense in the line during the Battle of Bastogne. I look at the pictures of the colonel, later the commandant of the Infantry School at Fort Benning, and I see a man with ramrod posture, a serious face behind wire-rimmed spectacles, the stature that sometimes comes with command, this officer destined to win the Silver Star. And I try to square those images with the frail figure across the room, a man now confined to a lounge chair powered by electricity. I feel sadness. I feel sympathy. I feel totally inadequate, witness to a soldier fighting his final battle.

I make one other stop in Atlanta, something I would not miss, the chance to pay my respects at the grave of the Rev. Martin Luther King, Jr. As I make my way from the car, I reflect on the great distance I have come in my perceptions of this man.

I remember driving to an Ohio amusement park in the summer of 1963, not long after I had completed my sophomore year in high school, and I recall seeing people along the road carrying signs about something called the March on Washington. My reaction was suburban white kid naïveté; I was filled with wonder about what their problem was, and what they possibly thought they could accomplish, this handful of black people along a road in Ohio who were headed, it later turned out, to join a quarter million people who would be gathered at the Lincoln Memorial and hear Dr. King proclaim, "I have a dream."

And I remember the summer of 1966, when I was living at my grandfather's while working at the *Detroit News*, and I remember when my grandfather flew into a rage about "that Martin Luther King." I can still see us seated around the kitchen table that morning and my grandfather buried in the newspaper until something caught his eye and he started to rail against Dr. King. I cannot recall what had prompted his outburst, but what he said went beyond disagreement into viciousness that left me stunned.

I also remember driving to National Airport in Washington, D.C., on my way to pick up a weekend date on the day after Dr. King had been murdered in 1968. And on the George Washington Memorial Parkway, I could see across the Potomac to a pall of smoke hanging over the city like a shroud, smoke obscuring the Capitol dome and the Washington Monument, smoke from the fires of rage that were sweeping through the city's black neighborhoods, leaving thirty-nine people dead. I recall fear over what was happening to this country and where it would lead, as well as grief over the loss of Dr. King, whom I had come to admire in my college years.

I would cite Dr. King's example as one of my inspirations when I wrote my application as a conscientious objector. My grandfather, as I had discovered in El Paso, would go on to criticize Dr. King in harsh ways. I read his television commentary in response to Dr. King's opposition to the Vietnam War, and he likens him to "a demagogue," "a propagandist" and even "P. T. Barnum." His vitriol is even more evident in a commentary delivered on the day of Dr. King's funeral.

Marshall's wrath is supposedly directed at the rioters and looters roaming the cities and how police power must be applied promptly "to put down violence and compel respect for law." Dr. King is not mentioned anywhere by name in the commentary, but Marshall's distaste for the man is transparent even on this day of his funeral. So Marshall cannot resist making a reference to King, edged with sarcasm: "I cannot claim to see all of life as from the top of a mountain. Such grace, such vistas, are not given to me." A firestorm of criticism results in Detroit, well-founded criticism.

So intense is the reaction that Marshall is moved to do something he seldom did amid the dogma and venom in the last phase of his life. He offers a televised apology, or at least his approximation of an apology: "When the other night I said I had never been to the top of the mountain, I meant no profanation of the memory of Doctor King. To any and all who so took it, and whose sensibilities were wounded, I say that I regret the phrase was so used, and am sorrier still that for even one moment I hurt them. Only a fool would naysay a prophet who is with full honor in his own country."

The remainder of Marshall's "apology" is a curious mix, a mention that he himself had climbed Mount Sinai, an obscure quote by Albert Schweitzer, a reiteration of the need for respect for the law, and only the faintest praise for Dr. King himself. That what the TV station obviously expected to be Marshall's apology proves to be something less foretells what will happen the following year when the station yanks Marshall off the air for his "unpopular views." His longtime relationship with WWJ ends in bitterness, just as had his long relationships with the *Detroit News* and his New York publisher, all these sad acts involving a vitriolic old man.

There are times on this trip when I think about how things could have turned out otherwise between my grandfather and me, how we might have patched over our differences in later years. But I have few such thoughts standing in front of the white marble crypt of Martin Luther King, Jr. Here, the differences between my grandfather and me seem absolutely fundamental, irreparably opposed, an impossible mix. Such thoughts conflict with Dr. King's own philosophy of unqualified love, even for one's own enemies. But I am also struck by what a difficult example he set, how few of us do manage lives that eloquently bespeak our ideals and beliefs.

The four-hundred-mile drive to Charleston does little to lighten my mood, this detour undertaken on the faint hope of seeing General Westmoreland. I endure my first near-accident on the road, almost forced into a drainage ditch by a semi. And the closer I get to Charleston, the more hurricane destruction I see.

Hurricane Hugo has roared through this area only a month ago, and the storm's devastation is visible along the Interstate. Toppled trees line the roadway, huge trees supported by the shallowest of roots. Tarpaulins are tied to the tops of houses, where roofs have been blown away. And holes have been punched through many elevated signs along the Interstate, those familiar emblems for gas stations and fast food spots now looking as though they have been the target of some antifranchise vandalism.

I arrive in Charleston in late afternoon and feel fortunate when I get the last room in a new motel on the outskirts. A siege mentality still grips the area, with residents forced out of their homes and fighting for scarce motel space with utility repair crews, construction workers, and insurance adjustors, many from out of state. The newspapers have been turned into Hurricane Hugo broadsheets, with much news still unremittingly grim—damage from the storm now expected to climb from $8 billion to $10 billion; an Air Force squadron of C-130s soon to begin spraying to eradicate mosquitoes bearing life-threatening viruses; one headline declaring "Child abuse on the rise since storm, official claims."

My own worries about seeing General Westmoreland seem trivial indeed, amidst all this ruin and heartbreak. And yet I still cannot stop thinking how important this visit could be to my search. I put off calling the general this evening, try instead in the morning.

"General Westmoreland, this is John Marshall, the grandson of S. L. A. Marshall. I called you several days ago about an interview, and I'm in Charleston now. I wonder if you might be able to spare some time today, sir?"

"I really don't think I have anything for you. We're probably just wasting each other's time."

"I only have a few questions to ask, sir. If you don't have answers, then we'll just skip over them."

The line goes silent for a moment before Westmoreland finally says, "All right. Why don't you come by here at ten."

On the drive into town, my mind replays the questions I want to ask Westmoreland, most centering on the accusations of David Hackworth. The retired colonel's autobiography, *About Face*, had gone on to become a surprising national best seller and its chapter savaging S.L.A. Marshall had probably reached a wider audience than the article in *American Heritage*. Never mind that Hackworth's portrayal of Marshall is so transparently nasty, especially after all Marshall had done to help Hackworth's career. Marshall had rescued him from a dreary Pentagon post and taken him along as his assistant on a three-month mission across Vietnam; he personally commended Hackworth's efforts to the Army chief of staff on at least two occasions and gave Hackworth title page recognition ("Assisted by Lieutenant Colonel David H. Hackworth") beside his own byline in his 1968 Vietnam book, *Bird*. There was a distinct mentor-protégé character to the relationship between Marshall and Hackworth.

Until Hackworth's Army career had crashed and burned during his last tour in Vietnam, a self-inflicted flame out. Hackworth had commanded a remote outpost where his version of military discipline somehow allowed the unit to operate its own whorehouse, its own gambling hall, its own slush fund, its own way of diverting military supplies. And the good colonel himself smoked dope with his men and ferried his Australian girl friend about in his command helicopter during her two-week stay, this tryst in the killing fields with "Hack." "I *did* have my own separate army in the Zone. And I *was* the law,"[1] Hackworth wrote in his memoirs. It was little wonder that Hackworth was said to have been the "model" for the outlaw Colonel Kurtz character in *Apocolypse Now*. Or that Hackworth exited the Army in a blaze of publicity, including an interview on ABC-TV's "Issues and Answers" which was taped before he left Vietnam and featured his pointed criticisms of the war.

S.L.A. Marshall probably watched that "Issues and Answers" featuring his former protégé—his disappointment deepened by the fact that it came the day after he had written his letter disowning his grandson. And he soon weighed in with his analysis of Hackworth in his column syndicated by the *Los Angeles Times* and the *Washington Post.* Hackworth's portrayal of Marshall in *About Face* seemed to be his way of settling that score eighteen years later.

I had interviewed the fifty-eight-year-old Hackworth for the *Seattle Post-Intelligencer* during his national tour promoting his book, an interview that oddly took place twelve hours after I had watched a broadcast of *Apocalypse Now.* Our hour together only further confirmed the impression of the man I had received from reading his autobiography. I found Hackworth to be a person marked by his limited education and intellect, someone used to going on gut instincts, with a certain messianic zeal, a simplistic good-guys-vs.-bad-guys view of the world, distinctly humorless, and with an unsettledness that veered into defensiveness. I did not tape our interview, but Hackworth did, and he also jotted down tiny notes to himself on three-by-five cards as we talked.

I looked at Hackworth's strong chin, his thin lips, his prominent nose, his broad forehead, but I kept coming back to his eyes, his most prominent feature, eyes cold and intent, and often fixed in a vacant stare that seemed to say he had seen too much death in his life, often from his own hands. Once proud to be known as "Sergeant Combat," Hackworth struck me as someone far better suited for the role of hard-ass master sergeant than as a full colonel entrusted with command. Something seemed missing in Hackworth somewhere. Yet he remained fully convinced of his own grandeur, this once-little-known Army colonel who had produced an 875-page autobiography, 437 pages longer than the autobiography of Gen. Douglas MacArthur.

Of more importance was the accuracy of Hackworth's recollections. His book made him appear to be a person who went through life wearing a concealed tape recorder, so detailed were his memories. Yet I had found errors in Hackworth's account of his time with Marshall, including his recounting of their Saigon meeting with Bernard Fall, the respected French writer on Indochina. Hackworth states flatly that Marshall "knew next to nothing of the history of the Vietnam conflict, having never read Bernard Fall,"[2] and he paints the encounter as a first meeting when "Fall gave Slam a quiet education on the Vietnamese."[3] The only problem with Hackworth's portrayal, I discovered in El Paso, was that Fall had visited Marshall in his Detroit home years earlier, giving him a copy of his classic Vietnam book, *Street Without Joy*, which he inscribed: "To Gen. S. L. A. Marshall, with my sincerest admiration, this book about a 'wrong war at the wrong place.' (But are there ever any right places?) Bernard B. Fall. Detroit. Nov. 1, 1961."

"Did you really think," I had asked Hackworth, "that the encounter between Bernard Fall and Marshall in Vietnam was the first time they'd met?"

"That's the impression I had," Hackworth replied. "I got that from the Navy lieutenant commander who introduced them and was all excited about bringing these two giants together. If Slam knew Fall before, I was not aware of it."

"He did. Fall was a guest in Marshall's home in 1961. He even gave him an inscribed copy of *Street Without Joy.*"

Hackworth considered this for a moment, then said, "Oh."

That was the problem with Hackworth. He might not be "aware of" something but was more than willing to present his "impressions" as fact. Hackworth—like his fellow Marshall critic and friend, Harold Leinbaugh—had been content to do his Marshall research from afar, writing a few letters to the Marshall collection in El Paso, but never bothering to comb the archives. And like *American Heritage*, Hackworth had not made the effort to contact those who knew Marshall best in order to assess the accuracy of his assertions.

Maj. Daniel P. Bolger was well aware of the problems with Hackworth's book. He is a former history instructor at West Point, the holder of a doctorate in history from the University of Chicago, and author of three books. Bolger had reviewed *About Face* for *Army* magazine and concluded that "examples of obvious untruths and half-truths jump from every chapter."[4] I had corresponded with Bolger, who wrote that Hackworth's "credibility in most of the U.S. Army is about zero, except with the 'Soldier of Fortune' fringe and some of his old subordinates. . . . Only the truly gullible believe anything in 'About Face.'"

Bolger added, "Marshall still stands, his core theses unchallenged. His body of published work has already stood the test of time. The U.S. Army remodeled its infantry units based upon 'Men Against Fire,' an action not taken lightly, and certainly reflective of a body of research work that agrees with Marshall. . . . Marshall's influence, in short, is pervasive in the very fiber of the Army. At my level (former West Point instructor, current student at the Command & General Staff College), I've found that most cadets and officers still trust Marshall, a respected and authoritative source for much course work and student research at both West Point and Leavenworth. Those aware of the controversy may or may not agree with Hackworth, but the majority argue that those charges have nothing to do with the tested validity of Marshall's work."

I myself had found more flaws in Hackworth's account of his time with Marshall during my second research visit to El Paso. Hackworth's memory, what had once seemed like total recall, had now taken on a very selective tint.

In *About Face*, Hackworth writes about how he changed his mind about accompanying Marshall on a second trip to Vietnam because, as he says, "I realized the purpose of the trip was actually to whitewash the effects of the Tet Offensive through Slam's considerable media power."[5] What Hackworth neglects to mention is that he wrote a letter to Marshall backing out of the trip because he was "fed up with the Army and Vietnam" and was in the process of retiring from the service. Hackworth also told Marshall: "I appreciate your friendship, past advice and constant assistance. You have been much like a father to me and I in turn like a son to you."

Even Marshall's syndicated column on Hackworth did not turn out to say what Hackworth said it said in his memoirs, as I found in El Paso. Hackworth referred to the column as "my public discrediting (tit for tat)" and asserted that Marshall "lied through his teeth to imply I was a coward."[6] Marshall did say that Hackworth "has had far too much combat" and "was given to episodes of moodiness and untriggered expostulation," but also wrote: "Hackworth is of a company with Alvin York, Sam Dreben, Audie Murphy and the lesser-known Harrison Summers. They are extremely rare, these American fighters who perform with almost desperate intrepidity time and again . . . . Hackworth has not only been outstanding as a combat soldier but also an inspired leader of troops under fire."[7]

If someone were lying through his teeth here, those teeth were in the mouth of David Hackworth. My interview with him provided yet another example of that. In *About Face*, Hackworth charges that

Marshall "for years and years did an incalculable, horrific service to the Army."[8] In person, Hackworth told me, "S. L. A. Marshall made a great contribution to our military."

I found I could dismiss many of Hackworth's charges against Marshall, including Hackworth's criticism that Marshall reveled in the VIP treatment that the Army accorded him. Marshall was a sixty-six-year-old retired general who had devoted much of his life to the Army, often with little or no compensation, and surely he was entitled to savor a few fruits of his labors this late in life. The real villain here was a grotesque Army system that allowed generals to dine on fine china and sip cognac in secure base camps while their men were fighting and dying in the jungles.

I could also discount Hackworth's charge that Marshall should have gone public with his criticisms of the Army's operations in Vietnam. It was stupid to expect Marshall to abandon his life-long support of the Army at the time when the Army was under attack from many quarters. Marshall—unlike Hackworth—was much too loyal to the institution. He stood behind the Army even when those views were causing his own reputation to plummet. For the first time, Marshall was starting to have difficulties finding a publisher for his books, and he later told an Army interviewer, "If I wanted to make a hundred thousand dollars in a hurry, all I'd have to do is turn around and write articles damning the military service and I could sell it anywhere I wished." But S. L. A. Marshall was not about to desert the Army, and especially not during Vietnam.

There could still be no excuse, though, for Marshall pulling his punches with the Army in private, refusing to share his thoughts about Vietnam operations with Army commanders behind closed doors. He had the influence to urge changes that could save lives, and perhaps avoid defeats. I found myself agreeing with Hackworth when he writes: "I felt Slam had a responsibility to tell Westmoreland and the rest of the establishment the truth about what was happening to the war effort. But instead he continued to play the distinguished guest at every unit, and ruffled no feathers."[9]

But is that what Marshall indeed did? This question should be answered by Westmoreland, this man I now approach while he stands in the driveway outside his house.

12

Westy & Slam

THERE IS NO MISTAKING William Childs Westmoreland. Seventeen years after his retirement from the service, now attired in civilian clothes, Westmoreland still looks like the man in command of United States forces in Vietnam, the general from central casting glimpsed so often on the TV news, the handsome face on an ugly war. There is still that ramrod bearing to Westmoreland, that charismatic visage worthy of sculpture, with his jutting chin, his bold forehead ending in the bushiest of eyebrows, and steely eyes so deepset that photographs often showed them in shadow.

Film stars and TV anchors are supposed to be the ones who benefit from good looks, but Westmoreland demonstrated that the military too was not immune to the persuasive power of appearance. Westmoreland's striking handsomeness had marked him as a Golden Boy when he was a boy; had marked him as a Golden Boy when he was an Eagle Scout, a West Point cadet, and a young Army officer; it still marked him as a Golden Boy at seventy-five. People had always taken notice of "Westy's" chiseled appearance—it seemed to set him apart, promise great things. And his authorized biography carried a title that mirrored how many people felt about the imposing South Carolinian; it was called *Westmoreland: The Inevitable General*.

I expect to share that reaction as I walk up and introduce myself to Westmoreland, who has been chatting with a man he seems to know. Westmoreland and I shake hands, then I wait for him to introduce me. He does not.

Westmoreland soon leads me around to the side of his house, a modest two-story box that is sandwiched among many larger homes, his house a relative newcomer to this historic street but designed in a timeless southern style, with pale pink stucco, white shutters around the windows, a tin roof. We pass through the foyer, proceed into the living room.

"Sit there," Westmoreland suggests. "The light should be good there, so you can see what you're doing."

I take a seat in the straight-backed chair and am immediately engulfed in sunlight. It streams in through French doors overlooking a small garden, reflects off the white pages of my notebook.

Westmoreland takes a seat in an identical chair, just out of the sunlight. Our chairs are side by side, with a small table between us where there is a telephone. The two chairs fit nicely into the symmetry of this large room, but conversing in them requires contortions much like talking to someone across the aisle of an airliner. Westmoreland, though, makes no such effort. He appears content to stare straight ahead toward somewhere in the middle of the room, while I am to talk at his profile. His eye contact with me is fleeting.

Westmoreland offers no encouragement when I try to make small talk. My questions about how long the Westmorelands have lived in this house, what impact the hurricane had, prompt little response other than the strong implication that he considers this time all business, and unpleasant business at that. I get the message.

I make a quick summary of the Marshall controversy since Westmoreland had shown little knowledge of it over the telephone. I stress the role of Hackworth in all this, and how he alone can answer some of Hackworth's charges.

"That Hackworth would not be kind to Slam is something I can't understand," Westmoreland offers. "Slam elevated Hackworth to a stature that he would not have been elevated to by himself."

"I think it is payback for Hackworth's perception of what Slam wrote when he fell out with the Army. I think Hackworth viewed his book as a chance to settle an old score."

Westmoreland considers this and says, "It may well have been payback."

Westmoreland is about as animated as a mannequin. His voice

S. L. A. Marshall and General William C. Westmoreland, 1971. Courtesy
S. L. A. Marshall Military History Collection, University of Texas at El
Paso.

is lifeless. He sits slumped in his chair, with his hands folded in his lap. His command presence must be hung in a closet somewhere along with his old uniforms.

I ask Westmoreland about his relationship with Marshall. They were not close, he says, but they were more than passing acquaintances, "getting together every once in a while over the years," some mutual back-scratching often involved, as I confirmed in El Paso. In 1959, Westmoreland, then commander of the 101st Airborne Division, had dispatched his personal plane to Detroit to bring Slam and Cate to Fort Campbell, Kentucky, for the premiere there of *Pork Chop Hill*. Ten years later, Marshall had dedicated *Ambush* to Westmoreland: "In honor of my friend Bill Westmoreland who like a General of Old Rome deserves well of the Republic."

Vietnam brought Westmoreland and Marshall together on several occasions. I had found a letter that my grandfather had written to Cate from Saigon in June 1966, a letter that recounts time with Westmoreland, a colorful snapshot of the way things were at the high command.

"I was moved out to Westy's residence at 3 p.m. today, delaying as long as possible, because I was comfortable in old clothes and relaxing," Marshall writes. "It took two field grade officers, two NCOs and one Viet driver to move me, not because I am that immobile, but due to the poor fact that certain pomp & circumstance seems required.

"Westy lives in a mansion . . . that occupies a full walled and carefully guarded block in Saigon. I am in a secondary mansion, two stories, stone-walled, a suite of four rooms and two servants. . . .

"Tonight's affair was a going away party for Lt. Gen. Joe Moore, Westy's deputy for air. But it was more than that: This was the day we bombed Hanoi's petroleum reserves, which action I have been crying for the past 18 months. So it became an extraordinary occasion—and an extraordinary night for all of us.

"Westy was giving the party . . . . We were at cocktails. Westy had to run in and out of the room to answer long-distance calls from Washington—Gen. (Earle) Wheeler (Army Chief of Staff), (Robert) McNamara (Secretary of Defense), then the President (LBJ). Twelve generals were there, also Ambassador (Henry Cabot) Lodge, whom I happened to be sitting with, and striking up a kidding acquaintance. Then suddenly comes a messenger with blown-up pictures of the bombings—and what pictures they prove to be. . . .

"We sat down to dinner, Moore on Westy's right, I on his left and across from Lodge. Then in popped the two pilots who had led the raid to give us a blow-by-blow description—and it was a stunner of a story. We finished up with champagne and Westy said: 'I want you all to note I am serving this for the first time at this table, and I will tell you why.' Then he talked first of our friendship, and of what my work had meant to the Army, etc., after which he talked about his friend, Moore. Then toasts were drunk. This morning we had breakfast together and most of today I will be accompanying him on a round of inspections."

Two years later, a brief flap marred this mutually beneficial relationship between the commanding general in Vietnam and the retired general with the syndicated newspaper column. It was the spring of 1968 and Westmoreland had written asking Marshall to visit Vietnam again, a personal invitation that would be difficult for him to reject, especially since it was laden with flattery ("In view of your complete understanding of the individual fighting man and of the war itself, I believe that some articles by you on the current situation would help put the conflict in its proper perspective.") The invitation was sent a couple of months after the Tet Offensive and a couple of months before Westmoreland would relinquish command to return to Washington: he would contend the invitation had been his own personal request. But Marshall was quoted publicly as saying that he had been summoned to make the trip for the Department of the Army, a distortion that irked Westmoreland. Several letters were exchanged between the two before the upset was patched over, with words from Westmoreland finally signaling a truce.

"It was my confidence in you that motivated me to ask you to come over during a time when it appeared that the situation in Vietnam was being portrayed to the American people in a distorted manner," Westmoreland wrote. "This confidence has not changed. You have been of invaluable assistance to the Army in the past, and I hope that you will continue to be disposed to lend us a helping hand. Needless to say, this does not suggest that you will always agree with the way that the Army or its Chief of Staff handles the many, complex situations that arise. Our batting average will never be that good. . . . The days ahead are going to be rugged ones, and I will welcome your counsel. I would therefore hope that whenever you visit Washington, you will let me know so we can get together. Best personal regards. Sincerely, Westy."

This is the savvy way with words that helped propel Westmoreland to the top rank in the Army. I solicit his impressions of Marshall.

"He had a very warm personality, he was an engaging individual, he was rather likable," Westmoreland says. "He was a good speaker and he was one of the most prolific writers on the American scene. I couldn't imagine how he could write as much as he did. He seemed to me to be a very down-to-earth person. A professional. A military scholar."

"What was the reaction to him in the Army?"

"Senior officials thought well of him. He had a lot of credibility with them."

"Did you think there were two camps regarding Slam in the Army, those who were his friends and those who were his detractors, people who thought he was only in it for himself?"

"I have no sense of that. Slam was viewed as a friend of the Army, not someone who would exploit the Army for his own aggrandizement."

What Westmoreland is saying is helpful, but he could be reading the phone book instead of recalling a former friend, so dull is his demeanor, so withdrawn his manner.

I would be more puzzled by this behavior if it did not mirror an impression of Westmoreland during his Vietnam days, as recounted by David Halberstam in *The Best and the Brightest*, that exhaustive account of American hubris marching into the quagmire. Halberstam writes of Westmoreland: "He was a reserved man with few close friends, terrible at small talk, totally committed to his work, his job of being an inspiring commander. . . . To his contemporaries he was a cold one, you did not get close to Westy, you kept your distance. He seemed to have no confidants; the system was his confidant."[1]

Mrs. Westmoreland suddenly walks into the room and I expect her to offer us something to drink, probably coffee at this hour, as so often happens during interviews in someone's home. But she withdraws without a word, her husband making no effort to introduce us.

And I am disappointed, desperate for someone else to interact with Westmoreland and get him to show a more human side, even a mild chuckle, anything beyond this stupor.

I feel a certain tension. Part of it comes from the general's short responses. Westmoreland appears to have a severe distaste for elaboration; he guards his words like rations. Part of the tension also comes from wondering whether he will suddenly ask me some unexpected question, as he had done when I called from New Orleans ("If the U.S. declared war on Russia tomorrow, would you fight?").

I move on to Hackworth and Westmoreland suddenly turns alert. "Oh yes," the general says.

In El Paso, I found a letter from Westmoreland to Marshall regarding Hackworth sent a couple of months before his appearance on "Issues and Answers." Westmoreland, Army chief of staff, wrote to Marshall: "I have your letter of 30 March 1971 and can appreciate your concern regarding Colonel David 'Hack' Hackworth. As we discussed previously, Colonel Hackworth's contributions to the Army have been most significant. Should he elect to retire, we would lose a real combat veteran with a wealth of experience. As for your suggestion that I might be able to convince him of the Army's need for his continued service, I am sure you can understand my hesitancy in projecting myself into his personal deliberations at this point in his career. Nevertheless, when he comes to the Washington area on his return from Vietnam, I intend to talk with him."

That planned talk never occurred, another casualty of Hackworth's scorched earth split with the Army. As Westmoreland says of Hackworth in his own memoirs, "Near the end, he developed an affinity for personal publicity, sometimes spoke irresponsibly, and conducted himself with questionable ethics."[2] But Marshall's suggestion that Westmoreland meet with Hackworth underscores that Marshall was still trying to help his former protégé years after he had backed out of their proposed second trip to Vietnam. That must have stung Marshall at the time, although he bore no grudge.

I run Hackworth's charges by Westmoreland one-by-one. He disputes Hackworth's criticism of Marshall for using notes garnered on an Army-sponsored trip to write his own Vietnam books. "I don't see anything wrong with that," Westmoreland says. "Slam was a professional writer—let's face it. It was not my impression that he was just doing this for himself."

Westmoreland also takes exception to Hackworth's contention that "Slam never broached the severity of problems when he was turned to for guidance." The general counters, "In talking to me Slam was very frank and forthcoming."

This is the entrée to the one question that has brought me to Westmoreland. I proceed to read aloud Hackworth's assertion: "I felt Slam had the responsibility to tell Westmoreland and the rest of the establishment the truth about what was happening to the war effort. But instead he continued to play the distinguished guest at every unit and ruffled no feathers."

"I can't agree with that," says Westmoreland, suddenly animated. "When Slam talked to me, he was more critical than praising. He dealt in tactics and I agreed with him. The whole point is that you can't have a one-year tour [in Vietnam] and have an expanded officer candidate program and then you put them out on the battlefield, which is totally foreign to them—you can't expect them to be masters of tactics."

"You're absolutely sure," I inject, "that Slam was critical of how the war was being waged when he was with you?"

"He was far more critical than praising, and I agreed with that. And he did not ingratiate himself to me; that was not his style. He wanted to be helpful, but he didn't hold back. He was frank. He couldn't pull punches with me if he was going to have credibility."

There is one follow-up question I must ask, another way of assessing what Hackworth knew of what went on between Westmoreland and Marshall. "Was Hackworth ever present during your discussions with Slam?"

Westmoreland pauses, then says, "I don't think Hackworth was there when Slam talked to me."

I touch upon Westmoreland's disagreement with Marshall over that trip to Vietnam in 1968, and inquire why he thought it was so important for Marshall to return to the war zone one more time in the aftermath of Tet. Westmoreland emphasizes, "Slam knew more about the military scene than many other reporters. Few knew anything like what he knew."

Suddenly, the telephone buzzes on the table between us. I expect Mrs. Westmoreland to answer it on another extension. But Westmoreland picks up the receiver himself.

"Hello," he says, his voice icy.

I look about the room for the first time, a setting so stiffly formal that it could be called a drawing room. I find myself wondering if the Westmorelands ever actually sit in here, and if they ever take off their shoes and put up their feet. This is a place I can only imagine demitasse and finger sandwiches. I would not be surprised to have a butler walk in here in a colonial Williamsburg costume, so stagy does this seem, with its gilt-edged mirrors, its delicate chinaware displayed in bookshelves, the antique Oriental rug, a grand piano dominating one corner of the room, the soft focus portrait of Mrs. Westmoreland above the mantel in a huge golden frame of baroque style. The only evidence of Westmoreland is his general's flag on a stand in a corner. Otherwise, the man of this house could be the conductor of a chamber music ensemble.

I try not to listen to the general's conversation, but find it difficult. Someone is obviously asking Westmoreland about the chance to meet with him, perhaps for another interview like this, and he is growing testier by the minute.

He is instructing the caller in just why it is that, as Westmoreland says, "what you want is certainly not a top priority with me and I will get to it when I get to it if I get to it at all." Westmoreland is almost shouting by this point and still does not quit.

"I've got so many people breathing down my neck from all over you wouldn't believe it!" Westmoreland exclaims. "I'm two months behind in my correspondence! I haven't paid my bills in a week!"

Westmoreland then slams down the receiver and immediately says to me, "I think that's enough."

I start to explain that I have only a couple more questions to ask, but Westmoreland is striding toward the front door. I grab my things and rush to catch up. Westmoreland opens the door, gives my hand a brisk pump, spits out "good luck" and shuts the door.

I walk away slowly, in shock. I stop at the sidewalk, searching my mind for anything I might have done to prompt this treatment. Thirty seconds ago, I was sitting beside Westmoreland and now I have been dismissed like some unruly subordinate, no elaboration, end audience, finis.

I look back at Westmoreland's house, almost to reassure myself that I have indeed been inside, and then my eyes drift to Westmoreland's car, a late model Buick, and I notice the bumper sticker affixed to the trunk, one last oddity in this odd encounter. Westmoreland's bumper sticker says: "I Am A Vietnam Veteran." Which is not quite right, I think. Westmoreland's bumper sticker should say, "I am THE Vietnam Veteran."

I did not know what would happen when I met the general who personified the war for so many in my generation. I certainly did not think the two of us would engage in any debate over Vietnam. I am aware of where he stood then, and where he stands now. Westmoreland has come to believe that the growing appreciation for Vietnam vets also extends to him and his role in the war. After all, he can march in parades these days without being subjected to abuse, and he receives standing ovations after talks to Rotary and Kiwanis.

So Westmoreland's justification of the war has turned more strident with the passing years. When he had written his memoirs in 1976, Westmoreland conceded that "history may judge that going into Vietnam was one of our country's greatest mistakes."[3] When he wrote a foreword to a new edition in 1989, Westmoreland describes the Vietnam War as "highly idealistic" and asserts "in no way can that be considered a defeat of American armed forces." He also reiterates his contention that "American aid to South Vietnam constituted one of man's more noble crusades."[4]

These words ring terribly false. But Westmoreland's pronouncements on the war often had that character. Time has made people forget his boundless optimism about Vietnam, his years of sunny reports from the front, how back in 1967 Westmoreland was saying that "The military picture is favorable"[5] and "The war is not a stalemate. We are winning it slowly but steadily."[6] These assessments came the very same year when Westmoreland had 470,000 troops in Vietnam and was pressing Washington hard for 210,000 more.

Or how back in 1968, right after the enemy's massive Tet Offensive, Westmoreland said, "I do not think Hanoi can hold up to a long war."[7] And two months later he said, "Militarily we have never been in a better relative position in South Vietnam."[8] And two months later he said, "The enemy has been defeated at every turn."[9]

Someone who voiced such rosy delusions should consider himself fortunate that people still want to hear what he has to say two decades later. For as Neil Sheehan writes in *A Bright Shining Lie,* winner of the 1989 Pulitzer Prize: "The financial and human costs of Westmoreland's war of attrition were so high that when the Tet 1968 Offensive exposed it as a fiasco, the inevitable result was a psychological collapse and a domestic political crisis of historic proportions. Westmoreland had brought about the kind of catastrophe MacArthur had perpetrated in the winter of 1950, but on a scale magnified many times by the extravagance of the failure in Vietnam. . . .

"What mattered to the American public was that this defeated enemy could attack anywhere and was attacking everywhere more fiercely than ever before. The winning of the war was not coming 'into view.' The war in Vietnam was never going to be won. Nothing had been achieved by the outpouring of lives and treasure and the rending of American society. The assurances the public had been given were the lies and vaporings of foolish men."[10]

I stand here on the sidewalk, thoughts on the war mingled with mixed feelings about my encounter with Westmoreland. I am grateful he was willing to see me, surely out of his respect for my grandfather. And I have come away with comments contradicting more of Hackworth's untruths. I should be satisfied with this.

But I cannot shake some disappointment. I guess I wanted the man who ran the war to be as imposing as his photographs, a towering presence commanding instant respect, as if that would make more sense of Vietnam somehow and why so many men my age fought and died under his command.

13

Passing through Eden

THE HISTORIC CHARLESTON STREETS are piled high with rubble, huge mounds of debris, mammoth tree trunks, large branches, pieces of roofing, decorative plants torn from formal gardens, remnants of wood shutters that once graced the windows of mansions. And the streets echo with the cacophony of construction: chain saws, circular saws, hammers, drills, radios blaring country music, the shouts of well-muscled men. A month after Hurricane Hugo, the city is clawing its way back.

The worst destruction is outside of town, particularly on the islands that line the coast, but the city's damage is awful enough, with more than a third of its trees damaged or destroyed, perhaps 80 percent of the houses suffering roof damage of some sort. But amidst the storm's disarray and disappointment, the stalwart grace of this place still endures, a grande dame who has managed to survive fire and flood, hurricane and earthquake, and even civil war.

On my way out of Charleston, I stop at an old plantation, where once-fertile fields are now reaping a bumper crop of suburban homes and cul de sacs. The stately house still holds its ground, but just barely, especially after the hurricane. Hugo has hit this development with particular fury, leaving few tall trees still standing. Workers are busy installing new roofs on the plantation house and its adjoining carriage house, while out by the curb stands a pile of dead vegetation eight feet high. It is here that I encounter the harried owner, Col. Walter B. Clark.

141

Pipe in hand, steady as he goes, Clark strides around this rush of activity, confronting the inevitable crises, barking instructions to the men on the roof with a brisk efficiency born of his twenty-seven years as an Infantry officer. General Harper had recommended that I visit Clark, who had once served as his aide, and it is readily apparent that I am now face-to-face with a full-blooded, unrepentant S. L. A. Marshall admirer. Clark had once spent four days ferrying Marshall about at Fort Benning, and he is not about to forget this brush with greatness. He has no use for Marshall's critics.

"Listen, I don't get excited about when Slam Marshall was commissioned," Clark says. "I met the man. I retain the impression that he was a damn good man, a great man. His *Men Against Fire* is an Army bible. And I never met a Marshall detractor. I knew scores of people Marshall wrote about and I never heard a disparaging word about him. I was General Harper's aide at the Infantry School, I worked in the office of the Army chief of staff, I was a senior aide to the commander-in-chief in Korea. I was more exposed to the senior leadership of the Army than most officers. Slam Marshall was everybody's friend! He was admired!"

Clark still proudly refers to himself as "a muddy boots soldier," this square-jawed, rough-hewn man who was wounded seven times during hand-to-hand combat as a rifle platoon leader in Korea and was awarded the Silver Star. His career ended up at the same place it had begun, at The Citadel, the South's own West Point, where as commandant of cadets he was still urging students to read Marshall's books just as he had done himself. Retired for twelve years, the fifty-nine-year-old Clark comes across like a bulldog unleashed.

"It pisses me off that anybody would throw a rock at S. L. A. Marshall," Clark spits out. "It's like attacking an icon, goddamnit! When I consider the attitudes of those involved in this, people like Hackworth, it becomes bullshit. Slam Marshall was an honorable man who had such an impact on the Army. I get pissed! I get angry! I'll defend Slam Marshall until the day I die!"

I listen to all of Clark's exclamations in support of Marshall and I keep thinking how many more men like this there probably are out there, men I will never get to meet, men of many ranks who were moved by Marshall's work and came to consider him a trusted friend, especially when it came time for combat. His lessons, they knew, saved lives.

Clark is the counterpoint to Albert Garland of *Infantry* magazine, the answer to why it was that so many in the Army "rolled out the red carpet for this guy, Marshall." I am touched by Clark's unquestioning devotion to Marshall after all these years and wish in a way that I could so readily summon up the same feelings. And I am touched even more by Clark's repeated comments about how "honored" he is to meet S. L. A. Marshall's grandson, but it also puts me in a quandary. I wonder if I should tell this hard-core Army man just what happened between my grandfather and me. Will it spoil this visit for him, even cause some sort of unfortunate scene? But the interview is almost over and the truth is what this trip is about, so I finally decide to mention it.

"I told you before that my grandfather and I had a falling out over the war in Vietnam," I say to Clark. "But it was more than that. I won discharge from the Army as a conscientious objector and my grandfather disowned me because of that."

Clark puffs on his pipe for a moment, then says, "I had heard that. Did the two of you ever get back together again?"

"No. Not really."

I proceed to offer details of what happened between my grandfather and me, and how things ended up. Clark keeps asking questions and our conversation continues as we head outside.

"I don't know if what you did about the war was right or wrong, I just don't know," Clark says. "But I do know that I have not been able to visit that Vietnam Memorial in Washington. The memories are just too painful for me. I'm afraid I knew too many men whose names are up on the Wall."

I notice how Clark is turning tense, his crusty veneer falling away, revealing a different side indeed. I had forgotten there is a tradition of such men in the service—men from the South, steel-tough, committed to duty, honor, and valor, but sentimental at the core, men who can chew somebody's ass as needed, and yet are still not ashamed to cry.

I try to steer the conversation to less difficult terrain for Clark, telling him about my visit to Fort Benning, how impressed I was with the lieutenants going through the Infantry School these days, and how much better their training was than for my own class. "Now, of course, there's no war on," I say, "so there's plenty of time for thorough training."

A grimace washes across Clark's face and he proceeds to recall his own time at Fort Carson, Colorado, during the height of the war, back in 1967–69 when he was commanding a mechanized Infantry battalion. He tells me about the vast numbers of lieutenants who were being rushed through Fort Carson on the fast track to Vietnam. What he says sends a shiver through me since I originally had been assigned to go to Fort Carson right after Fort Benning in late 1969. And Clark relates how there were just not enough command spots to go around for these Carson lieutenants, so their real training would have to come after they had arrived in Vietnam.

"They would rotate in and rotate out of Carson," Clark says, his voice growing softer, "and I knew they were poorly equipped to handle the demands of combat."

Clark's eyes are moist now, his voice halting: "And the best ones, the ones who were really gung-ho, the real leaders, they were the ones who never came back alive."

Clark's sorrowful words press in on us both. We stand in his driveway a while longer, making small talk after this moment of unexpected communion between a career soldier and a conscientious objector. For we both mourn so many lives lost for so little effect, and we feel Vietnam's lingering legacy—anger and regret.

Dense pine forests line the Interstate later in the day when I pass my six thousandth mile on the road. I am into the thirty-seventh day of the trip now, speeding through South Carolina toward Charlotte, and I wonder how many more miles and how many more days the trip will take. I do not want to ponder that much because then I start feeling helpless about what I keep hearing from Anne. She reports that Thatcher is having problems adjusting to my being gone, waking up most every night crying "Daddy! Daddy!" Anne tells me this more in hints than complaints—that is her nature—but what she does say tears at my heart as I listen to her voice in some motel room. And then come the feelings of guilt about being gone so long, although I can see no way to speed what I am trying to accomplish. We had once thought that I would return home for a few days about now, flying back to Seattle from Atlanta or perhaps Washington, but Thatcher's problems now preclude that. Returning and then taking off again would only make things harder for him. So we have decided that I should press on, arriving home whenever the trip is completed, maybe months ahead. And in the meantime, I send home two postcards every day, hoping that somehow helps.

I soon cross into North Carolina and approach Charlotte, this city where my brother lives. I have visited him here only once before, almost a decade ago, just passing through town, a reunion which featured frantic minutes in the airport cocktail lounge, shouting through the din and the smoke. Since then, I have seen Sam only one time, at our impromptu family reunion in San Antonio three years ago. Otherwise, it has been brotherhood-as-usual for us as adults—occasional telephone calls, usually late at night, presents at Christmas, cards at most birthdays, and 2,739 miles between us.

But more than distance separates us, as it always has. There is the five-year difference in our ages, a gulf we seldom could bridge as children. We shared the same bedroom but little else, the straight arrow older brother in the letter sweater, the mischievous younger brother who had the looks and the charm. It was as if we had deliberately set out to be the other's opposite, so contrary were our interests and aptitudes, from grades and sports to guitars and cars.

We were destined to grow into much different men, I suppose, although I still am mystified by just how different we have become. I listen to this male voice on the telephone that everyone says sounds like mine, but there is this Southern drawl on the other end of the line, often relating various good ol' boy attitudes, and I wonder if any two brothers anywhere could be more different.

I am inching along with Friday rush hour traffic on Independence Boulevard, the clogged highways one of the signs of Charlotte's astounding growth, this boom town of 373,000 which nobody outside the South much noticed until it was awarded a new franchise in the National Basketball Association. My brother's livelihood is dependent on Charlotte's growth. He is a project superintendent for a custom homebuilder. He is still on the job when I arrive at his house in a neighborhood of modest brick homes and shady oaks, an enclave just off a commercial strip lined with car dealerships.

Katie welcomes me warmly at the door. I have met my brother's wife once before, at the reunion in San Antonio, and after that there was never any doubt about where my brother has been acquiring his Southern accent. Katie is Carolina magnolia to the core, pretty and blond and sweet-talking, with an air of Southern propriety about her, a woman who is my age but has a knack for disguising that very well. Her children arrive home soon afterward—Melissa, a twenty-two-year-old head-turner, a vision of her mother's youth, yet with a sassy streak; and Bill, fifteen, a soft-spoken young man at that gangling age, just coming out of being called Billy, his room plastered with posters of heavy metal bands, rap groups, and motorcycles.

Sam comes home not long after they do and we hug by the doorway. As always, I am struck by how thin he is, how he alone has escaped the Marshall physique. I also notice how exhausted Sam is from his long hours on the job. That winning smile does not flash from under his mustache as readily as it once did, and his eyes seem particularly tired. Obligations at work and at home seem to weigh on him. There are few hints of the goof-off little brother I remember.

We search out common ground again. We talk of our sister and our father and we laugh aloud when Sam mentions that Dad might drive here from St. Louis for the weekend, since we are together here and Monday is his sixty-eighth birthday.

"He might just do it," Sam says.

"I know—he's a regular driving fool. He drove out from St. Louis to our wedding in Seattle, stayed a couple days, then drove straight back. He loves to drive, for some reason."

Sam and I head to a place called The Scoreboard to watch the World Series. This is also supposed to be our time alone to talk, presumably of family matters and what I have found on my research trek, but this sports bar has all the intimacy of a high school gymnasium. This is a place where male bonding is conducted on that traditional level—the raising of beers and cheers while TV screens flicker with millionaires playing the games of our youth.

We still make some attempts to discuss our family through the clamor and especially our famous forebear whose name Sam shares and whose initials grace his Chevy Blazer's license plate (SLAM III).

"So was Poppy a good guy or a bad guy?" I ask to get things

going, a remark of such stunning inarticulateness that I wish I had it back as soon as it is out of my mouth.

"Is this on-the-record or off?" my brother asks in response. "I'm not used to talking to reporters."

I can sense that Sam is not exactly joking—and I am taken aback by his comment. After all, he had been the one who was so insistent that I investigate the charges against our grandfather back when I was wracked with doubts. Now, I have spent months on S. L. A. Marshall's trail and my own brother seems far less interested in what I have uncovered, and wary of me besides. I can understand that in some ways, but it still hurts.

We retreat to our beers and our dinners and the World Series. But the game is turning into a rout and Sam gradually comes back to talking about Poppy, although he admits his memory is not that good about what went on in his youth, the act of blocking out the bad somehow having blocked out much of the good as well. There are many things he often wishes he could recall, but cannot.

Sam talks some about the influence of Cate on her husband, how that seldom brought forth his better traits, especially late in life when Poppy was, as Sam puts it, "her pawn." Sam also talks about how heartbreaking it was to visit Poppy in the hospital near the end, his robust figure reduced to skin and bones, and curled up in a fetal position, sometimes lucid, often not, and an absolute terror to the hospital staff, making countless demands, giving orders even, perhaps grasping desperately for the authority he once had. And Sam recalls his funeral, that impressive military ceremony, and how the one thing he will never forget is the sight of soldiers throughout Fort Bliss snapping to attention when the funeral procession slowly passed.

We return to Sam's house not long after that and our conversation continues around the kitchen table, now joined by Katie. The kitchen is meticulously decorated in the style of American Country, such a profusion of hearts and wreaths and geese silhouettes that it seems as if all meals should be prepared here over a fire in a brick hearth. We are chatting amiably over late night coffee when we are startled by a knock at the back door.

"It's Dad!" I joke.

"Right," says Sam.

And then the door is opened and in walks our father.

And I look at Sam and Sam looks at me and our faces belong on characters in some episode of "The Twilight Zone." It is almost 11:00 P.M. and our father has just driven straight through from St. Louis, only too happy to inform us what a piece of cake this was, covering 730 miles in one day. Why if his Audi did not require oil so often, he would have made it much earlier.

By the next morning, Sam and I have recovered from our astonishment and this display of bravado by our father showing what he can still do at his age, quite a wondrous performance if it did not entail flirtation with exhaustion and dangers of the road. No one raises this point with Dad over the breakfast coffee, although someone probably should. We ache to just get along with each other, three strangers from the same family. There has been only one other time when just the three of us Marshall men have been together as adults and that was in Oregon fifteen years ago.

Now, we bury ourselves in a host of activities in hopes that they will produce something approaching normalcy. Sam takes us for a tour through Hurricane Hugo's devastation, so unexpected in Charlotte with its inland location, this monster storm that roared into town in the nether hours before dawn. The destruction in some of Charlotte's most expensive residential neighborhoods is even worse than Charleston.

We drive north to Lake Norman, a reservoir with over 520 miles of shoreline, and we inspect some of the new $350,000 waterfront houses that Sam is overseeing. To see him move about these houses, discussing construction problems and their resulting solutions, is to watch my image of my little brother crumble before my eyes, replaced by a grown man who commands new respect.

"I am very impressed by all this," I say to him.

I still cringe when Sam unleashes another Southern cracker comment about why he considers it so necessary to own guns, or how hard he has been trying of late to break himself of saying "ain't." But at least I can see my brother as he is, not the hazy presence I attach to the voice on the telephone. I see the dedicated craftsman turning disparate materials into well-built houses. I see the caring and solicitous stepfather and feel the emotion when he admits, "You expect them to call you Dad and all that, but they just don't."

S. L. A. Marshall, Jr., flanked by his sons, S. L. A. Marshall III *(right)* and author *(left)*, during their Charlotte reunion. Photograph by Katie Marshall.

But there is little time for such reflection, perhaps by our design and maybe to our relief. Hours rush by, days fly past, meals and conversations are grabbed on the run. We race about trading quips and snippets of thoughts, intent on avoiding what had too often been poison before—long discussions that disintegrate into debate and then march inexorably toward outbursts and regret.

Our last night together includes presentation of a surprise birthday cake for our father, a cake ablaze with sixty-eight candles, which leaves him touched and a little teary. He is bent over and about to blow out the candles when someone says, "Make a wish, make a wish" and others pick up the chant.

"My only wish," our father says finally, "is for everyone here to have all their wishes come true."

The next morning, I am about to set out again, but first there are some photographs to take. Katie has the camera in hand and Sam and I stand close together, our father pressed between us. She then raises the camera but there is no need for her to say "Cheese!"

or any such thing. We Marshall men are already wearing smiles, the broad smiles of three survivors finally overcoming past mistakes.

Back on the road, it is suddenly fall. I have made my way around the country for almost six weeks now, basking in the warmth of Indian summer, sunny days, warm nights, cotton sweaters in October, my amazement with the weather growing with each new morning on the road. I feel as though I am defying the calendar on my journey, blessed with endless summer. It gives the hours at the wheel a languid feel.

Then, on the Interstate in North Carolina, speeding along on the eve of Halloween, I cross into the land of autumn. The trees along the highway wear leaves of red and gold, and a few trees are already bare. I can sense winter coming on for the first time on the trip. And I shudder when I think about what winter might be like when I am trying to make it back to Seattle, across the Midwest, over the Rockies, and in a car which has terrible traction in the snow.

Snow in the Rockies has always been my greatest driving fear on this trip. I still have nightmare visions of driving across Wyoming in a blizzard in 1971, somehow proceeding right past a roadblock that was supposed to have closed the Interstate, the worst drive of my life, huge drifts across the highway, swirling winds, a clenched steering wheel, a look of near-terror on the face of my first wife.

This morning, I am on a sentimental detour, heading toward a border town called Eden where I was first married in 1969. That summer I graduated from Virginia and I was feeling the press of my upcoming entrance into the Army. The war was no longer a distant threat, now maybe months away. I had stayed in Charlottesville for the summer, working as a construction laborer to pay the bills, while the woman I loved was attending Harvard summer school.

We had seen each other a couple times during the summer, separation afterward always painful since our future seemed out of our hands. She had another year of college to complete. I had to report to Fort Benning. So we were stuck, our love stymied.

Then, she sat down one night in her Harvard dorm room, and wrote me a letter on yellow legal paper that said in part: "I have been thinking about making a deal with you. I don't think you'll go for it in a big way. But anyway the deal is to get secretly married and not tell anybody until I graduate. It's sort of a hair-brained idea. It just sounds like a good idea now."

I had not received her letter that Tuesday night when I picked up the phone and called her in Boston. I was nervous because I had this idea we had not discussed before, something I thought I might raise, depending on how the conversation went. Finally, I could hold off no longer. "I've been thinking," I said, "why don't we just elope?"

She laughed and told me about her letter then in the mails somewhere along the East Coast. That we had both come up with the same proposal made our reasoning impossible to resist. Besides, the first two men had walked on the moon only a few days before. It seemed such an auspicious time.

We could not get married in Virginia, it turned out, because she had a few weeks to go until she was twenty-one. So we set out for North Carolina the last Saturday in July, our good friends, Al and Brenda Vermeire, in the back seat of my Mustang, a bottle of French champagne on ice in the trunk.

It was like some riotous field trip on the road that morning. Laughter and loud music ricocheted inside the car and sometimes we all sang along. The suddenness of what we were doing made us giddy. We were in love, we were seizing our future, we were getting married and doing it our way, with no complicated plans, no exhaustive guest list, no parental scenes either, just a groom in blue jeans and a bride in a Marimekko dress. We blew across the Carolina line with a cheer and entered Eden, a mile or so beyond. Even the name of the town signaled this was the right place to start our married life.

Now, I am back in Eden twenty years later, driving streets that look unchanged, except that the Globe Variety Store is nowhere to be found. Justice of the Peace Andrew Collins had his office above that store, up old wooden stairs that creaked under our feet, our exchange of vows on hold while a couple of town troublemakers were booked for an indiscretion the night before. I now search in vain for the storefront before getting directions from a friendly old-timer in the hardware store.

I head up the old steps, which still creak, and arrive at what looks like the waiting room of the Justice of the Peace, although no sign of his office remains.

"May I help you?" asks a man, from beyond an open door to a law office.

"I was looking for Andrew Collins' place."

"He moved to the Municipal Building years ago. He's probably over there now if you need to talk to him."

"Oh no, that's not necessary. I was married here twenty years ago and I just wanted to confirm that this was the place."

"It sure is," the lawyer says. "There used to be an awful lot of weddings up here; I served as a witness at many. Maybe even yours."

"Perhaps you did."

There does not seem to be much else to say. I walk around for a moment, trying to conjure up the elation I once felt in this hallway, the future full of unknowns, but at least it would not be faced alone. Now, I had a wife.

"The old building has held up pretty well," I finally say to the man. Then I add for some strange reason, "Better than the marriage, I guess, since that ended after thirteen years. But thirteen years is not bad these days."

"Not bad at all," he says.

My new wife had returned to Boston after the weekend we eloped and she had written me a letter a few days later following an exchange of harsh words on the telephone.

"I refuse to become stodgy just because I am married," she emphasized. "We are young and I think we should be lighthearted, so to speak, while we can. I am just as serious and willing to accept my responsibilities toward our marriage as you are—I just refuse to let our situation get the best of me. I wish you would stop thinking only the bad parts—and being influenced by skeptical people—I am convinced that we are going to be happy forever and if we aren't it's our own fault."

And it was "our own fault." We weathered the year of separation while she finished school; weathered the days of uncertainty when I was trying to get out of the Army; weathered the poverty of graduate school when her clerical work and my G.I. Bill barely kept us afloat; weathered a move half way across the country, too, and starting careers in Oregon. But somehow when we had surmounted all those challenges and had settled into a comfortable life, we found we did not love each other anymore. We had grown up and grown apart, and not much seemed to hold us to each other, least of all the determination that we must make things work.

So we were not "happy forever," although we did have fine times, many I remember still. And I am married to someone else, the mother of my first child, source of satisfactions I could never have imagined two decades ago. But standing where I was first a married man, I still feel sadness mingled with loss, aftermath of a love that did not last despite vows in Eden, what now seems ages ago.

14

The Demise of Coats & Ties

THESE ARE STAIRS I climbed many times as a college student, stairs up to the fifth floor offices of the *Cavalier Daily*. I first entered this hubbub early in my first semester, a hesitant lad in new college clothes who inquired as to whether I could write for the student newspaper. I had been put to work that very day, or the next, and I kept working here three years, spending most afternoons and many evenings until I had become co-sports editor and columnist. I came to love this hectic place, the ready camaraderie, at least until I finished second in the staff election to become editor in chief, the worst disappointment of my college years.

But that experience never soured me on the University of Virginia. From my first visit, I was enthralled by this school founded by Thomas Jefferson, one of the three accomplishments he wanted remembered on his tombstone: "Here was buried Thomas Jefferson, author of the Declaration of American Independence, of the Statute of Virginia for Religious Freedom, and father of the University of Virginia." Jefferson is still revered here, so much so that generations of students have referred to him as "Mr. Jefferson," as if he might drop down from Monticello again for a chat at any moment.

Jefferson's design for the university—the Lawn and its centerpiece, the Rotunda—was honored by architects in 1976 as the greatest accomplishment in two hundred years of American architecture. But it is no museum. Students still walk to class along Jefferson's pathways, where his presence is felt amid the stately white columns, the handsome brick buildings, the formal gardens, the stone steps worn smooth by the feet of students all the way back to Edgar Allen Poe. Beauty and civility still linger here, with a student-run honor system still revered. At U.Va., there is an enticing mystique, the university as a special world apart, a notion that still has a hold on me, especially when leaves turn color in the fall.

But my two visits back to Charlottesville after college have left me stunned by all the change. Virginia's enrollment has doubled from the seven thousand students during my years, women have been admitted and the university has added several encampments of mediocre modern buildings, the sort seen on campuses anywhere. Charlottesville itself is even more altered, with strip shopping centers stretching halfway to Washington, D.C., fast food outlets on the university's doorstep, a revived downtown, boutiques, galleries, pricey restaurants, an undercurrent of hunt country pretense. For Charlottesville has suddenly been discovered by the celebrity set and is now home to Jessica Lange, Sam Shepard, Sissy Spacek, Ann Beattie, Rita Mae Brown. The hilly countryside is alive with new money, giving Charlottesville an unusual character—cap and gown meets Ralph Lauren in college Polo town.

The offices of the *Cavalier Daily* remain the same old raucous confusion. The wastebaskets overflow, half-finished Cokes are left here and there, weird bumper stickers abound. Too many phones ring in too small rooms and too many staffers scramble for too few desks. This is newspapering at its most basic, messy, gutsy, great fun, the way it used to be before the business grew up and modeled itself on the insurance industry. I feel immediately at home back here, except that everyone seems frightfully young.

I have not come back to relive memories. I have come back on a research mission to insure that I am not guilty of looking back at the 1960s through the granny glasses of nostalgia. What I experienced at Virginia seems to have set me on a collision course with my grandfather, or at least that is how I have chosen to remember it. But so much seems hazy in my memory. I think I recall the first Vietnam demonstration at Virginia on a chilly winter afternoon my first year. I can see a handful of protestors parading in front of the library, while a gathering crowd watched and jeered. But did that demonstration occur then, or have I got the details wrong? I turn to the leather-bound volumes of the *Cavalier Daily* to test what I remember against what took place.

I have only started to make my way through the first issue of my first year, dated September 1, 1965, when my attention is captured by a headline that proclaims, "Gentlemanly Attire: Meaningful Tradition for University Students." There follows this report: "In an atmosphere where tradition is a respected and meaningful way of life, the custom of wearing coats and ties is, next to the Honor System, the tradition most cherished by the students of the University. The coat and tie (when worn, of course, in conjunction with shirt, pants, underwear, shoes and socks) is not considered to be in any way a sign of that dreaded word 'conformity.' University students conduct themselves as gentlemen and their dress reflects this attitude. Thus, the coat and tie, being the everyday dress of the student, conveys the idea that at this stage in his life, the student accepts his role as a young adult and a gentleman."[1]

I smile. These words and sentiments now seem quaint—like some nineteenth century Englishman expounding on the virtues of colonialism—especially in light of how many U.Va. students soon came to view coats and ties as a symbol of The System, spurned in favor of Army field jackets and jeans. And then it occurs to me that these old U.Va. newspapers are an invaluable record of what the 1960s wrought at a college steeped in conservative tradition. This was not Berkeley, Cornell, Columbia, or Madison, one of those hotbeds that garnered the headlines, with students turned quasi revolutionaries. These papers recount what it was like at many more places, a record of the real 1960s as experienced by the majority of American college students, not at the barricades, but not on the sidelines either. Too much was going on then to escape unscathed.

I make my way through these pages of yellowing newsprint, intent on comparing what happened my first year at Virginia with my last, 1965–66 versus 1968–69. This seems a convenient barometer to measure changes in the weather during that stormy decade.

Vietnam is asserting its presence on campus even before I have bought all of my first college textbooks. The war is still distant, but it hangs over our heads, ominous dead weight. There is no need to name the country where students could end up when the Registrar's Office reports finding errors in some Selective Service forms from registration; it is sufficient to warn, "Delay in sending in these forms could affect your draft status." And the next day's *Cavalier Daily* carries a story that begins, "Ten thousand former airmen and other ex-servicemen are being sought to fill the active duty enlisted ranks being increased by the Vietnam crisis."

This is a much different Vietnam from the one which would come later, and not just because it is called a "crisis." This is a Vietnam where American certitude still reigns, and those who protest the war are seen as a lunatic fringe. The burning of a draft card in New York prompts the *Cavalier Daily* to editorialize: "It is just another one of the myriad and irresponsible ways by which an infinitesimal minority of the American population has captured a national platform from which to speak. . . . It is about time our non-believers in the Viet cause realize that these men serving in the Asian nation are there to protect our interests, our security. Those who embrace pacifism as a credo should have learned that it was this same attitude which led to Munich."

Twenty years later, the Vietnam War has been so discredited that it is easy to assume such hard-line views were only voiced on campuses in the South and perhaps the Midwest. But the *Cavalier Daily*'s editorial stand on Vietnam was in the college mainstream, as a national poll of students finds in November. The "Playboy Survey on College Opinion" reports that 82 percent of college students agree the United States has an obligation to aid Vietnam and 90 percent agree that Americans have an obligation to serve in the military even if they disagree with government policies.

My first months at Virginia do see the first clouds of the gathering storm. An associate of Timothy Leary lectures on "LSD and Sober Reflections on the Ecstatic Experience." Writer Tom Wolfe talks on California surfers and bohemians. A Vietnam symposium pits a film produced by the State Department against one done by the Viet Cong. And a second-year U.Va. student named Jonathan "Lance" Gainsbrugh is fined fifty dollars and sentenced to twenty days in jail because a judge in Charlottesville Municipal Court finds him in contempt for failing to comply with his order to get a haircut. Gainsbrugh had come for a hearing on a traffic charge with his hair neatly combed and clean-shaven, only to have Judge Allan Spitzer rule that his appearance was "a deterrent to the orderly proceedings of the court." "The whole thing," Gainsbrugh is quoted as saying, "was like something out of William Faulkner."

The second semester starts and Vietnam is again in the news. In November, the conservative Young Americans for Freedom has sponsored a drive to send Christmas cards to soldiers in Vietnam, evidence that those in the service were not always the object of scorn from college students. One of the recipients of this U.Va. mail is a Marine enlisted man named Cecil W. McClellan who writes a thank-you letter to the newspaper and includes this message from the war zone: "I would like to say if there is anyone who cannot see why the U.S. has involved itself in South Vietnam, I have this to say. A man or woman who thinks he has the right to question the actions of the United States President is not a true American and should not consider himself as such."

I would like to be shocked by McClellan's ill logic, how his patriotic fervor eclipses any understanding of dissent or the guarantees of the Bill of Rights. But our generation had been raised on Davy Crockett and JFK; we had no heroes who had dared to say no. So we lashed out at what seemed so foreign to us, our ridicule bred by ignorance, even at Thomas Jefferson's university.

That is underscored when I do come upon the account of that first Vietnam demonstration at Virginia. The front page of the *Cavalier Daily* on February 15, 1966, carries a photo of some demonstrators, most in coats and ties, marching in front of the library. Two women are part of the demonstration, and two children, one an infant in a stroller. Except for their hand-written signs ("End War Before War Ends Us"), this group looks about as threatening as a monthly meeting of campus Young Republicans. But that is not how these demonstrators were viewed, as a news story recounts:

"An hour-long demonstration was held Saturday against the War in Vietnam by the Students for Social Actions (SSA). Twenty-three marchers circled before Alderman Library carrying placards attacking the present policy of military involvement in Vietnamese affairs with various slogans: 'Support Our GIs; Bring Them Home,' 'Draft LBJ,' 'Support Mental Health in the Pentagon.'

"A crowd of about 100 spectators formed to view the march, an occasional few jeering and pelting the marchers with snowballs. The general opinion of the crowd was that the march was ridiculous and laughter was the most common reaction to the demonstrators. Preston Syme, fourth-year College, remarked that 'once you notice what a pathetic group they are, it is hard to take them seriously.'

"One student, after tossing a snowball, declared that 'The University is not the place for such a protest. The University has gentlemanly traditions—this belongs in California.' A few students sang a chorus of 'Mickey Mouse' while a few others yelled 'Gobble, Gobble' and threw pennies.

"One of the organizers of the march said that the purpose of the demonstration was to show the press, The University community, and the people of Charlottesville that the entire student body is not mesmerized into believing in the Johnson policy." A graduate student, William H. Leary said, 'It is ridiculous not to negotiate. I want the war to end in the most expeditious way possible.'"

So my recollection is correct. I had come upon this demonstration and it did seem to me like something from California, if not Mars. I did not jeer, and I did not throw anything, but I do remember wondering why those weirdos were marching around and just taking it when subjected to catcalls and snowballs. Now, I start to discover that what they had done was light the first candle in the darkness, not changing U.Va. overnight, but illuminating the way for much of what was to follow. This tiny demonstration on a Saturday afternoon—what seemed a parody of a real protest—is a watershed event at Virginia, as its aftermath shows.

Great controversy flares. The Student Council is moved to investigate whether the demonstration was an "unauthorized assembly," conducted in violation of university regulations. A record crowd of three hundred people turns out to hear the council debate. The *Cavalier Daily* weighs in with a massive editorial ("Trouble on the Left") which defends the right to demonstrate peacefully and criticizes "the inexcusable conduct of a few ungentlemanly spectators."

The paper's Letters to the Editor section erupts in debate with a new-found passion.

David Bonds-Kemp, a second-year student, asserts: "A university has a place for forums, lectures, debates, and dissertations to

facilitate the contemplation of the derivation of truth . . . but there
should be no place within the ivory tower of thought for distracting
activist propaganda which belongs in the streets."

William J. Sragow, a first-year student, counters: "It seems that
Virginia is the only university of importance which has chosen es-
capism as its reaction to the pressing, and unusually frustrating problems of today. The intellectual ferment present on other campuses is
sadly lacking here. . . . The linen service excites more emotional
fervor than the killing of soldiers and civilians in Vietnam. . . . If
World War III began during a 'Big Weekend,' the Virginia gentleman would not want to know about it. So while we, supposedly the
future leaders of this country, shirk our responsibilities, we condemn
and ridicule those who meet theirs. Only the joke is on us."

The spring of 1966 winds down toward finals. The first fires of
controversy die down. Calm returns. Gen. Lewis Hershey, director
of Selective Service, godfather of the draft, lectures to a packed Ca-
bell Hall with no protest. A Student Council drive collects two hundred fifty pounds of books for students of English in Vietnam. And
the *Cavalier Daily* assesses Vietnam and concludes, "This is a war
worth fighting."

A news story in March foreshadows another element of the hurricane ahead. "University Students Arrested after Police Stage Dope
Raid" is followed by a story that begins: "A joint raid by the University and Charlottesville Police, along with federal narcotics agents,
Saturday netted about an ounce of what is believed to be marijuana
and led to the subsequent arrest of two third-year College students at
the University." That "federal narcotics agents" could be concerning
themselves with an ounce of marijuana seems comic now, a throw-
back to "Refer Madness" days, but not then. Not when the newspaper feels compelled to tell innocent readers that the search of a
student's sports car yields enough grass to "make up about 100 cigarettes which may sell for 75 cents to $1.00 each."

I am just finishing the 1965–66 papers when a reporter comes
into the room and sits next to me. This reporter is a black woman
and I welcome the change that twenty years has brought to Virginia.
For we had no women and no blacks working on the staff during my
C.D. days, although we did come to recognize those glaring deficiencies. One of my last acts as sports editor was devoting the entire

sports page to an in-depth examination of why no blacks had yet received athletic scholarships at Virginia. "Recruiting Negro athletes obscures the greater problem," I wrote in a column, "of just getting Negro students here."

Two decades later, I find myself listening as a black reporter calls the president of the university for a comment on a story, then leaves her name and number.

"Does he ever actually call back?" I ask her, voicing a familiar reporter's complaint.

"Most of the time," she replies. "He's a pretty good dude."

The bound copies of the *Cavalier Daily*'s from my last year are missing from the newspaper office, so I must go to Alderman Library instead. I descend to the basement of the mammoth building where the *Cavalier Daily* is stored on microfiche. I stare at the lighted screen where the newspaper pages are displayed in bold relief, the high-contrast so appropriate for what is going on in the fall of 1968.

A draft counseling service operates daily at the student union. A local chapter of the radical Students for a Democratic Society (SDS) is holding its second meeting. Two self-proclaimed anarchists sit on the Student Council, after last year's campaign featured the slogan: "Vote Anarchist: What Has Order Gotten You?"[2] The dean of students has felt compelled to send a letter to first-year men, warning them of the dangers of hallucinogenic drugs. A store just off campus called Xanadu is offering "Whatever Your Head Desires," from water pipes to black lights. Beta Bridge, where the scores of Virginia's athletic triumphs have been painted for years, is now covered with peace signs. And, buried in a story ("Accidents Claim Lives of Four During Summer"), this news from the war—Henry Luke Warner III, class of 1966, former president of Beta Theta Pi, has been killed in Vietnam. The twenty-five-year-old Army first lieutenant from Alexandria is dead from shrapnel wounds.

Army ROTC has become a particular target of protest at U.Va. Enrollment is dropping and the Army staff is trying to blame the decline on something other than the war. Vandals ransack the display cases outside the ROTC offices, stealing medals and photographs, prompting the FBI to be called in. And a Letter to the Editor charges that ROTC is "incompatible with The University's function" because it "is an instrument of the government for training killers."

My head spins, confronting these times again. I wonder how we ever managed to study in this intoxicating atmosphere of so much change. Every day brings forth some development unimaginable at Virginia only a year or two before. Activism bursts into full bloom and not even the Student Council can remain immune.

The council suddenly goes on record urging students and faculty to boycott local barbers who say they will not or cannot cut the hair of "Negroes." The *Cavalier Daily* responds by calling this "one of the boldest moves we have ever seen the council take." Only six days after the council's action, the barber chairs are liberated for all.

Drug use has mushroomed. Two unnamed student users are interviewed by the *Cavalier Daily* and tell the newspaper that "pot was just coming into its own in 1967 at Virginia" and things have escalated from there. "Is there much acid available in Charlottesville?" asks the newspaper. "You can get it," replies one user, "without much trouble."

Student activism builds to a crescendo second semester with the appearance of a new student group called The Coalition, which presses demands for greater integration (only eighty-six black students are enrolled), plus changes in the way the university is governed. Leading The Coalition is Robert Rosen, who rockets into prominence with a massive tome in the *Cavalier Daily*, "A Prospectus for the University," serious words for these serious times, quotes from Camus even, and including this Rosen conclusion: "The man who best expressed how I—and hundreds more 'free-thinking' students—feel about the issue of student activism was none other than Thomas Jefferson, local founder, sage and (by the way) Revolutionary."

The Coalition soon rallies four hundred students on the Lawn. The Coalition formulates its "Proposals to End Racism." The Coalition garners support of local ministers. The Coalition prompts the university president to state that equal opportunity is "the firm commitment" of the university, yet he offers no specific plans. The Coalition promises "a year of protesting." The Coalition takes its proposals on to the governor, who offers "no support" for The Coalition's goals. The Coalition runs out of steam. The Coalition cannot hold.

There are several last gasps of activism in this spring of 1969.

Two hundred students walk out of the annual Founder's Day ceremony, disrupting the celebration of Thomas Jefferson on the 150th anniversary of the university's founding. "An air of tenseness" prevails, according to the *Cavalier Daily*. Thirty-five students invade a closed faculty meeting of the College of Arts & Sciences, demanding that the meetings be open to students and two students be appointed to the board.

And the annual Military Weekend review, my last march in my ROTC uniform, is conducted in Scott Stadium, where the football field sports a mammoth peace symbol drawn in lime. Protesters, some wearing bandages, chant "Peace Now! Peace Now!" and brandish signs that accuse us of being "Fascist Pigs." There are many conflicting feelings among those of us in uniform, as we listen to these angry chants while wondering about what our military service will bring, how soon we will see the war, and what that will entail.

Jackson Lears, my best friend, is marching in his Navy ROTC uniform this day and we share some of the same doubts about Vietnam and the military. Our four years at Virginia have given us decidedly liberal views. Jackson, a member of the Student Council, has just coauthored an op-ed article in the *Cavalier Daily* that attempts to rally students with a clarion call. "The University is ripe for revolution" is how the article opens and it concludes with "now is the time to act." But these words have a hollow ring late in the school year when graduation looms and so much student activism has already been expended with so little effect.

As the year-end editorial in the *Cavalier Daily* summarizes: "Looking back at the past year, at its failures and disappointments, we are tempted to express our disdain for what went on here—the incipient attempt to galvanize a University that had lain dormant for, lo, these many years. But then we reflect on the old University, wrapped in its tranquil cocoon as it was not that long ago, and perhaps more than we sometimes realize, The University is moving, is changing, is, in its own way, struggling to meet the challenges of the times."

But the editor cannot resist one final postscript, so U. Va. in its concern, but still indicative of all the change. "We mourn," he writes, "the apparent passing of coats and ties."

I was no activist my last semester at Virginia. I was no leader of The Coalition. I had time to myself at long last. Behind me now were my days at the *Cavalier Daily* and *Rapier* magazine, my part-time job as an ad copy writer for a Charlottesville radio station, my service as vice-president of my fraternity. I was free of these obligations and I decided to enjoy being a college student while I still could. Before the Army.

So I spent those last months in love with two women, a semi-successful juggling act of dating a nursing student in Charlottesville and an art history major at a college down the road, the woman who became my wife. And I studied, studied so hard that I managed the best grades in my four years at Virginia, a 3.375 grade point average.

No course that year affected my thinking quite like William Henry Harbaugh's History of the United States in the 20th Century. At first, his class seemed a stretch; I was an English major and this was a graduate-level history course. But the reading was fascinating and Harbaugh was one of the best lecturers I had ever encountered. He mesmerized his class, this solid-set, square-jawed man with a ruddy complexion, prematurely white hair, and fiery eyes behind thick glasses. Harbaugh had the ebullient spirit of an Irish poet, the soul of a revolutionary, with strong convictions, broad sympathies. His perspective was liberal, unrepentantly liberal even at Virginia, and this challenged many of my long-held perceptions of history, especially America as Hero on the World Stage.

Harbaugh summarized his philosophical approach in a letter he later wrote in support of my application for C.O. discharge: "Although my course was not designed to inculcate pacifist attitudes, all my students know that I subscribe to Walter Lippman's view that 'the majority of wars in which any great power engages are not life-and-death struggles in which its existence is at stake, but little wars of policy, interest, or accident.' That theory, among others, was elaborated during the course. We studied the decision to acquire the Philippines after the war with Spain. We studied American atrocities during the guerilla war against Aguinaldo. We studied the decision to drop two atomic bombs on Japan despite the fact that we had intercepted and decoded Japanese messages indicating that they were

THE DEMISE OF COATS & TIES   165

on the verge of surrender. We studied Nuremberg. And we studied the origins of our involvement in Vietnam."

Now, I am seated in Harbaugh's book-filled living room, with the professor looking virtually unchanged by two decades, and I am telling him how much his course affected my thinking, especially when Vietnam loomed, and how much I appreciated his C.O. support letter, one of three I received from U.Va. professors. Harbaugh tells me how many such letters he wrote back then, not only to the military but also to draft boards, his course obviously a crucial foundation for many of us who took stands against the war.

Teachers are such strange creatures to their students, people we usually glimpse only in halftones. They come into our lives for a time, share their insights into Eliot's *Waste Land* or guerilla movements in the Philippines, and yet we have no understanding of how they came to their perspectives, what forces shaped them, or what they had hoped to accomplish with their course. We students usually do not care that much about those who stand before us while we scribble notes. Harbaugh was one of those rare exceptions and I use our conversation to explore the person behind the professor.

Harbaugh turns out to have been the commander of an antiaircraft battery in France during World War II, who returned to the United States, entered Columbia University, and began teaching soon afterward. His specialty has been public policy and twentieth century America and he has written two biographies, one of Theodore Roosevelt. Now, nearly seventy, he has tired of teaching.

"In a sense, I have lost my fire," Harbaugh says. "I've always been prematurely gray, but I'm really tired of trying to simplify issues that defy simplification. The longer I live, the more complex they seem. And since I am not the teacher I once was, I should quit."

"I wonder how Vietnam affected the teaching of your American history course back when I was a student?"

"What was on my mind regarding Vietnam," Harbaugh responds, "was having been in World War II and having witnessed the opening of one of the Nazi concentration camps in Austria. I had read enough to know that the German intelligentsia had put its head in the sand—a great many professors had become instruments of the state. I didn't want it on my conscience that I had been an instrument of the state in what I considered a wrong and immoral war. World War II had been 'a good war' and it did influence me. But I didn't want to be like those German professors who rationalized Hitler."

"Were you ever thinking that the students who listened to your lectures could end up in Vietnam?"

"I was torn by that all the time. There were guys who would come to my classes in their ROTC uniforms and it was most difficult for me. Here I was, a former battery commander, and I was marching and protesting in Washington—why I gave one or two speeches there. To go on those marches, with my background, was a painful experience. And it was compounded by the fact that a lot of those who went on the marches wanted to change everything. I didn't endorse that and I had to keep reminding myself that stopping the war was preeminent."

"How did you come to your perspective on the war?"

"The study of history changed my view. I still believe in national defense; I am not a conscientious objector, not a pacifist. But the study of history persuaded me that we were overextended in the Pacific. We misconstrued, to a great degree, the Communist threat. As a great power, we exceeded the limits of a responsible defense."

"I take it you have no regrets about what you did then."

"I've never felt guilty or regretful about my involvement in the antiwar movement. History has confirmed that we had no national interest in Vietnam. For us to lose those boys killed and to kill all those Vietnamese was a pure tragedy—what good came out of it?"

"Did you speculate on what you would have done if facing possible service in Vietnam as your students were?"

"I had a family during the time of Vietnam," Harbaugh says slowly. "I felt that if that war continued, I would take a job in Canada to free my children from facing that kind of decision about the war."

We spend an hour together talking about the past we shared. There is little nostalgia. We recall too many hard dilemmas, too many horrible scenarios, too much frustration confronting the war. There was a desperate urgency to things then, as if daily life came with a score by The Doors.

And yet I cannot stop myself from asking Harbaugh to compare what it was like teaching back then versus now, my presumption transparent—that it was certainly better during the 1960s when I was a student.

But Harbaugh demurs from making any such comparison. As he has said, he has grown weary of easy answers. What he does respond could serve as an epitaph for the 1960s and what I have rediscovered in the pages of the *Cavalier Daily*.

"Those times were unique," Harbaugh declares. "They had a dynamism that cannot be reproduced."

15

Rising Star

CHARLOTTESVILLE GIVES WAY TO GUM SPRING and Sandy Hook, back on the Interstate once again. I am on the way to Fort Monroe, this Army headquarters which is in the process of publishing an official book detailing S. L. A. Marshall's influence on the Army. I am thinking about my grandfather and our split as I speed across the lush Virginia countryside.

Rereading those *Cavalier Daily*'s had reawakened buried memories, as had visits with Harbaugh and professors John Coleman and John Graham. "I damn well remember those 1960s," Graham had told me over lunch. "I remember walking up the Lawn and seeing students who liked me and wouldn't meet my eyes because of the politics of those times. That hurt, that hurt damn bad." My time back in Charlottesville has confirmed what a crucible my college years had been and how so much of what I did—the courses I studied, the professors I admired, the friends I treasured—all seemed to be leading me on a collision course with my grandfather. Maybe if there had not been a war on the clash could have been avoided, but the war awaited soon after college, with hard choices to be faced.

Urban sprawl now scars the landscape as I near Newport News and Norfolk, the local hero recalled by the Patrick Henry International Airport and the Patrick Henry Shopping Mall. I soon drive across a bridge spanning a moat, then pass through the massive stone walls of Fort Monroe, this historic old fort guarding the harbor of Hampton Roads, in continuous use since 1823. I park near the quarters that once housed a U.S. Army lieutenant named Robert E.

Lee. I walk into the office of the command historian for the U.S. Army Training and Doctrine Command (TRADOC), which is deep within the fort's walls, a cool place perhaps better suited for a wine cellar.

I am greeted by Susan Canedy, a thirty-five-year-old Army historian, one of six assigned to TRADOC headquarters. I have corresponded with Canedy and talked on the phone; we meet now for the first time. She is a tall woman with frizzy, shoulder-length hair, and a pretty face. The product of an Army family, she has a doctorate in history from Texas A. & M. She also has a puckish wit.

One of Cannedy's first tasks at TRADOC has been the editing of a book on Marshall written by Maj. F. D. G. Williams, a career Army officer now stationed in Germany; he had originally submitted this as his master's thesis at Rice University. Canedy has checked and rechecked Williams' work, tightened his writing, suggested some changes in what will become a 138-page book distributed throughout the Army. Although Canedy was not familiar with Marshall at first, that changed during months of full-time work on the project. As she says, "I turned into a Marshall scholar real quick."

Williams has done more thorough research into S. L. A. Marshall than any of Marshall's critics and his conclusion is highly favorable to what Marshall accomplished. Williams does discuss Marshall's personality flaws, but also dismisses much of the criticism of the man and his work. Examining the sometime complaint about Marshall's accuracy, Williams conducted a "spot check" of three Marshall books from different wars. He compared the texts with Marshall's notes on which the books were based. William's study of *The River and the Gauntlet* (Korea), *Night Drop* (WWII), and *Ambush* (Vietnam) found that Marshall did, on occasion, increase the number of men involved in an action or distances, but Williams concludes, "Most often, however, the story followed the notes exactly . . . the changes were never significant in any way."[1]

Williams' favorable assessment of Marshall might give rise to suspicion that his book is the Army's response to the current controversy, the circling of wagons around an embattled Army legend. But Canedy assures me that is not the case. TRADOC had decided to publish Williams' book before the controversy broke and nothing revealed in the controversy caused the Army to reconsider publication. So I should not be surprised when I ask Canedy for her assessment of the controversy.

"I thought it was petty, not relevant to anything; the charges are not relevant charges," she emphasizes. "And it was poorly researched by historians or writers out to make a name for themselves on the tail of another. Marshall's *Men Against Fire* finding that only one of four soldiers fired their weapons in World War II is not that important because there is no way to know whether the correct figure is one of four, two of four or three of four. Nor will we ever discover his motivations for choosing that.

"And I find it odd that *Men Against Fire* was well received when it came out and real queer that those who had the memories of World War II fighting did not raise a flap then. Instead a flap does come up forty years later. Marshall's current critics are like gnats—I don't listen to them."

Canedy goes on to tell me how she has come to admire Marshall's savvy as "a major actor" within the Army, his tenacity in working toward change, his devotion to the institution, too. And she has also come to like him as a person; she finds him a fascinating character. She says she would not mind meeting him in a bar someplace and sharing conversation over a few drinks.

"And what would you ask him?" I say.

"I'd ask why he stretched the truth in his autobiography and I'd like to have him say, 'To make a better story.'"

"Then that's why you think he lied about some things?"

"Right. To make a better story. But what he thought he was stretching was insignificant really. It doesn't necessarily mean that he lied about big things."

Canedy accompanies me out to my car. It is quitting time on a Friday afternoon, most of the fort's offices have already emptied, the sun is starting to set in a burnt-orange sky. We have not talked that long and what I do not mention, although it is much on my mind, is how Canedy's perspective on S. L. A. Marshall is, in many ways, one I am coming to share.

Washington is next, certain to be one of my busiest times on the trip. There is research to be done in the National Archives, friends and critics of S. L. A. Marshall to be interviewed, other mat-

ters to be tracked down, and during this time I am to be living with
my grandfather's brother, this man I hardly know. Charles Burton
Marshall had been a great help when I was writing my newspaper
series, offering insights into his brother that seemed startlingly can-
did. He has been more help since, supplementing his 1977 letter to
historian John Keegan with a letter to me, both letters discussing his
brother in great depth, a total of twenty-seven pages single-spaced.

His relationship with his brother, Burt had written, was
"marked by mutual esteem, but reserved rather than chummy," a
relationship that certainly did not preclude his recognition of his
brother's foibles, and sometimes pointed criticism. There had later
come Burt's surprise invitation to visit him in Washington and listen
to all he has to say about his brother, an invitation tinged with the
unspoken recognition that the days for doing this may be limited.
Burt is eighty-one, and I was not about to let this chance pass, but I
also wonder how he and I will get along without the easy intimacy of
telephone and letters.

Now, I am walking up the sidewalk to a brick rambler in a tree-
shaded neighborhood of Arlington and I ring the doorbell and Burt
opens the door and I almost gasp. He looks so much like his brother;
it is eerie, unexpected. I feel as though my grandfather were suddenly
greeting me for the first time since my mother's funeral eighteen
years ago. Granted, Burt is five inches taller, but the family resemblance is unmistakable, especially that pronounced Roman nose.

But then I go to embrace Burt, as I always did Poppy, and Burt
draws back, awakening me from this strange sense of being with my
grandfather again. Burt introduces me to Betty, his second wife, slim
and pretty at seventy, utterly charming, sweet-tempered, so unlike
Cate, my grandfather's wife. We settle into the living room. Burt
and Betty want to hear all about my trip and I produce an abridged
version, while also noticing that Burt actually resembles the British
actor Robert Morley more than his older brother.

Burt has that harrumph quality about him, that rarefied air of
civility, sophistication, and reserve. His sense of humor is as dry as
Bombay gin and his laugh is a chortle that causes his jowls to quiver.
And he has this habit—so disconcerting to me at first—of punctuat-
ing his humorous stories with a probing stare and a quick little "huh,

huh?" that comes across as a way of making sure the listener has grasped the story's full glory. The aura of academia still clings to him, even seated in an easy chair in his living room. His humorous stories are intellectual, filled with word play, rife with irony, yielding lessons. He bespeaks Harvard doctorate. And I find myself liking the ways that he is so different from my grandfather, less coarse, more circumspect, less incendiary, more thoughtful.

But oh how they like to tell their stories, both Burt and Slam, stories that become monologues, ten minutes long, sometimes fifteen or longer, monopolizing conversation while firmly ensconced at center stage. Slam's stories of wars are Burt's stories of stints at various foreign policy posts or advising the prime minister of Pakistan. Slam's Army generals are Burt's Washington insiders, friends like Paul Nitze, other members of the elite Cosmos Club, where one wall is reserved for pictures of members who have won the Pulitzer Prize and another is reserved for those who have won the Nobel. Both Slam and Burt's stories give knowing glimpses of the power game and how it is played, behind the headlines.

Burt continues his stories through most of our first afternoon together, then into the evening, including dinner. Betty is the perfect partner to his tale telling, adding an occasional detail, supplying a missing date or place on request, acting as if the story is every bit as fascinating as it was the first time she heard it. They complement each other so well that I can believe Burt when he proclaims their thirty-one years of marriage have been untouched by acrimony. "I swear this is true," he says. "Every day is like Christmas for us; we have pleasant conversation the moment we awake."

I retire to the spare bedroom, where I try to plan my time in Washington. There is so much to do that I finally give up in frustration and go to bed. The clomp of Burt's wing tips on the hard hallway floor awakens me the next morning at six-thirty. He is on his way to make a pancake breakfast, which is served promptly at seven.

I wait for the morning rush hour to clear, then head down the George Washington Parkway along the Potomac and into the city. Washington, like Paris, never fails to exhilarate me, even on a cement gray day like this. To revisit Washington is to be reassured by broad avenues, great monuments, pleasing vistas. Much remains as I remember it from my first trip to the city with my parents, a youngster posed in front of various tourist sites, and looking so serious in a man's sort of overcoat, heavy, scratchy, wool.

I pass through the city this morning, cross the District of Columbia line and enter Suitland, Maryland, where a massive federal complex of nondescript buildings sits behind a chain-link fence topped with barbed wire. Somewhere in one of these buildings, my brother developed reconnaissance photos of Vietnam during his days in the Navy. The headquarters of the U.S. Census Bureau is located here, too, its computers tracking everyone in America. Other buildings here carry no markings about what is being done here or by whom, although maybe one would rather not know since the complex has a certain George Orwell air.

I finally locate Entrance No. 9 and drive into a federal compound so vast that signs soon warn: "No Golfing on Government Property." I pass a huge heating plant surrounded by ponds that emit steam in the morning air, and at last come upon the Washington National Records Center, a low-slung building that sits atop vast underground storage rooms, this newer annex to the original National Archives building downtown, both straining under the crush of federal paperwork, that prime product of the bureaucracy.

Some of my grandfather's records are supposed to be found at both of these locations—World War I records downtown, World War II here in Suitland—and I am about to begin my search. But first I must check in, a process not unlike gaining entry to a small foreign country, and not a hospitable one at that.

Show identification and sign in at the front desk. Show identification and sign in at the research room down the hall. Receive Researcher Identification Card, plastic debit card which operates Xerox machines, the fifty-page booklet setting forth "Regulations for the Public Use of Records in the National Archives." Deposit all personal belongings, including notebooks, in locker in the hallway. Return to research room, be granted access, pick up free paper on which all notes must be recorded, be shown to assigned table with assigned seat. Fill out research materials request and take it to the front desk. Return to assigned seat. Wait.

I scan the room. It is much like a library at a small high school, bookshelves lining the walls, large tables with chairs taking up most of the space, windows with a view of a parking lot. About fifty researchers are seated at the tables, scouring through pages and pages of paper, much of it yellowed with age. The researchers are an intriguing mix; some look to be lawyers, outfitted in their well-tailored suits, others look to be graduate students, the men wearing that perennial grad student uniform, faded blue jeans, wool shirts, the oldest pairs of Clark's desert boots still in use in America.

My research compatriots include: Cindy Hahamovitch, a twenty-seven-year-old graduate student from the University of North Carolina, who is doing research for her doctoral thesis on the farm labor movement on the East Coast, from 1880 to 1950; Will Lundy, a seventy-two-year-old Californian, who is the historian for his World War II bomber group and is copying all the unit's war records; Albert Diegmann, a thirty-five-year-old graduate student from the University of Aachen, West Germany, who is working on his doctoral thesis on the United States and the control of the Ruhr district after World War II; and Kenichi Hoshi, the forty-three-year-old leader of a team of five Japanese researchers who sit at small computers copying the records of the American occupation of Japan after World War II, a compilation being done for the Japanese equivalent of the Library of Congress, a laborious project that has consumed several years and will take at least two more.

A library cart is soon brought to my desk, filled with those gray boxes so familiar from El Paso, nine boxes in all, the records of the Historical Office of the European Theater of Operations where S. L. A. Marshall served as deputy and later chief. I am seized by intense curiosity, wondering if this is the place where I will finally discover his missing field notebooks. I open one box and see no such evidence. I open another box.

"Mr. Marshall," booms a voice from the front desk, "you are only to have one box open at a time!"

"Sorry. I didn't know."

I return to the first box after my breach of research protocol. It does not take me long to come upon my grandfather's name amid these tables of organization, weekly reports, requests for information, field interviews, correspondence. His name is almost everywhere,

S. L. A. Marshall making notes while interviewing two soldiers in the Pacific Islands, World War II. Courtesy S. L. A. Marshall Military History Collection, University of Texas at El Paso.

and then I even come upon his Army 201 personnel file. There may be none of his missing field notebooks here, but there is a treasure trove of information about his service in World War II. I devour the material, fascinated by voices from the war effort almost half a century ago.

Marshall is clearly a comer, first noticed far off the European stage, on assignment covering island operations in the South Pacific. Makin Island is the first, late in 1943. It is a small operation, perfect for study, like a lab experiment, except there is no set procedure to follow. So Marshall decides to record everything about the operation, from the inception plans to the final shots; he even makes sure that all the equipment for the operation is catalogued and weighed. Out of Makin comes Marshall's chance discovery of his pioneering group interview technique. Also born here is his conviction that these interviews will produce crucial lessons to be learned, the very reasoning that will motivate *Men Against Fire*.

Marshall reports to Washington: "The real need among ground troops is for 'briefing officers' who can put details of operations together, enable troops to understand what they have gone through and the lessons therein, and finally, to provide a sound basis for the writing of tactical history."

Kwajalein Island is next. Marshall hones his interview technique, producing another small-unit combat narrative. Copies are soon forwarded to the historians in Europe. It is turned into a book called *Island Victory*, which is published by the *Infantry Journal*, with a foreword where the editors proclaim: "No book like it has ever appeared before. And it is most probable that no days of battle in this or any previous war have ever been described as accurately as *Island Victory* describes the combat on Kwajalein."[2]

Marshall begins to garner a reputation. The commanding generals of two divisions whose operations he has covered think so highly of his work that they ask him to detail what he has found and what changes in training might be warranted. Marshall responds with a classified report of nine pages filled with pointed observations about combat that can be seen, in retrospect, as a virtual blueprint for *Men Against Fire*. Even the paper's first tactical area discussed comes under this heading: "1. EFFECT OF FIRE."

Brig. Gen. Arch Arnold, commander of the Seventh Infantry Division, is one of the two generals who requests the report and makes sure Marshall remains in the Pacific two extra months to complete it and work with his troops. Arnold later writes Marshall: "I don't know if you appreciated the tremendous impact of your past battle critiques started on Kwajalein and completed at Schofield had on the combat efficiency of the Seventh. The individuals realized during the critique how little each had contributed to the success of their units. Squads, platoons and companies were welded into hardhitting fighting units by each man's contribution to the team work. . . . Past battle critique had a very considerable influence."

Marshall's technique draws more interest among Army historical officers. Lt. Col. Charles H. Taylor, a colleague in the historical branch, a Harvard historian before the war, concludes that Marshall's work "justifies saying (and I am saying it) that he has created a new form of military literature." Taylor makes this observation in a letter to the chief of the Historical Branch in Washington and adds,

"Nobody but Sam could have done it. It required a man with his battle experience, knowledge of what to look for, aggressiveness, and reportorial skill. . . . Sam is really doing, in a remarkable way, what all the elements in the Information and Historical units are supposed to do. His product is at once history, battle stories that bring out the job and heroism of ground forces, and direct analysis for tactical lessons—and statement of same. It is in the third feature of this that it will be hard for anyone to follow in Sam's footsteps. It takes both knowledge and confidence to go as far as Sam does in this respect. . . . I am going to start out with Sam, but how long I can keep up with him is another matter. That guy is a wonder."

Col. William Ganoe, chief of the historians in Europe, is so impressed with Marshall's work that he asks him to provide a summary of his methods. Marshall responds with another nine-page report, a veritable how-to handbook on conducting group critiques after combat. Ganoe promptly distributes copies to all of his historians in June 1944, along with his notation: "Not only do I regard it as masterful but most extraordinarily helpful to all of us."

I read through these pages filled with Marshall's minutely detailed instructions until I come upon a passage that says: "It is not enough to ask at what time troops landed at a given point. Did they land wet or dry? Did they lose any equipment on landing? Did they go to the ground immediately? How did they feel while they were pinned down by fire? It is not enough to ask what kind of radio or other communications facility the company had. Did it work? How well did it work? When was it supplemented by runners? If communication failed, why did it fail? It is not enough to determine, in connection with a local episode, that M-1s [rifles] and grenades were used. How many men actually fired with M-1s or threw grenades? Answers can be had with a showing of hands."

My eyes screech to a halt. My eyes backtrack. My eyes read again, "How many men actually fired with M-1s. . . . Answers can be had with a showing of hands." I would like to let out a cheer in the archive at this moment. For this passage confirms that weapons firing was indeed a concern of Marshall's, a line of inquiry from early in his war service as a combat historian. This passage is crucial evidence. Maybe his field notebooks will never be found. Maybe they do not contain exact computations on firing anyway. But firing was indeed on Marshall's mind, a problem he had noted and pondered in the Pacific, something he would then have tracked during his interview sessions in Europe. He certainly did not invent this after the war when he began to write *Men Against Fire,* as some of his critics charge. Their allegation is wrong. And I feel profound relief.

I return to my research and watch Marshall continue his ascent. He arrives in Europe several weeks after D-Day, demonstrates his technique with some of the units involved in that action, convinces skeptical historians about the worth of what he is doing, joins forces with Westover, sets off on a frantic round of postcombat interview missions. He goes wherever he needs to go, with a military pass card that stipulates: "It is requested that this officer be given as complete freedom of movement as is practicable, that he have free access to all military areas and installations, and that he be permitted to interview all persons as are deemed necessary. All Service Authorities are requested to assist this officer in the discharge of his official duties in every way practicable."

Marshall is supposed to be on temporary duty in Europe, but soon proves himself so valuable to the historical mission that he is named Ganoe's deputy. Later, he becomes de facto chief under an agreement he has worked out which allows Ganoe to maintain his title, despite his ill health. Later, Marshall replaces Ganoe as chief.

Copies of Marshall's letters to his friends at the *Detroit News* are included in these files and they give a glimpse of his thinking at this time. He is feeling his oats in some of these letters; is contemplative, even worried, in others.

His promotion to full colonel prompts Marshall to write: "As you will see from the outside of the envelope, they made me a colonel some weeks ago and will no doubt discover their mistake in time. However I am not letting that concern me. I know many officers of my grade who should be generals and that makes me very humble. Also I know some few of my grade who should be dog catchers and' that eliminates all my humility. Thereby I manage to stay on an even keel, being quite as preoccupied and unpleasant as ever."

Marshall also summarizes what he has learned writing combat reports, foreshadowing the narrative form that will be seen in his many books. "At first I was bothered by the fact that each of these stories seemed to work up to a very strong dramatic climax because it seemed to me that I might be pressing to make the point," Marshall writes. "Then with growing experience I came to realize that it could not be otherwise since the greatest drama in life is death. In battle the plot builds up gradually through a few men getting killed and then it must have a high climax either through a great number of tragic deaths resulting in defeat or in some other turning which means death and defeat to the enemy. I believe that any company story in battle, where the company plays a strong part, will almost always have perfect dramatic sequence."

And Marshall reflects on his new job heading the historical operation: "I became theater historian which puts me in charge of an operation with about 60 officers and 70 NCOs. Frankly, it is a job somewhat beyond my abilities."

Ganoe knows better. Marshall has written perhaps half a million words as an Army historian and he has held together a historical unit that has faced a staggering assignment with monumental obstacles. So one of Ganoe's last acts as theater historian is to write a lengthy, confidential letter to division headquarters providing, as he puts it, "Factual Statement of Outstanding Contribution of Colonel S. L. A. Marshall, To the War Effort and Practical History."

Ganoe's letter glows with praise for Marshall, this man whom some will later charge had brushed Ganoe aside in a grab for power. Ganoe cites Marshall's "vast energy and acumen," and how he "displayed that great rarity among men of having as much moral courage as physical." Still, Ganoe saves his strongest words for Marshall's innovation in the recording of military history. Ganoe writes: "As one celebrated professor said when I offered that we had changed the gathering and writing of history in general, 'If you've done that, you've changed the face of history.' Colonel Marshall has done just that. Not only has he produced the most accurate and complete experience tables for future effort, but has been able to pass along progressive changes on the battlefield so that other units could profit, with the maximum dispatch. I haven't a doubt that many lives have been saved through his inventive efforts."

I am in awe of my grandfather's work in World War II. His life then has such a steep trajectory, rising fast, nearing greatness, reaching greatness, and he is my age at that time. My own age. Amazing. I find myself wishing I could have spent a day with him then, watched him do his combat interviews, ridden in his jeep, entered Paris. Or later in his life, he had once taken the time to tell me about those times, a few stories from then, nothing elaborate, maybe an hour or so from his busy schedule. But he never did. So I am left to discover this on my own in the National Archives, family history buried in official government documents, revelations about my grandfather long after his death.

I can now see there is no boast in his 1947 letter to his New York editor regarding his just-completed book, one he plans to call *These Valiant Few* or *Men Against Fire*, although he hopes the publisher "will have a better idea." He has no doubts, though, about the book itself. Not after all he has discovered during the war, the lessons he has drawn, the way he has presented them in these pages. It is several months before *Men Against Fire* will be published and my grandfather confidently writes: "I know what this book represents and what place it fills in the professional need. The way has already been greased for it. It will become a standard text and required reading in the service schools. It will sell for many years."

16

Tempting Trouble

DAYS PASS IN RESEARCH, evenings in interviews, nights listening to Burt talk, and sometimes sing, one night when he stands in the corner of the living room and belts out childhood songs, also operatic arias, all a cappella, loud enough for the stage. Some of these he sings in his own singing voice, powerful, clear, direct. Others, at my prompting, he sings in his version of his brother's singing voice, unschooled, laboring, imprecise. It is a virtuoso performance, and Betty and I break out in applause.

Seldom in Washington do I have time to myself. I am always on the move, rushing from this place to that. I listen to well-known historians express their debt to S. L. A. Marshall, compatriots who served under him during World War II and were proud to be considered "Marshall Men" for the rest of their careers. There is Forrest Pogue, biographer of General George C. Marshall, and Martin Blumenson, biographer of General George S. Patton, Jr., and author of more than a dozen books. "I still adore Sam," Blumenson tells me. "I always will."

My emotions are taken on a wild ride all over the territory. Exhaustion predominates, but there are also moments of fascination, or boredom, or elation. Surprises about my grandfather still crop up.

I am researching in Suitland, looking through a box labeled "Office of Quartermaster General, Cemeterial Files, 1915–1939" when I find the file belonging to "Jones, William C.—Sgt. 2236578, Ft. Worth, Texas." Charly Jones, my grandfather's buddy, whose death prompts that poignant inscription in my grandfather's scrap-

181

book. That was my great discovery on my first trip to El Paso, convincing proof of my grandfather's combat experience.

Now, I hold Charly Jones' final Army papers in my hands and read his first sergeant's account of his death: "On the morning of the 8th of November, Sgt. Jones was in charge of a detail repairing the Villers devant Dun-Montigny road. Sgt. Jones' detail was working on the road forks leading to an old German ammunition dump, a point about one kilometer southwest of the town of Montigny. About ten o'clock, a HE [high explosive artillery round] came over and dropped pretty close to where my comrade was working. The second shell hit right in the midst of Sgt. Jones' gang and I saw the men fall. I ran towards them and when I got there, Sgt. Jones was lying face down by the edge of the road. He was dead when I got there, evidently having been instantly killed. Upon examination I saw that he had been hit by several shell fragments in the chest. He was buried about fifty yards from the edge of the road, on the East Side opposite the spot where he was killed."

This eyewitness account of Charly Jones' death suddenly confirms my worst fear—that my grandfather lied when he wrote his inscription. This account shows that all the crucial details of Charly Jones' death are wrong in his scrapbook. Jones was not killed "near Bantheville," as my grandfather wrote; he was killed close to Montigny, seven miles away. He was not killed "going forward"; he was killed while working on a road. And he was not killed by "three machine-gun bullets in his head"; he was killed by artillery fragments in the chest.

In my newspaper series, I had written that "I cannot imagine a returning doughboy lying about a fallen comrade in his war scrapbook." Now, I confirm my grandfather did exactly that. There were clues I missed then, things I should have caught, it occurs to me in the evening. I had made no connection when I read the letter home to his father with its mention of having been in the Argonne campaign "for a few days." Charly Jones was killed more than two weeks into that campaign, so why didn't that click in my mind months ago? Why wasn't I more skeptical, more cautious, less eager to be convinced by my brilliant research?

But the real question that bedevils me is: Why did my grandfather do it? Did he just want to appear braver when he showed his war scrapbook to pals in El Paso? Or was something more going on? Did he feel guilt about not being there when his best buddy needed him most? And was he trying to cover his guilt by making them comrades-in-arms right up to the end, at least in his scrapbook? Or is this teenage inscription evidence of a character flaw arising from some deep-seated need, and resulting in something more sinister than the usual embellishments we all resort to every now and then? I do not know. I wish I did. I may never know. But I will always wonder. Reading my grandfather's writing is so much easier than reading his mind.

I find further evidence of my grandfather's status at the end of the war when I am in the National Archives in downtown Washington. This is a stately edifice, a Greek Revival temple with massive pillars and these words carved on its exterior: "THIS BUILDING HOLDS IN TRUST THE RECORDS OF OUR NATIONAL LIFE AND SYMBOLIZES OUR FAITH IN THE PERMANENCY OF OUR NATIONAL INSTITUTIONS." The Declaration of Independence is kept within these walls, the Constitution, the Bill of Rights, the Watergate tapes, too.

Historian Barbara Tuchman has written about researchers who never leave the National Archives, or at least never want to leave the National Archives, so enthralling is the grand presence of this place. Researchers may walk in the back entrance of the building, without the broad stone steps that grace the front entrance along Constitution Avenue, but they soon find themselves in a central research room that looks like a film set. A ceiling two stories up, made of carved wood. Huge chandeliers hanging down. Walls lined with large bookshelves, filled with weighty old volumes. Solid wood tables with individual study areas set out by glass dividers, the writing surface covered with worn leather, small lamps made of brass. All talking done in whispers. The guard by the door wearing a uniform and a gun.

I take my seat and feel a part of history myself, thinking about the flow of knowledge that has come from this room, all the dissertations, all the books, and the researchers themselves who have preceded me, spending months, even years here in solitary quests through old documents. My grandfather himself came to this room late in life when he was writing his last book, *Crimsoned Prairie*, his revisionist history of the Indians and Custer at the Little Big Horn.

Now, I am following his footsteps here while tracking his trail through World War I.

I examine many records of his 315th Engineers in this archives, monthly reports of operations, lists of men killed and wounded, more indications of the dangers of the engineers' work when my grandfather was with this unit. His critics may dismiss the engineers for doing "road work and building delousing stations" but these official reports state: "The first week of the month [October 1918] found the entire Battalion in front line position in the St. Mihiel sector, engaged in laying out positions and wiring [barbed wire] for the 179th and 180th Brigades. This work kept the Battalion under practically constant shell fire. The wiring of the outpost positions involved the operations under direct machine gun fire at all times."

I search in vain for any mention of my grandfather's name in these reports. Finally, in another box, amidst many personnel files, I come upon a folder marked "Sgt. Marshall, Sam L." I open it gingerly and find a single sheet of paper. I read it slowly. It is a letter dated December 6, 1918, from the Personnel Adjutant of the 315th Engineers to the Commandant, Army Schools. "Inquiring," it begins, "as to *Sgt. Sam L. Marshall (2236673)*, Company A, 315th Engineers, who was ordered to Langres for examination for West Point by par. 9, S.O. [special order] 251, Hq. 90th Division, 11 Oct. 1918. Nothing further has been heard from the sergeant and information is requested as to what disposition was made of him."

The response from the Army Schools' Commandant is typed below on the same sheet of paper, dated December 15, 1918. "This soldier," it states, "failed to qualify for assignment to the United States Military Academy at West Point, N.Y., and, in accordance with instructions from G.H.Q. [General Headquarters], was assigned to the Army Candidates' School (Infantry) at La Valbonne (Ain), per paragraph 4, Special Orders, No. 301, these headquarters, dated November 1, 1918."

I feel a rush of relief, then sadness. If the 315th Engineers had not seen young Sergeant Marshall since he went off to the West Point exam, sometime in mid-October, then he certainly could not have been beside Charly Jones when he was killed on November 8. Nor could he have been, as his critics have pointed out, where he often said he was at the moment of Armistice, that account repeated in his memoirs: "I finished the war at 11:11 a.m. on 11 November as a lieutenant of infantry in a foxhole not far from Stenay."[1]

Again, I am beset with guilt about my failure to figure this out sooner. And the guilt only increases later when I go back to Marshall's letter to his father and discover words that I somehow passed over before: "When taking exams for West Point, we were stationed at Fort-du-France near Langres, from there we were sent south thru Dijon to La Valbonne."

Later, I even find a clue to his Armistice location in Marshall's own work, *The American Heritage History of World War I*. This book had prompted an unsolicited fan letter from an unexpected source, George Kennan, the noted foreign policy expert and Princeton professor. He had written Marshall: "I know of no other short history of the War that approaches it in sharpness, balance and intelligibility. My own experience in the writing of history has taught me what a difficult thing it is to summarize in this way. . . . I have recommended the book to my graduate students in modern diplomatic history, as the best thing they can read on the subject."

The American Heritage History of World War I is grand in scope, history far beyond the scale of what Marshall usually wrote, but it is still filled with the telling little details that enliven his accounts of small-unit operations. Marshall uses one of those details in his retelling of the World War I Armistice, that moment when the guns of the Great War fell silent. "In La Valbonne, France, which was an American officer candidates' school," he writes, "the aspirants became so delirious that they bombed one another with live grenades, barracks against barracks. A dozen men got flesh wounds, which but added to the joy."[2] This is a fine scene, great color, but where would such a small incident far from the front have been recorded? Official reports? Not likely. War histories? Hardly. In the memory of someone who was at La Valbonne himself? Exactly.

So Marshall went ahead and inserted the incident—or at least some version of what occurred at La Valbonne—in his World War I history. There was nothing to link him to that Armistice celebration, no first-person pronoun used in the account, no footnote either. It was something from his own experience, but who would ever bother to check that out?

Another evening, I am sitting in a high-rise condominium in

Alexandria, listening to Hugh and Joan Cole talk over drinks about their "special relationship" with my grandfather. "Doc" Cole is an academic historian who served as Marshall's deputy, and later his replacement as historian for the European Theater. Now seventy-nine, he has the look of a slimmed-down version of the late Sen. Everett Dirkson and has the habit of referring to his wife as "Momma." Joan Cole, then a British citizen, had been Marshall's secretary when she married Doc in France. Now seventy-two, she is a trim, stylish woman who wears a very short skirt and devilish look in her eyes behind oversized glasses. She still works as a public affairs officer for the Smithsonian.

The Coles had been close to Marshall during the war, closer than probably anyone other than Westover, and they had stayed close friends in the years after, observing with some sadness the change in him in later years, especially after his 1960 heart attack.

"I thought he became more aggressive for self-aggrandizement," Joan observes.

"Sam kept testing himself after his heart attack," Doc adds. "We were together at Gettysburg once and we went to Little Round Top and climbed up to the top of that hill and came right back down again, almost without stopping. Sam did this to test himself—he wanted to know 'can I still make it anymore?'—and later, it got worse. He got more pompous, more full of himself, beyond the bounds of reason. The last time I saw him, though, he just said, 'We'll go have a hamburger,' which was so unlike him. And I almost didn't recognize him. He had gone dark in the face, there wasn't a human spark in his face. This was right before he went into the hospital, and he was morose that night. Our main conversation revolved around whether I would go get him some Metamusil."

Our talk turns toward more pleasant times the Coles recall sharing with my grandfather, operas they attended, nights they celebrated, family visits. A half hour passes. I grow drowsy. Finally, I decide I had better bring up *Men Against Fire*, center of the controversy, asking, "Did Sam ever talk to you about how he came up with that 25 percent firing finding, where he got that number?"

"Christ, I warned Sam!" Doc snaps. "I said to him, 'You're out of your fucking mind to pick out a percentage like that!' Sam replied, 'You don't understand. I'm just making a point.'"

All of my senses suddenly kick in. I feel as though someone has just plugged me into an electric socket. "You mean," I say, "he didn't really have any statistics to back up that percentage?"

"No, he agreed that he didn't. He picked out something, some figure; he was making a point. He had a perception of things that other people lacked, but he was not trained in that kind of research."

"So he just picked out a number, based on his perception of firing problems?"

"Listen," Doc replies. "Sam had gotten bedeviled by the idea you had to have a number. Now, it's important to consider that if you took away the number, was Sam right? What he found became accepted and it affected the Army."

"But he did just make up that figure?"

"He did what a lot do—he gave a number and believed people would believe him. And maybe he wouldn't have gotten as far without that number. He said, 'Doc, you stupid bastard! I'm just saying that the first time troops go into combat, this is how they react.' We both thought about that number and finally figured, so what? But that, of course, is what they are pinning him to the mat for now."

I leave the Coles soon after that. It is late, and I have finally found what I have driven thousands of miles to discover. I head back to Burt's and Betty's house, but stop at a Japanese restaurant along the way. It is almost closing time and the place is deserted. I take a seat, order a beer and some sushi, sit alone with my thoughts.

Damn him, I think, goddamn him. Just when I gain a new respect for my grandfather's work, I get bushwhacked by another sorry revelation. If it is not some aspect of his World War I service, it's that damn statistic in *Men Against Fire*. Which was, it turns out, picked out of the air "to prove a point."

These revelations are never of the same magnitude as S. L. A. Marshall's accomplishments. But they are so needless, so stupid. I have seen how *Men Against Fire* is the culmination of his search for combat lessons that began in the Pacific and continued in Europe. I have become convinced there must have been firing problems during the war or he would have been ridiculed when *Men Against Fire* was published. And studies by impartial observers in Korea would not have supported his conclusion. Nor would the Army have ordered sweeping changes in its combat training as a result.

But why did he have to be so goddamn brazen about the way he stated things, so cocksure that his observations were evidence enough and nobody would ever investigate further, this utter carelessness, so damn dumb. I am not looking for a hero to put on a pedestal. I am far beyond that now. But some of my grandfather's failings seem so avoidable. A few different words here or there, a little less unbridled bravado, a somewhat different story, near to the truth, and his hard-won reputation might still be intact, unimpeached, or close.

My mind is crowded with "what if's" and "what might have been's." If only my grandfather, in writing *Men Against Fire*, had replaced "systematic collection of data" and "company actions we brought under survey" with something like "this is my conclusion based upon my own extensive observations and interviews." Instead, there is the bold-faced assertion, the 25-percent figure paraded as truth, this questionable means to an important end.

And so in keeping with the way Marshall had described himself in the unedited manuscript of his memoirs. Contrasting his approach with that of Sir Basil Liddell Hart, the British military historian, Marshall had written: "He was a scholar and profound technician, I think of myself as a hard-nosed practitioner, concerned mainly with what can be established out of proved experience and having little time to concern myself with theory." These words now convict him—"having little time to concern myself with theory." "Theory" is for "scholars," academic types, footnote users, people of that ilk. No, my grandfather's approach was the bold assertion, open to debate but who would dare? Playing chicken with the truth.

He brought that same approach to recounting his World War I service. I am left thinking how much of the current controversy could have been avoided if he had stuck to what he did in World War I, no battlefield commission, no ending the war in a frontline foxhole—rather, a sergeant selected for officer training, after some pretty rough engineer duty at the front, and still only a few months past the age of eighteen. Why wasn't he satisfied with that? Why wasn't that enough? And what I keep thinking is how he was a small man with little education who wanted desperately to be heard and figured he damn well better shout.

"I always felt there was a bit of braggadocio about him, what we at West Point call the Runt Complex," one of Marshall's general friends tells me. "A lot of times, I had the impression that he was making himself the hero of stories involving himself. But I accepted that, because I liked the guy very much."

Lt. Gen. Harry W. O. Kinnard had first met Marshall soon after the D-Day parachute drop into Normandy, had met him again after the Battle of the Bulge, had watched him do his group interviews, had been interviewed by him, too. Kinnard came to consider Marshall a friend, but also respected his work. "I liked the fact that he was fascinated by how people fight and that he got a handle on the inner workings of the infantryman," Kinnard says. "When he got through interviewing people, he knew more than the participants. He had the whole picture. His book *Bastogne* was extremely accurate."

Kinnard was later the commander of the First Cavalry Division (Airmobile) in Vietnam, one of the Army's elite units, and he had been instrumental in getting his old comrade to come have a look at that war. Marshall had returned the favor, dedicating *Battles in the Monsoon* to Kinnard and his large family. Kinnard, now seventy-four, is a trim man with carefully combed hair atop a young-looking face with few lines, a reserved person who speaks in clipped sentences, a cool presence, controlled. But Kinnard is unsparing in his criticism of Marshall when he feels it is warranted, times when his excesses would get embarrassing, times when he "could get obnoxious, pretty garrulous."

So I keep inquiring how Kinnard gets beyond that, why he still liked and respected Marshall, looking for help out of my own dilemma with my grandfather—what I admire versus what I detest.

"I feel you have to take a man as complete and entire," Kinnard responds, "not just the drinks, the brags. Sam did important things; you need to look at the whole."

"Even when what he did is sometimes so disappointing?"

"Yes. After his heart attack in 1960, he was becoming more argumentative, his fuse was shorter, he fulminated more quickly. It hurt me that he drank as much as he did after his heart attack. I saw him when he needed to go to bed, but didn't, and he was not getting the most out of his medicine. And he put on weight—a fat man who drinks is asking for a six-foot farm. But that was part of his charm; he used to imply that there were these exploits with women, that he was one hell of a Lothario. He did everything balls out."

A smile briefly crosses Kinnard's face at that recollection, this little man as a big Lothario, such an unlikely Lothario. But Kinnard soon focuses on another image.

"I also remember Sam in World War II with his reporter's notebook," Kinnard continues, "and I can still see the light on late in his tent, with him hunched over, doing that little tortured finger-writing of his—he must have made very good notes. I remember Sam as very dynamic, hard-working. It was not easy to do what he did."

There is a slight pause, maybe a second or two, before Kinnard concludes, "Sam did monumental things."

I try to keep such thoughts in mind when I meet with Harold P. Leinbaugh, prime force behind the Marshall controversy. I know what to expect of him, having talked to Leinbaugh on the phone several times, including one coast-to-coast call for over two hours, much of it consumed by Leinbaugh's rantings, his hatred for Marshall burning white-hot.

Leinbaugh is a former World War II infantry company commander who spent most of his working life as an obscure bureaucrat within the FBI. Then in 1985, Leinbaugh had his first taste of fame when he and a fellow company officer had coauthored *The Men of Company K*, a well-received account of their unit's service in World War II. Unlike Marshall, who did his postcombat interviews within days or weeks after a unit's battle action, Leinbaugh and John D. Campbell had gone back to their own men four decades later and asked them to recall their actions. Their technique may make for a dramatic narrative, but it has definite shortcomings as a way to capture history—interviewing former colleagues at a time when, as even the authors admit in *The Men of Company K:* "Tales are told, events embellished . . . the familiar ones—often amusing, sometimes poignant, occasionally accurate."[3] Nonetheless, Leinbaugh had enjoyed his brief stint in the spotlight and started looking for a second act.

Leinbaugh found it in the person of S. L. A. Marshall, this Army legend with the untarnished reputation. Leinbaugh had never met the man, had not really read his work either, but some research in the Washington area, plus a friend's examination of Army records in St. Louis, convinced Leinbaugh that he had the scoop on Marshall. Why there was not any need to make a research trip to the Marshall collection in El Paso; he had this fraud figured out, nailed.

So Leinbaugh was soon spreading his revisionist word on Marshall to anyone who would listen, friends, associates, fellow veterans, journalists, David Hackworth, Army classes at Fort Benning and Fort Leavenworth. Leinbaugh fired away at Marshall and his reputation, using such words as "fabricator" and "charlatan," such phrases as "that guy perverted history" and "he didn't understand human nature in combat." Leinbaugh would say that his animus toward Marshall was the result of his finding in Men Against Fire and how that "maligned" the efforts of brave infantrymen like himself and his men. Never mind that Leinbaugh had discovered Men Against Fire decades after it was published or that Marshall had blamed firing problems on shortcomings in training and not the soldiers themselves ("they were not malingerers," he wrote). "It's either my book or his book," Leinbaugh told the Associated Press. A macho approach not unlike Marshall's. Dueling authors at twenty paces, mano a mano.

Marshall and Leinbaugh would have loved to go at it. I am a poor substitute, having little interest in their breed of debate, a hurling of absolutes accompanied by chest beating. But I still feel a responsibility to hear what Leinbaugh has to say in person, present what I have discovered about my grandfather, and let him respond.

I readily recognize Leinbaugh when I walk into the cocktail lounge of the Key Bridge Marriott. He is seated in the far corner of the room, this sixty-six-year-old man who looks just like the news photo I have seen, slim of build, with a hound dog face and a countenance so dour it appears he has been sucking on a lemon. I had assumed that Leinbaugh and I would meet alone, but he has brought along Earle Hart, an imposing figure who introduces himself as "a leg man" for Leinbaugh. Hart turns out to be a fellow World War II veteran although he hardly looks old enough, this terribly tan, terribly blond man who could play tight end for the Redskins, or a bodyguard in a James Bond film.

Hart flips open his briefcase, pulls out a tape recorder, switches it on and deposits it in the middle of the table. Then, he pulls out a sheaf of papers and hands some to Leinbaugh, who already has a considerable stack of papers and reference materials spread in front of him from his own briefcase. I get out my notebook and we are, apparently, now set to begin.

The subject immediately becomes *Men Against Fire*.

"I don't know a single engagement in World War II where there was a failure to fire!" Leinbaugh asserts. "And we've read everything in German or English! I think if it would have happened I would have known about it."

"There's no way of quantifying that," says Hart.

"And besides," adds Leinbaugh, "indirect fire dominated the battlefield. We did something called testing by fire when you could smell the enemy and hoped they would fire back."

I try to insert a point about how *Men Against Fire* led the Army to study firing problems in Korea with independent scientists, and how their findings supported Marshall and helped lead to changes in Army training.

"I don't know they did," snaps Leinbaugh.

"It's bullshit," adds Hart. "I would like to see one document with quantitative numbers on who was firing and who wasn't."

"He never did a study," adds Leinbaugh. "This is a greater hoax than the Hitler Diaries. It is all fabrication."

I try to inject something about how Marshall spent years interviewing soldiers in World War II, and afterward, and certainly had a sound basis on which to draw some conclusions about how they operated. The words barely have time to get out of my mouth before Leinbaugh pounces.

"He didn't know about combat," he says.

Leinbaugh proceeds to name some film documentaries that prove everyone fired their weapons in World War II. And then he is tossing Xerox copies of war photographs across the table, photos that show individual infantrymen, or sometimes groups of two or three infantrymen, firing their weapons, or at least pointing their weapons. It's tough to tell which.

"See!" says Leinbaugh triumphantly.

"You can't be serious," I say. "All these photographs show is that these guys were firing weapons when a photographer happened to take their picture. That's all."

Leinbaugh is undeterred. He pulls out copies of more photographs, horribly gruesome photographs of war wounds caused by rifle fire—what this "proves" eludes me—photographs that carry such captions as "Multiple wounds of pelvis, lower extremities, and genitalia" or "Single wound of neck" or "A. Wound of entrance. B. Wound of exit." And Hart keeps chiming in with comments like: "Firing a weapon is a high; out there, it's a moment of truth."

Leinbaugh and Hart charge on. I try to insert a point every now and then, but it is trampled by these two in full stampede. I start to feel like I am debating American foreign policy with Iranian militants. Finally, I have had enough.

"Listen," I almost scream, "I did not come here to have the two of you play some two-on-one game on me. I came here to talk with Bud Leinbaugh. What you, Hart, are here for I have no idea. But I do not have to sit here while the two of you gang up on me. So if you keep it up, I'm leaving."

Leinbaugh seems shocked, defensive. He offers an apology. Things simmer down for a while, before they heat right back up again. The main impact of my outburst is to remove Hart from the discussion. Now, Leinbaugh rails on, an angry monologue prompted by some perceived hurt. It is as if S. L. A. Marshall had singled out Leinbaugh by name in Men Against Fire, had said Leinbaugh was the worst commander leading the worst troops in the entire European Theater. I cannot imagine Leinbaugh being any more furious.

"We weren't all cowards," he emphasizes. "We did our bit, we didn't want to, but that's the reason we're not speaking German here in this cocktail lounge today. We're not claiming to be heroes, our Army was very adequate, but most of the times, we out-fought the Germans. I just don't think Marshall had the slightest idea of how we functioned as company commanders. Men Against Fire never even mentions how a rifle company works."

I am tempted to say that is not what the book is about, but I don't bother. I simply let Leinbaugh have his say, his jowls shaking, his finger sometimes pointing right at me, the man looking more Nixonian by the minute, with his crimped posture, swarthy complexion, dark-set eyes.

"You fire from the hip, you keep moving, you hit the ground, you roll over—that's the way it was done," Leinbaugh continues. "We fired! Marshall was terribly wrong! He maligned us! By the time we got to the Elbe, we were very good!"

This has gone on for an hour now. While the rest of the crowd in the cocktail lounge has been unwinding after work, our table has been re-fighting the Second World War.

Leinbaugh finally burns out. I put away my notebook. Hart picks up his tape recorder. Leinbaugh orders some more white wine and pretzels for himself. Curt good-byes are said. I get up to leave.

Leinbaugh's last words to me are: "You can't get out that way." His arm gestures toward where I am heading.

"Oh yes I can," I say, striding out a side doorway. My exit is a little show of defiance, silly really, but satisfying.

I walk to my car, relieved to be free of these zealots, people who seize on one point like pit bulls, and then disregard everything else. S. L. A. Marshall's entire career reduced to one assertion. End argument, case closed. And then I remember Marshall's letter in El Paso, written back in 1963. A sergeant had written a Letter to the Editor of *Army Times* and made accusations not unlike Leinbaugh's. Marshall had been so incensed that he threatened a libel suit.

"The whole implication of the letter is that I am personally and professionally a fraud," Marshall wrote to *Army Times*. "Second, I am a scoundrel in that, despite my oath as an officer, I have willfully denigrated and vilified the American soldier, which is basely incorrect and wholly counter to the course I have run, which course may be documented in published works, TV tapes and recorded lectures given at the various staff colleges."

The documented course of a long, public life—not without flaws by any means, but still accomplishing "monumental things." The whole picture of the man and his work, what the likes of Leinbaugh choose to ignore.

17

Bedrock for a General

THE NIKE RUNNING SHOES on the front stoop belong to Lt. Gen. Sidney B. Berry, retired. Berry greets me at the door of his handsome brick home in Arlington and this sixty-three-year-old man looks much like he did the last time I saw him, back at Fort Benning when I was a lowly second lieutenant and he was a brigadier general, the assistant commandant of the Infantry School. Even when glimpsed from afar on the stage with my grandfather, Berry had an unmistakable presence for a general, not magisterial like Westmoreland, just battle-hardened, intent, wired. Berry was not a particularly handsome man, but his chin was set, and he had a withering gaze, especially when something or someone failed to attain his lofty standards. "Hard Charger" was the hushed description that preceded an appearance by General Berry at Benning; "Hard Charger indeed!" followed in his wake. Even we lieutenants knew that this was a rare general riding the express elevator to the very top.

Life magazine confirmed that a year later when it published a ten-page profile of Berry, "Case Study of an Army Star." Personal publicity was not Berry's style; he was an Eagle Scout from Hattiesburg, Mississippi, who believed in unselfish hard work and other traditional values instilled in small towns in the South. But *Life* had approached the Army about profiling a general and Chief of Staff Westmoreland had thought this offered the service a rare chance for some good press in the waning days of Vietnam. Westmoreland had chosen three brigadiers for *Life*'s consideration and the magazine had

195

selected Berry who reluctantly agreed to go along with the project, despite his wife's warnings against it.

What resulted was a profile of a man who seemed too good to be real, but also self-possessed, a man who kept copies of all the letters he wrote, compiled elaborate scrapbooks of his life's progress, as if he always knew he was destined for greatness and wanted a historical record to show how it had been achieved. Headlines hammered home the magazine's themes about Berry—"The rise of 'an ideal American soldier,'" "In his letters, only rarely does he mention war's horrors," "Fearless, he is dangerous to be near in combat," "A man's record must ring with 'the sound of guns.'"[1]

Berry's record was truly remarkable, a succession of high peaks, makings of a legend: A Cadet Captain at West Point described in the school yearbook as "Our Leader, The Owner of the Place." Two Battlefield Promotions in Korea and Two Silver Stars for Valor. A Master's Degree from Columbia University. A Return to West Point to Teach History for Three Years. One of Two Military Assistants to Robert McNamara, Accompanying the Secretary of Defense on Four Trips to Vietnam. A Volunteer for Vietnam Who Contributes More Distinguished Leadership in the War Zone. Wounded by Shrapnel from a Grenade, His Second Purple Heart. Awarded His Third Silver Star. A Fellow at The Council on Foreign Relations in New York City. Assistant Commandant at The Infantry School. Another tour in Vietnam.

It seemed understatement when *Life* proclaimed: "Pentagon insiders say nobody looks more like a future chief of staff than Sid Berry." And things continued that way, for a while. Berry had become the fiftieth superintendent at West Point, that revered post held by so many of the Army's greats, but then the academy was rocked by the worst cheating scandal in its history, with fifty Cadets expelled, what Berry considered the toughest test of his career. His bright shining general's stars were forever tarnished. Berry rose to lieutenant general, a considerable accomplishment, but not higher. He came up just short of climbing that final rung to four-star rank, and never became chief of staff. "A Case Study of an Army Star" turned out to be "A Case Study of Expectations Thwarted." It may have been good public relations for the Army in a troubled time, but it was something that Berry, in later years, wished he had never done. *Life*'s reporter did not seem to grasp some of the important distinctions he had tried to make and there were those who assumed that Berry had sought this attention. Worst of all, such a public prediction of future success was, in some strange way, a kiss of death.

Now, I follow Berry down the stairs to his basement den, a large open room with his desk and personal computer, some of his books and mementos, the Infantry motto of Follow Me! emblazoned over the fireplace. The room is bright white, organized, resplendently spick-and-span, spotless enough for a formal dinner to be served on the linoleum.

We take seats opposite one another, I ask Berry some questions and his command-ready voice is soon booming off the basement walls. I have a hard time reconciling this vibrant military man with these casual civilian clothes, gray corduroy slacks, a gray herringbone sportcoat, a blue flannel shirt. I keep imagining a well-tailored uniform hugging his trim body.

I ask him about his acquaintance with S. L. A. Marshall and Berry reaches behind him to a bookshelf with a worn copy of *Men Against Fire*. He opens the cover and notes it was bought on "10 Nov 1947," only months after publication.

"I graduated from West Point in 1948," Berry says, "and there were two important books to me then. One was *Company Commander* by Charles MacDonald; the other book was *Men Against Fire*. This had more influence on my young career; this was extremely important to me. I had never thought about the volume of fire before. Two things came out of Marshall's book that greatly influenced me when I was in Japan, right before I went to the war in Korea. One is that you have to emphasize teaching soldiers to fire their weapons. And the other is that, at the small-unit level, you've got to get your men talking and not let them become a group of isolated individuals. They've got to talk to each other in combat like they were in a ball game."

Berry keeps flipping through *Men Against Fire*, pausing to scan the notes he wrote in the margins forty years ago.

"Here's one of those places I wrote, 'I agree with Marshall,'" Berry says, pointing to the page. Then he continues, "I read *Men*

Against Fire before combat and it influenced the way I approached combat, and it made me more effective. I read it after combat, and that experience confirmed the validity of what Marshall had written.

"You know, I recently reread that *New York Times'* article about the Marshall controversy, but I still believe that Marshall had a unique value. He was very important in the shaping of young officers of my generation. Marshall's writing was helpful to us. It got us thinking: What would I do in this or that situation? He reported, as well as anyone could, how units reacted in combat, and that stimulated professional thinking. He did that better than anybody else for those in my generation. And *Men Against Fire* significantly influenced training at Benning. Throughout my service, people responded to your grandfather's writings, particularly this book."

"Did you meet him?"

"Later in my service, I heard him speak at Benning. But Marshall was always a given in my professional career, someone whose writings had the sound of truth."

"You realize that questions are now being raised about the accuracy of some of what he wrote."

"Listen," Berry says, "I was a company commander thirty-nine years ago and those actions always seemed frozen in my memory. But lately, I've been trying to write a record of those events and I find that I can't get the details of what happened; they turn out to be different from what I remember. That's the problem I have with [Leinbaugh's] *The Men of Company K,* a book written forty years after the action. Written that much later, there is a lot of room for error. The old soldier's mind is fertile. But that is irrelevant to *Men Against Fire.* I hold this book up as a real trailblazer. If this were Slam Marshall's only book, it established a major contribution to the increased combat effectiveness of American units."

"Then you don't feel his reputation has been diminished by this controversy?"

"People I know have had enough dealings with the press to realize it is a tempest in a teapot. The controversy, in my judgment, is not particularly important."

"You're not bothered by the fact that Marshall may not have been in combat, as he often claimed?"

"It does not make any difference to me if he was in combat. The guy who wrote *The Red Badge of Courage* didn't know combat either, but I don't give a damn. The book stands alone; it's irrelevant whether the author has been in combat. It's much more important if he can write with validity, accuracy, and that's what Marshall did in *Men Against Fire*. Whether Marshall was in combat is irrelevant."

Berry reaches behind him again and pulls another book off the shelf. Then, he turns the tables and asks me a question.

"Tell me, did Slam Marshall write this? Did he write *The Armed Forces Officer?*

"He did. His authorship was credited in a later edition."

"OK. My memory is correct. Now, this book, I still go back to this. This is one of the best statements of the military ethic ever written. I've got two or three copies of this. I would add that—did he write this alone?"

"Yes."

"I will tell you I have several copies of this, filled with asterisks and underlines. *The Armed Forces Officer* is a support book, the equivalent of which is simply not to be found. That defines it as a classic. This and *Men Against Fire* are two classics that your grandfather wrote. I would frequently go back to these two books. They're sound; they provided the bedrock of my professional training. And I am not alone in that, by any means."

A telephone call interrupts and I am thankful for the chance to catch my breath. Berry is a potent speaker; his defense of Marshall has the force of a steamroller. And I am gratified by what he has to say; no one of such prominence in the Army has so eloquently described the pervasive influence of S. L. A. Marshall. And Marshall's critics, when compared to Berry, seem minor league.

But there is more going on here for me than just hearing praise of my grandfather's work from someone of great accomplishment. I find that I am coming to relish this encounter with Berry; his discourse is eloquent, his energy infectious. He is turning out to be everything I thought Westmoreland might be, but was not.

Berry seems to be enjoying our conversation as well, although perhaps he is always this enthusiastic. But I have finished my questions about Marshall, and yet I have no desire to get up and leave.

So while Berry is still on the telephone, I decide to venture into what he now thinks about Vietnam, even though I have sent him my newspaper series and he knows of my stand against the war.

Berry gets off the phone and I ask him about that time when we were both at Fort Benning and the My Lai massacre burst into the news. I tell Berry how distressed I was by all the instructors who kept saying that such a thing just could not have happened. That response seemed such a company line, a conspiracy of denial.

"I didn't believe it could happen either," Berry says. "At least, I do not believe it would have happened in a unit I commanded without my being aware of it. I would have jumped on it with both feet. I got around. It was unbelievable. Incredible."

"What is your view of the war now? There seems to be a common view among some from the military that 'if those darn civilians had just unshackled our hands, then the war could have been won.'"

"I don't hold to the view that we lost because civilians tied the hands of the military. In retrospect, we may have gone into a situation that was simply unwinnable. What had happened before in Vietnam had forewarned the triumph of the other side. It was a civil war, and we took a side. Plus we had a short span of patience. The North had a will that was lacking in the South. Unless we were prepared to stay there forever, we went into a situation that was probably impossible to win."

"And who was to blame for that?"

"I fault the Kennedy advisers. *The Best and the Brightest* has a lot in there about that. And the characterizations of the people I know from my time with Secretary McNamara are quite accurate in that book. The Kennedy advisers thought that Vietnam could be handled with surgical precision, and that was a bad assumption. They didn't understand their opponent or the American people either. The argument that we could have won in Vietnam if only the military's hands were untied is an oversimplification. It does not show an understanding of the deep forces that were at work there."

I am surprised. Before this trip, I would never have believed that someone who served two tours at high rank in Vietnam would espouse views so similar to my own.

Berry continues, "Vietnam was a failure. I have a bad feeling about what our country did in Vietnam, especially after we pulled out. If I were the head of a small country and saw that, I certainly would not trust the United States. But let me emphasize, too, that I have a great admiration for American servicemen who served over there, particularly the young draftees who were sent into a war they didn't understand. I grieve for the American soldier. I admire his steadfastness in a situation not of his own making, particularly the draftee. They gave service that was actually undeserved! And I'm still angry at the Jane Fondas. We've got to have freedom of expression in this country, but . . ."

I suddenly realize that Berry does not remember that I was a conscientious objector. I feel compelled to tell him.

"You were a conscientious objector?" Berry says. "I guess I had forgotten that."

"What is your reaction to people who did what I did during the war?"

"If you had gone to Canada, I would not have respect for you. But you dealt with the issue. I have a son who is about your age—how old are you?"

"Forty-two."

"Well, he's thirty-seven. And while I was in Vietnam, my son was protesting the war, in conscience. Later, he apologized for his intemperate language back then. Anyway, he got his draft notice, but he never had to face that decision."

"But what would you have done if he had done what I did, if your own son had become a conscientious objector? Would you have ostracized him from the family?"

Berry does not pause. He answers straight out, "The way my wife and I view that is we have three children who went through the terrible period of the 1960s and were more liberal than we were. And Lord! We disapproved of some of the things they did! BUT THEY WERE OUR CHILDREN!"

Again, I hear those same words I had first heard from Lucian Truscott III, the preemminence of family, love taking precedence over politics, even in the most trying times.

I have no more questions for Berry, until I think to ask if he has visited the Wall. I know there are Vietnam veterans, career military especially, who feel the memorial to their fallen comrades is nothing but a scar in the earth.

Berry confirms that he has many friends from the service who have not been to the Wall, and may never go for a variety of reasons. But then he surprises me again.

"I've been to the Wall many times," Berry says, "and it's emotional every time. And every house guest we have, I take them to the Wall. I know a lot of names there, and I can go to a date and see the names of men I remember, men who were with me when I was their commander. It is a very moving experience. And it is exactly the right memorial for that war."

I follow Berry upstairs soon afterward, out the front door, down the steps. We talk on the sidewalk for a time in the chill morning air. Then, we shake hands.

I drive away reflecting on where were the Sid Berrys in the aftermath of Vietnam. These tested leaders, so readily discredited, so quickly forgotten. Might some of them be yet another valuable American resource that we squandered with the war?

18

Elegy at the Wall

TWO DAYS LATER, I visit the Wall.

I first visited the Vietnam Veterans Memorial a year ago and it had not been a time for much reflection. The September day had been a late blast of Washington's steambath summer, and Anne and I had been trying to complete a whirlwind tour of the city's tourist sites with a one-year-old in a stroller.

Now, I am back at the Wall again when there is a special ceremony. Thousands of people have come to pay tribute to nineteen men whose names have just been added to the Wall, their sacrifice previously overlooked for various reasons, usually how much time had passed between their injuries in the war and their deaths.

It is also Veterans Day, what seems an appropriate time for me to visit the Wall. I am a Vietnam-era veteran, after all. I wore my country's uniform for one year and nine months, was promoted to first lieutenant when the time came, received an honorable discharge at the conclusion of my service.

Yet I am one who served but later said no to any further participation in the armed forces. And I am painfully aware that I am one of the fortunate conscientious objectors, able to express myself well on paper and in person, a decided advantage in the arduous C.O. process. So my application was approved, while many others were rejected. There were even those C.O.s who were sent to military prisons after they refused to fight, far braver men than I, true heroes of the war.

All this conspires to make me feel desperately separate. Vietnam ripped apart my generation, dividing us into those who went to the war and those who did not, causing an estrangement that lingers two decades later. That may be why I, a war objector, feel compelled to make a pilgrimage to this memorial to the war dead. The Wall is the war's symbol and perhaps this is the place to seek a truce.

But this will not be easy, I discover after I park the car and set out for the Wall. I must pass through a gauntlet of stands selling Vietnam memorabilia, campaign pins, sloganeering T-shirts, bumper stickers, military paraphernalia, photos, wall plaques, rugs, ashtrays. I am repulsed by seeing the war experience, cause of so much agony, now turned marketable commodity, hawked with curios and souvenirs.

I am set on edge even more by one of the first conversations I overhear near the Wall. It is a guy simply saying, "I was a plain ordinary grunt, I did what I was supposed to do." That makes me think about how many others did what he did and what they endured because of it. I have read many of the Vietnam veterans' memoirs and novels, seen most of the best films about their experience, interviewed many vets and chronicled their stories. I know too well what vets faced when they went to what the military called "a short tour area," or the much longer tour of life in the States afterward.

But this comment by a "plain ordinary grunt" also causes me to ponder what might have happened if more had not gone along, doing what they were supposed to do. Might fewer names be on the Wall if more soldiers had somehow managed to take a stand against the war. Going along can be so insidious. A 1971 survey of enlisted men on their way to Vietnam found that 47 percent believed the war was a mistake and still they went anyway, maybe to their deaths, when there were other options.

This is the heart of the dilemma that I face when I consider Vietnam veterans. I have great empathy for what Vietnam vets have gone through, but also wish they had not gone at all. I can respect the choice they made, as long as they made a choice, just as I can respect those who chose not to go. The Vietnam War is the true villain, fucking over most of the men and women in our generation in one way or another, presenting endless no-win options, ruined plans, family crises, actions born of desperation, death, loss. And Vietnam vets often had it worst and still do.

I walk around this peaceful park in Washington, with its green lawns, groves of trees, Reflecting Pool, and I keep encountering war wounds of all kinds. I see Vietnam vets in wheelchairs, Vietnam vets who can only hobble along with canes, Vietnam vets missing arms, Vietnam vets missing something, their eyes fixed in "the thousand-yard stare," a vacant look that says this person is still preoccupied elsewhere, not yet arrived home.

I see some Vietnam vets who look like they just came off patrol, outfitted in full camouflage regalia, minus only weapons. I see other Vietnam vets who look like they still live in the 1960s, with scruffy beards and scraggly long hair and faded blue jean jackets, vets still stuck in Sergeant Pepper time.

The effect of all these Vietnam vets on me is: RELIEF. I am so thankful that I never went to the war. I do feel a slight twinge of envy at the vets' camaraderie, as they pose together for pictures, clasp hands, pound backs, embrace, greet each other as "brother." I feel this slight envy because I have met only four or five conscientious objectors in my life and we share none of the vets' badges of a special fellowship, no conscientious objector handshake, no conscientious objector uniform, no conscientious objector salutation. We share no conscientious objector literature either. The memoirs of hundreds of Vietnam vets have been published, often to great acclaim. Few memoirs of conscientious objectors have become books. C.O. Gerald Gioglio found so little publisher interest in his *Days of Decision*, an oral history of military C.O.s during Vietnam, that the New Jersey man had to found his own company to publish it, Broken Rifle Press. Gioglio has said, "The antiwar movement has somehow been written out of history."

But my touch of envy for vets in no way translates into a wish that I were a Vietnam vet myself. I am definitely not one of those men my age who found a way out of the war only to later lament having missed out on "the war of our generation," the rite of male passage. I do not buy that shit. I feel no "Viet guilt." I think I am a better person for having not gone to war, for having acted on my beliefs in the sanctity of life.

Now, the loudspeakers fall silent, the powerful strains of Dvorak's *New World* Symphony fade away. The large crowd quiets. Jan Scruggs steps to the microphone, this Vietnam vet who was one of the prime movers behind the Wall, a man who saw *The Deer*

Hunter in 1979 and was so moved that he stayed up much of that night, thinking and drinking, and then the next day told his wife that he was going to find the way to build a Vietnam War memorial, one to display the names of every American killed in Southeast Asia.

Just three years later, Scruggs stood proudly in front of the finished granite monument as it was dedicated before a throng of 100,000. The Wall was soon to become Washington's most-visited historic site, drawing 12,000 to 15,000 people every day, a crucial salve on the nation's tortured Vietnam soul, our unexpected Lourdes.

"This is a very special day for us," Scruggs begins. "With us today, we have seventy-five people from families whose family members have just had their names added to the Wall."

There is an immediate outpouring of applause, perhaps the first public recognition these seventy-five people have ever had for what their husbands and fathers and brothers and sons did two decades ago, their tragic sacrifice. The applause falls off, after military honor guards troop forward with the colors. A bagpipe wails. Some in the crowd salute.

The "Star-Spangled Banner" is soon sung, followed by "God Bless America." My eyes wander across the crowd, often saddened by the sight of vets still angry after all these years. There is a guy in front of me wearing a field jacket with a bumper sticker slapped on the back that says, "Vietnam vets are not Fonda Jane." Not far away, the back of another jacket has a patch with Snoopy, that beloved Peanuts character, giving the finger, accompanied by the words: "Fuck Jane Fonda."

Then there is the man who has brought his young son to the memorial, a fine impulse, except that this youngster is outfitted in a fatigue uniform, combat boots, insignia, the works, this little G.I. Joe, this Rambo-in-the-making at this place that shows the ultimate cost of such "adventures."

My unease only deepens when a female star of the television show "China Beach" is introduced, prompting loud applause, even a few whistles. Next come a few words from the sponsors, the head of a rare coin company that has contributed $75,000 to the memorial, then the CEO of a tobacco company that has contributed $90,000 to inscribe these new names on the Wall.

Sen. John Warner follows with the keynote address, this senator who comes from the Old Dominion but looks to be from Hollywood, with his craggy face, his shock of hair, his strong presence. The start of Warner's speech seems to promise thoughts tailored to this day at this place, with his mention of how "This memorial where we gather today conveys the message, victory is ours—not the traditional military victory, but a nation approaching victory over itself. A nation gradually healing from the enormous sacrifices made by the young people, and their families, of the Vietnam generation."

But Warner soon veers Right, launching into a stump speech, winning the day's heartiest applause for his mention of the crumbling Berlin Wall, then warning of the continued Soviet threat and emphasizing "Gorbachev has not become a pacifist," before finally urging continued reliance on "peace through strength."

The experience at the Wall has been one disappointment after another. This whole visit may be a mistake. Then Mrs. Eva Eldredge of Mills, Wyoming, steps to the microphone.

Hers is one of those terrible tales of family heartbreak wrought by Vietnam, the tragedy compounded by the bunglings of the government bureaucracy afterward, insensitive people, outrage after outrage. Jose Lujan, Mrs. Eldredge's brother, was an Army enlisted man who had flown 250 combat missions in Vietnam and was in the midst of his second consecutive tour in the war zone when he was severely injured in an airplane crash. He later died of his war wounds in a Veterans Administration Hospital in Albuquerque, but the hospital failed to notify the Army, forcing the family to buy a casket it could ill afford, then make their own arrangements to have the body shipped back to Wyoming. Without an Army casket, without an Army uniform, without an Army honor escort for the body, without an Army survivor assistant to aid the family with the funeral arrangements, without the Army's payment of $550 for funeral expenses— all these things the Army should have provided, but did not. Mrs. Eldredge soon found herself locked in a battle with the bureaucracy to get it to admit its mistakes, no easy task.

Then this July, Mrs. Eldredge had discovered that her brother's name was not inscribed on the Wall, as she had always assumed. Another battle with the bureaucracy followed, with Mrs. Eldredge, a fifty-three-year-old wife and mother of four, feeling all the burden of proof of her brother's death was being left to her, with various agencies demanding she provide this paper or that. "I was bitter, terribly bitter," she would later recall. "At night, I couldn't go to bed and I couldn't sleep. I kept thinking why are they putting me through this? Everybody wants some proof—why don't they get it from the Army? It's a good thing I kept everything, all the paperwork. But I went through all those papers with tears in my eyes, having to read all over again about my brother's injuries."

The strain on Mrs. Eldredge became so intense that she was constantly in tears, even had to be hospitalized at one point, and finally heard her daughter remark, "I'll be so glad when this is over and you can be my mother again."

Now, the Eldredges' nightmare is ending. She and her daughter arrived in Washington a week ago and had made their first visit to the Wall, just in time to see her brother's name being inscribed. "The war is over for us now," Mrs. Eldredge told a Wyoming reporter. "It's over for our family. We want to let our brother rest in peace."[1]

Now, Mrs. Eldredge is introduced to the crowd and her voice is trembling slightly when she says, "I consider it an honor to have been asked to call out the nineteen names that have been added to the memorial. Today we are here not just to honor the nineteen new names that have been added to the Vietnam memorial or the 58,175 names that are now on the memorial. Today we honor all the men and women who fought the war in Vietnam. We never want to forget the war or what it did to the men and women who fought it."

Mrs. Eldredge proceeds to read the new names: "Robert Bruce Annas . . . John Frederick Anthony . . . Michael J. Bosiljevac . . . Robert Dennis Brown . . . Robert C. Cothran . . . Tom Joseph Cress . . . Charles C. Curtis, Jr., . . . Billy D. Hooper . . . Freddy Paul Heugel . . . Jose Leopoldo Lujan."

Mrs. Eldredge reads her brother's name just as she does all the others, in a clear voice, but definitely a mother's voice, and that only underscores the loss. A black man in front of me has removed his hat and has tears rolling down his cheeks. Other men in the crowd are standing stiffly at attention. No one anywhere is even whispering now.

I feel my chest tighten as Mrs. Eldredge continues reading: "Philip V. MacKinney . . . Richard D. Mattson . . . Paul Francis Newman, Jr., . . . John Nishimura . . . David James Pugliesi."

This small list is a reprise of the Vietnam War, those who bore the war's greatest burden, those who paid the war's greatest price. These are frightfully young men, boys just becoming men, average age twenty-one, almost half of them dead before they are old enough to cast a vote or buy a drink. There are three officers among them, one major, one captain, one lieutenant, but the rest are enlisted men, many from the lowest ranks. And many come from small towns across America, places named Granite Falls, Mount Pleasant, and Pinehurst, where their deaths reverberated through the community since so many folks knew Billy or Freddy, Bob or Jose.

Mrs. Eldredge reads on through the final new names: "William C. Strevel, Jr., . . . Melvin E. Taylor . . . Paul Isaac Vegas . . . Wilbert Walton."

Wreaths are soon laid at the Wall, "Taps" is played by a solitary bugler, the mournful notes incredibly drawn out, the crisp November air now laden with grief, the sun finally breaking through gray clouds, people openly sobbing.

I walk around aimlessly following the ceremony, aching and numb at the same time. I still see things like patches that say, "Vietcong Hunting Club" and "Vietnam—If you haven't been there, shut your mouth!" But I also see scenes that grab my heart, tender private moments played out on a public stage—generations of one family posing in front of a name on the Wall. A man in a blue jean jacket and a four-star general in uniform, standing side-by-side and saluting the flag. A man and his wife standing alone in an eddy in the crowd, the two in a clenched embrace, tears streaming down his face.

I wander about for a half hour, maybe an hour. I have lost all track of time. The crowd has finally started to thin. I decide it is time to walk along the Wall myself.

The first few feet are not that difficult. There are so few names here and so low to the ground that I walk along well in control of my emotions. But the Wall grows taller, now at my knees, now at my waist, now at my chest, and I sense the pull of Maya Lin's inspired design, the weight of so many names of so many dead. Mementos have been left at the base of the Wall along here, as there are every day—small American flags, photographs, notes, medals, flowers.

One note says: "Hello, my name is Serene Rodin. When I was a young girl in the mid to late 1960s, I used to write to servicemen in

Vietnam. If anybody here who's visiting reads this letter and by a miracle remembers writing to me, I'd really like to know how you are doing and to know that your letters meant a lot to a child who at that time did not have ANY friends I could trust."

Another note says: "To Cpl. Donald R. Pritchard, 4th Bn., 11th Marines (Pops). Don: I'm leaving this picture here so that everyone who knew you can remember you and tell everyone that I'm proud that we were friends in Vietnam. You told me, 'I want to see more action than John Wayne.' The only difference is your name is on this Wall and his is not. Your buddy, Cpl. Jerry Riley. Louisville, Ky."

Another says: " 'Doc' Allen Groshong. Newport News, Va. Corpsman, U.S. Navy. Killed April 8, 1968, Hill 504. Silver Star. Dear Allen, It took me 20 years to contact your parents. I couldn't find a way to say your son died saving my life. I finally did. I talked to your father on the phone. It was difficult for both of us, but my load is so much lighter now. Johnny, Chip, Ted, Gerald, Bob and Sgt. Jackson are here with you. I miss you all. Love brother, Lynn. Lynn Witt. Rockville, Md."

And there is an Army fatigue cap, a baseball cap in olive drab, on which is pinned a Purple Heart and a note that says, "Rick, I didn't forget! It just took me a while. Jack." And across the bill of the cap are written two words: "NEVER AGAIN."

I continue walking until I have covered the Wall's entire length, almost five hundred feet of black granite, and these names are only the Americans who died in conflict, part of the tragedy of the Vietnam War, but an abridged version.

I am overcome by the enormity. But I also feel empty, strangely unconnected to what I have just seen. I realize after a time that the war is still faceless to me at the Wall. These are just names, no one I knew or remember. There must be the name here of someone who went through officer training with me at Fort Benning, probably several of those lieutenants, although I forgot the names of my classmates long ago. Then I remember Pete Gray.

I remember Pete Gray from the University of Virginia, not because he was a friend, but because he was someone everyone knew, a star of the school, a politico, a jock, a great guy. I decide to find Pete Gray's name here until I recall that Pete was only his nickname.

I approach one of the guides stationed near the Wall with huge books that catalog all the names and their locations.

"I am looking for someone I knew in college," I say to the young woman in the Park Service uniform. "Except I didn't know him that well, and I only knew him by his nickname."

"What was that?" she asks.

"Pete Gray."

"I'll see what I can find."

She opens the book and soon confronts a very long list of people with the last name of Gray. She appears stumped as to what to do next, how to proceed.

"I think he had one of those long Southern names, maybe followed by a numeral," I offer. "Perhaps you could start reading down the list and a name like that will jump out."

She reads one Gray name, then another, and another, and soon I interrupt, " I think that's it. Read that name again."

"Arthur Powell Gray IV."

"And what does it say with his name?"

"B. July 5, 1946. K. July 19, 1970. 1st Lt. Marines. Richmond."

"That is definitely Pete Gray."

She gives me directions and I walk down the Wall again, near the vertex of the V, where the Wall is the highest and names of the last casualties in the war link up with the first. I look up on the Wall to a place well above my head and I squint as I try to read the names. The granite is so shiny it reflects the clouds and the sky. I read: "Mark J. Webb . . . Edgar I. Crouse, Jr., . . . Joseph A. Seaman . . . Arthur P. Gray IV."

I focus the camera, I take a picture of Pete Gray's name to remember this moment. Then I step back and reflect on the loss of Pete Gray.

Arthur Powell Gray IV. Class of 1968, the class ahead of mine. President of the College of Arts and Sciences. Chairman of the Honor Committee. National Advertising Manager for the *Cavalier Daily*. Member of the varsity football and track teams, not a natural athlete, but dedicated, driven. Named by the Alumni Association as winner of the Distinguished Student Award for 1968. Rhodes Scholar Nominee. Pete Gray. Respected student leader, but still unassuming, an example to us all, what incredible potential. Who knows what he might have accomplished if only he had lived longer.

This is what I had been seeking in my visit to the Wall, a chance to ponder on what the war truly cost, although now my heart is thrust in my throat. My eyes fall from Pete Gray's name after a while, down to a wreath at the base of the Wall, and a ribbon on the wreath that says, "Not in Vain."

My anger flares up. Pete Gray's promise was snuffed out at twenty-four, and for what? "The Domino Theory?" "The Light at the End of the Tunnel?" "Peace with Honor?"

No, Pete Gray's death was totally in vain. Pointless. Wasted. Every one of these 58,175 deaths were. And that's why the only message that belongs at the Wall is scrawled across that soldier's cap: "NEVER AGAIN."

19

His Brother's Witness

MY TIME IN WASHINGTON is almost finished. I have been with Burt and Betty for a week, have called their home my home, have grown accustomed to the habits and rhythms of their lives, breakfast at the same hour around the kitchen table, dinner in the dining room, accompanied by one glass of wine, a cheese course at the end of the meal in the European manner. I have treated them to dinner at their favorite Chinese restaurant, with Burt in a Levi's jacket and rare humor, recounting the time when a woman asked him what fish curry was and he replied, "That's the curry with the fin on top." Burt and Betty have treated me, too, with Sunday brunch at the Cosmos Club, generations of old-line Washingtonians in a gilt-edged setting, hearty handshakes between longtime friends in the buffet line.

We have had a fine time together, with no disagreements or tense moments, three relatives who have gone from being strangers to friends. I have appreciated their hospitality—they take care of a guest with true grace—but more than that, I have valued the chance to forge a link with my family's past. Thanks to Burt, I now have a mental scrapbook filled with images of ancestors I never knew.

Caleb, his father, a hulking short man with a 17½-inch neck, known for his brute physical strength but also a man of the mind, pursuing his self-guided study of theology and logic throughout his life, a pessimistic man, austere, religious, no machismo about him, a sense of humor whose main focus was the dispensing of twisted aphorisms ("He who is lost hesitates," "Leap twice before you look").

213

Alice, Burt's mother, who had met her future husband when she was seventeen and he was twenty-two, the two of them attracted to each other in a Baptist congregation in St. Louis and married soon afterward. Alice is his opposite in many ways, optimistic, intuitive, sentimental, a woman who, during the Depression with troubles of her own, happened to learn about malnutrition among the children at a school near El Paso and set in motion a feeding program that began in her own kitchen and later grew to provide 2,500 meals every week for two years.

And the Marshall household, working class, seldom well-off, but always with good books and magazines, and usually a piano as well, although there was a time in Niles, California, when they had to do without a piano and Alice, Burt's and Sam's older sister, "practiced" her piano chords on a plain table top instead. A home often visited by tragedy and grief, with three of the six Marshall children not surviving past childhood, but still a home where there would always erupt one riotous water balloon fight every year, water balloons loosed from the second-story windows, wallpaper inevitably ruined, much hilarity, even Caleb joining in.

Burt's older brother is often mentioned in our talks together, especially his formative years. Burt tells me how susceptible Sam was to sickness and mishap as a child, his early years a succession of diseases and broken bones, leading his sister, Alice, to later remark, "If a mad dog had come to town, Sam would have been the first victim." This may help explain why Sam was so taken with testing himself later in life, why he became so enamored of the Army and its manly rigors, truly loved the Army in a way that Burt considers romantic, idealized, the Army as "some sort of spiritual fulfillment."

Sam was so bedeviled by illness as a boy that Burt's fondest memory of his brother is not of some boyish hijinx. It revolves around one of Sam's illnesses, this time at sixteen, some horrible swelling of his glands, diagnosed first as syphilis, the family shocked. A visit to a second doctor was ordered, Sam returning home terrified, young Burt peering through the keyhole of his brother's room and then returning to his own room where he prayed and prayed that whatever was the matter with his brother would go away.

"The next morning, Sam woke up and went to the bathroom and shouted for his parents," Burt recalls. "All the swelling was

Three generations of Marshall men, shown on the roof of the Detroit News, around 1937. *From left*, Charles Burton Marshall, S. L. A. Marshall, Caleb Marshall, S. L. A. Marshall, Jr.

gone—it must have been a cold—but what I remember most fondly about this was just sharing Sam's happiness. I was delighted that the burden seemed to have been lifted from him."

Like so many of Burt's stories about Sam, this one may tell as much about the narrator as it does about the subject. This incident is certainly that way, with its overtones of little brother as big brother's savior. I sense Burt's longing to be recognized by this brother who is eight years older, treated as an equal instead of an underling needing a mentor, a scenario that will persist through much of their adult lives. Sam would regularly come up with plans for Burt's future, joining the same newspaper (which he did for a time), or the two of them taking over some small-town paper, or working together in the Army at the outset of World War II, collaborations of one kind or another, but always with Sam leading and Burt following, which is why Burt usually demurred. "Making a career as little brother," Burt has said, "did not appeal to me."

What I had taken as Burt's remarkable candor about his brother over the long-distance lines now seems more complex. There is an undercurrent of disappointment, hurt and resentment in what Burt remembers about Sam, unstated at times, or denied, but there. Burt does have a phenomenal memory, but too many bitter occurrences are recalled a little too readily. Such as several of their reunion dinners erupting in verbal fireworks and hasty exits, especially when Cate was part of the equation ("With Cate present, Sam was picky and combative . . . defensive," Burt says), these flare-ups far more common after Sam has his heart attack in 1960, that time when Burt believes his brother began exhibiting signs of early senility.

Burt points out how such incidents left him "puzzled, not devastated," and how there should be "no implication of grudge or anything of that sort." I do not doubt his sincerity when he says such things; it's just that the experiences he describes seem so hurtful in ways that only loved ones can be.

People often remarked how different S. L. A. Marshall and Charles Burton Marshall were; surprise was the most frequent reaction to the discovery that the two were brothers. Their differences created distance between them, and surely some envy. For Sam, Burt was the younger brother who had the height, who had the education, who had a happy family, a man on such an even keel, his emotions under control, above the fray, impervious. For Burt, Sam was the older brother who could never quite abandon that role, and the more famous older brother as well, someone of such remarkable dedication and drive, a prodigious worker, but needlessly careless with his reputation, careless with his personal life too, often ruled by emotions, his need to be loved, such highs, such lows.

Now, Burt and I take seats in a living room that I have told him looks much like his brother's living room in Michigan, the sofa placed beneath the large picture window overlooking the street, the fireplace at the end of the room surrounded by built-in bookshelves, easy chairs set about, a comfortable place to talk.

Our own talk has a new edge this morning, a certain formality. I have my notebook out for the first time, I am asking specific questions and Burt is taking his time to answer. We both seem very aware that this could be the last chance the two of us may ever have to discuss S. L. A. Marshall.

I begin by asking about what seem like Sam's "lies" to me, but what Burt refers to as "fibbings" instead. And what, in his view, prompted this trait of his brother's—to sometimes play so loose with the truth?

"I wonder if it wasn't a tendency to shape his dreams into realities," Burt replies. "We all do that, but there seemed to be more of that in him."

"But why don't you call them 'lies?'"

"I suppose the word 'lie' is more resonant with malice than 'fib.' But the idea that there is an absolute in truth is not correct. There are, for example, times when it is appropriate to lie to the enemy. I would say that a lie is when someone deliberately concocts an untruth that has huge consequences for someone else, such as a government deception. I have to mitigate this—I think Sam had some psychic needs, a certain estimate of himself that he wanted to support and others to believe. Sometimes, goddamn, he made me a little sore with this. But we all have our psychic needs, I have some, too."

"Then that's what caused him to act that way?"

"I think Sam was terribly sensitive about being short, about being fragile—he had to make it up, to act cocky to cover it up. I can't be—I can't find it in my heart to be—contemptuous of him for doing this. All of us have our own peccadillos. But what Sam did is the kind of thing you can get addicted to."

Burt has left the sofa and is walking about the room as he talks, his hands at his side, his responses turning soliloquy.

"Sam went beyond what I consider legitimate," Burt emphasizes. "There was a dangerous thing he told me—nobody checks up on these things. He was getting beyond prudence then and, posthumously, he pays the price. But I still have great affection for him. I do not want to kick him around for it. I think my brother, with his great accomplishments, is more of a plus than a minus in the life of the republic. I regret that he had that defensiveness, that he had to compensate that way. But if he had such psychic needs, I'm glad he met them.

"I also think his powers were failing, his health slipping away. He aged very rapidly. That senility quote—that morning after a tantrum with me in 1976 when he apologized, saying, 'I made a fool of myself. You must know what brought all that on. I have been striving for years to fight off senility, but sometimes it gets the upper hand.' That was very genuine to me. I told Betty about that when she met me at the airport; that had a great impact on me. Sam that morning had a face like a whipped puppy. He was abject, he was a deflated fellow begging me to forgive him. It was a sight I didn't relish. I felt very compassionate toward him."

I inquire about Sam's strengths and weaknesses and Burt replies that they both sprang from the same thing: "I think there was a compensatory streak in his character. That's what made him a striving and succeeding person in his life, but, at the same time, he had to have manifestations of approval. He too much loved to be loved—I think that sums it up."

We talk about Israel and Vietnam and other places Sam would travel as military critic, columnist, author, with his tab often picked up by the government, ferried about as a VIP, and how, in my mind, that contradicts his claim of being an "objective observer." Burt says he can see "the shadow of a conflict of interest" with Israel perhaps, but nothing more than that: "Sam was more inclined to suspend initial judgment on his own side, as with Israel, as with Vietnam. Sam was more of a true believer in the cause than I would be. And I think Sam's work in Vietnam exposed his weakness, his concentration on tactics. He was too preoccupied with tactical techniques and that made him receptive to the fatal mistake of putting forces in battle without legitimizing it, recognizing there was a need to have declared war first. And Sam was certainly charmed by 'Westy,' his professional judgment was a little off. Westmoreland went along with a fatefully bad mistake—persevering in a war of attrition. The body count was a terrible development and it had a terrible effect on the military. My Lai comes directly out of that."

I figure this is the time to bring up my stand on the war and what his brother did in response. I pull out the letter disowning me, ask Burt to read it and give his reaction, but first try to explain a reference in it to my calling Sam a "liar." That comment was made not to him, I explain, but to a member of my family, prompted by my grandfather's complaints about no one paying attention to him at my mother's funeral. Yet he and I had spent a half hour that day discussing writers and writing, what I thought was the best conversation we had ever had. I was badly hurt by his complaint; it implied our conversation meant nothing to him.

Burt listens patiently while I try to rationalize all this, reads the letter, then comes right back to my "liar" comment.

"You may have earned this letter somewhat by calling him a liar. For him, those were fighting words. Maybe I would reprove you a bit on this. It is better to avoid fighting words—you can stand your ground without them."

"You have to understand what mother's funeral was like," I say, feeling defensive. "The shock of her suicide, everyone's emotions so raw. And the point is—who's to blame here? Sam for complaining about his treatment? Or me for making a comment about his complaining? It wasn't his funeral."

Burt grasps the letter in one hand and shakes it, saying, "This is melodrama—this whole damn thing!"

The room falls silent for a very long moment. Then, Burt continues, his voice lower: "Cate should have talked him out of this letter. I prayed for the perfection of my children, but I always understood the point of mutual dependency—they on me, me on them. That would be lessened if I defaulted on that relationship. But even if I wished for the perfection of my children, I knew they would not achieve it. And I also knew they will still be my children, no matter how abhorrent they may be. I am not going to renounce my allegiance. Their mistakes may be tragic in scope or in consequence, but if that happens, I would not renounce them. For I would be highly diminished myself by doing that."

Burt pauses, then adds, "I am put off by their saying they rule you out of the family. I'm tempted to say I hope you forgive them."

"I guess I must somewhat by now."

"It would have been better for them to say, 'We're disappointed by what you've done, but you're still our grandson and you're still welcome to come by our house.' This was a disturbing letter. And that Vietnam thing was a damn bad thing for young people."

I change the subject to the *American Heritage* article on his brother. I show Burt some of the letters I had written to the magazine, attempting to get them to correct their errors, attempts met with stonewall.

Burt skims over the materials, then says, "That's good lawyer's paper, what they wrote. Sam does make it a law of firepower (with what he wrote in *Men Against Fire*)—they have a point there. Sam didn't have a statistical appreciation. But it's painful for me to have this whole damn thing come out, these revelations. But, in a substantial part, these are things I have known about Sam for a long time.

"I was put off by the *American Heritage* article. It had a kind of snippy, sniping tone, as if somebody were bearing Sam a grudge. For example, pointing out that he made up part of his name is a lawyer's trick in the courtroom when you're trying to get a jury to snicker at the defendant. Thomas Woodrow Wilson had a right to drop Thomas from his name, if he wanted to. Winston Churchill had a right to add an S. Maybe it was silly for Sam to add an Atwood but it wasn't significant. I just don't think the thing in *American Heritage* was written with a very compassionate understanding of Sam. He was a creative thinker about many things. He understood a lot about the moral climate of military relationships."

Burt catches his breath for a moment, then resumes, "Character is the mark our experience has left on us, and experience left a lot of marks on Sam. Some were not marks of perfection, some were marks of creativity, there were some bad habits, too. But when you add up all these marks, I still give him a plus. I loved him, I didn't worship him. I saw his attributes, I saw his genuine faults—and some of them were unnecessary. He was a self-made man and he made some of those faults. I wish there had been someone around to admonish him more.

"I came to recognize that I did not have the same degree of creativity he did; mine was different from his. But I also did come to feel that I was inwardly more self-assured than he was. I felt luckier than he felt."

This leads me to ask Burt about the last time he saw his brother. It turns out to have been in the hospital in 1977, about a month before his death.

"Sam looked up at me with a vacant stare," Burt says, "and

then his face lit up. 'I'm so happy, so happy,' he said. Then he drew me close to him, kissed me, and said, 'I love you so.'"

"Sam was having a difficult time with the continuity of his thoughts, saying, 'I'm trying so hard to think.' We tried one thing and another. He said he had better recollections of World War I than World War II. 'World War I was *the* war,' he said, 'World War II was *a* war.' His recollections were about that early period."

"Did you think," I ask, my own voice halting, "this would be the last time the two of you would talk?"

"I had that sense. We discussed something for a couple minutes, something about the World War II battle of Arnhem, the only thing he could recall in any depth. Then Sam told me he was going to stay in this room and he was going to die in this room, and he wanted no heroic measures taken on his behalf. His work was finished, he was content to take his leave of life. That was better than lingering in a situation of dependency.

"He was tired, in terrible shape, immobilized, perhaps suffering imbecility. He was a sad thing to behold. It got to the point, after an hour or two, that he was tired, even with his greatly medicated limits, and there was nothing more for him or me to impart. So we hugged and we kissed and that was it.

"I had anticipated his collapse in a certain emotional way, and it may be self-centered to say this or be able to say this, but I know now that Sam was a sick man, near the end of his rope at the time of his outburst against me the year before. I can account for that episode; I can say he didn't mean it.

"It had been a traumatic experience for me being assailed by Sam. But there was a healing ingredient for me in the idea that this was a collapsing man, not a whole man, who assailed me. That was a liberation from the bearing of any grudge.

"'Fighting a losing battle with senility' was what Sam had said to me and I thought you poor chap, you've been trying too hard. So my resentment was purged away."

I still have several more questions, but Burt appears spent by all he has just said, the memories recalled, the emotions, the pain.

"I think that's enough," I say. "I appreciate how much you have shared with me."

I close my notebook, cap my pen.

"We enjoyed having you," Burt says.

"I enjoyed being here, too."

I expect to let things go at that, but other words tumble out of my mouth, almost on their own.

"I felt being here with you was as close as I will ever get to Sam again. And I guess I was hoping he would have seen that I didn't turn out so bad after all."

20

Brothers in Conscience

WE MET OUR FIRST YEAR at Virginia on the soccer field during phys ed. I teased Jackson Lears about his "cat-like movements" and we soon became fast friends. We had many classes together over the next four years, including Harbaugh's History of the United States in the 20th Century. We shared all-nighters of study, had intense talks about matters profound, made each other convulse with laughter, grew to question the war, despite being in ROTC. And when we each submitted applications for discharge as conscientious objectors, some of our strongest support came from a best friend first encountered on that soccer field behind Memorial Gym.

We have met again in many places since college, in San Diego, Boston, Columbia, Missouri, and Washington, D.C. But in all those reunions, for some strange reason, we have never discussed our C.O. stands. Tonight is our chance to change that, this time in Lambertville, New Jersey. Once the Delaware and Raritan Canal brought the industrial revolution to this town on the banks of the Delaware River, just across from Pennsylvania. Now, tourists are the trade, drawn by Lambertville's collection of historic buildings, its antique shops, restaurants, slow-paced streets, the aura of the past.

I join the Lears' family for dinner in Lambertville's only Thai restaurant, the kind of small ethnic eatery they always find wherever they live. Jackson is ever-Jackson, my least-changed old friend, his sandy hair always worn short, his beard well-trimmed, that open, gentle face with the prominent nose. He is intent, proud, resoundingly earnest and scholarly, a serious-minded man. After the Navy,

223

he had gone on to a distinguished career in academia, a Woodrow Wilson Fellowship, a master's from Chapel Hill, a doctorate from Yale. His dissertation on antimodernism in late nineteenth-century America had been published as *No Place of Grace,* and became a nominee for the National Book Critics Circle Award. He is now a visiting professor at Princeton. This former member of the U.Va. Student Council—who urged fellow students that "the time is ripe for revolution" in the spring of 1969—still displays his leftist beliefs on bumper stickers plastered on his Toyota station wagon.

Karen Parker Lears, Jackson's wife since college days, is a dark-haired woman with a striking inner beauty and considerable talent as a visual artist. She is an earth mother in the best sense, not the cliché, grounded, spiritual, giving, a fine compatriot for Jackson and often the perfect foil, playing on the droll sense of humor that his seriousness sometimes obscures. Their two daughters—Rachel, twelve, and Adin, seven—are seated at the table with us. They are energetic talkers, free-spirited accomplices, pals.

The Thai food is pleasingly spicy this chill evening and the table conversation is pleasantly nostalgic, at least at first. But talk of our times together at Virginia soon gives way to talk of our time afterward, when Jackson went into the Navy and I went into the Army. Karen, who may have been a pacifist long before we were, recalls what women often endured because of the men they loved and the war. She had hated the Navy and everything about being a "Navy officer's wife." She had hated the inequities of the service, the differences enforced by rank, even during the application process for discharge as a conscientious objector.

"I was painfully aware of the difference between Jackson, an officer, and an enlisted guy who was going through the same thing," Karen says. "We knew we had the law on our side, and had a lot of personal resources. And we were very lucky for all the support we had, support from me, support from his family, from my family."

Karen's comment brings it all back, what it had been like trying to become a C.O. in the military, the nights of fitful sleep, the tormenting uncertainties, alternate scenarios, endless discussions with our spouses. And how thankful we men were that someone was willing to share that with us, thankful and yet guilty as well.

"I had long conversations with Karen," Jackson says. "I'm sure I drove her crazy. I told her how desperate I was, how I had to get out of this thing. She was influential."

"I don't think I could have done it without my wife back then," I add. "Especially knowing the animosity I was sure to receive from my own family. She made such a difference."

Dinner takes two hours. Karen heads home with the girls afterward. Jackson and I walk back to my hotel. Snow seems imminent. Our breath is illuminated by old street lamps. We turn up the collars on our coats and move swiftly along deserted sidewalks.

The smell of wood burning in the fireplace greets us inside the Inn at Lambertville Station, a countrified motel on the riverbank. In my room, I pour bourbon on ice, some Virginia Gentleman I have saved from Charlottesville, then Jackson and I settle into chairs, prop our feet on the coffee table and begin to talk. When Jackson and I are together, our humor usually feeds on each other's, breeding rapid-fire repartee until we get giddy. But there is none of that now. We want to recall exactly what it was like two decades ago.

"I was on a nuclear-armed ship, a guided missile cruiser, the USS *Chicago*," Jackson begins. "I was to be one of the officers in the chain of command who would have authorized the use of nuclear weapons. This had led to a series of interviews with people, including the chaplain who asked if 'I had any ax to grind for or against nuclear war.'

"The nuclear issue overshadowed Vietnam for me. I was first assigned to the ship when it was coming back from Vietnam. What really focused my discontent was the nuclear issue—did I choose to be a participant in nuclear war? The thought was appalling to me."

Jackson's discontent had remained exactly that, discontent, until he returned to the States and a grad student told him that he did not have to just sit around and complain, that the Navy did not want officers around who "thought your kinds of thoughts" and there were ways to get out of the service, including being a conscientious objector. That comment was "an Epiphany," Jackson remembers, something he knew nothing about, but would soon investigate. Jackson's application for C.O. discharge later had the same effect on me. It caused considerable thought, then spurred action.

We both sought assistance from counseling groups, the Pacific Coast Counseling Service in Jackson's case, the Central Committee for Conscientious Objectors in Philadelphia in mine. There followed many weeks of intense reading and reflection, the study of non-violence along a path that was well mapped—Gandhi, Albert Schweitzer, Henry David Thoreau, Martin Luther King, Jr., Rein-hold Niebuhr, the Bible, Richard Gregg's classic 1934 work, *The Power of Nonviolence.* The readings helped focus belief, provide assur-ance that conscientious objection was part of a strong tradition, and not some 1960s' fad like tie-dye.

Then came the writing of the actual application, what seemed then like a graduate thesis where the grade might be Life or Death. The application required laundry lists of various kinds (every school ever attended, every address ever lived at, every job ever held), plus lengthy essays on the most complex of questions:

"1. A description of the nature of belief which is the basis of claim. 2. Explain how, when, and from whom or from what source the applicant received the training and acquired the belief which is the basis of claim. 3. A statement as to circumstances, if any, under which the applicant believes in the use of force. 4. A description of the actions and behavior in the applicant's life which, in his opin-ion, most conspicuously demonstrates the consistency and sincerity of the convictions which gave rise to his claim. 5. A statement as to whether applicant has ever given public expression, written or oral, to the views expressed in his application as the basis for claim. If so, specify when and where."

Jackson remembers struggling over the writing of his application for a week. His challenge was explaining how he had come to paci-fist beliefs from a Catholic background. Among the crucial passages he wrote was: "Christ's commandment to 'Love thy neighbor as thy-self' was meant to apply to *all* men—not just to those of one's own nationality or political ideology. I believe that my obedience to this commandment is crucial if I am to keep faith with the Spirit of Life which orders and presides over the universe, and with my own inter-pretation of Christian teachings. For this reason, I feel that contin-ued service in the military, the instrument of war, is unacceptable."

I managed to write my entire application in one frenzied week-end. One of my greatest challenges was proving that my belief in conscientious objection had developed *after* my entrance on active duty, a point all military C.O.s had to prove. So a centerpiece of my application was my recent commitment to the Unitarian Universalist faith. I tried to explain how that faith had affected my thoughts on military service: "War deprives man of his greatest attribute, his humanness. And in order to be ready for war, armies constantly require man to view his fellow man as his enemy. Hate for man in another uniform—the complete antithesis of love and respect, denial of the supreme worth of the individual—is a requirement of military discipline and order. All I believe tells me that I cannot be a part of ANY ORGANIZATION which requires hate of my fellow men as an operational necessity. However small and insignificant my contribution to the overall military effort may be, it is still all me and all my contribution. And it is a contribution that all my strongest, most fundamental, most deeply held convictions and beliefs compel me to stop right now. I cannot do otherwise."

The C.O. application had to be supplemented by letters of support from people testifying to the applicant's sincerity. Jackson included ten letters of support with his application, I included twenty-seven with mine, letters that still touch the heart after two decades, so far beyond the usual reference letters that people write. I am still amazed by the eloquence people summoned up, even when they were in the service themselves or were veterans, people definitely not conscientious objectors. I still feel in their debt to this day.

There followed that long-awaited moment, submitting the application. I remember the great relief that morning, the feeling of pride tinged with uncertainty, shocked looks on some faces, emotions on edge. Jackson's memories are more graphic.

"I was scared as hell," he recalls. "It was right after we had mustered out Monday morning, that time when you line up in formation on deck. I went down to my department head in his office and he turned around and said, 'What is it?' I had a sheaf of papers in my hand and I just said, 'I'm going to lay my cards on the table. I want to apply for discharge as a conscientious objector.' He said, 'You're kidding.' Then there was thirty seconds of silence before he said, 'We're going to have to go see the executive officer.'

"That was Watt W. Jordan III, so we went up to his office and my department head said, 'Mr. Lears has something he wants to tell you.' Jordan looked over my application, fuming, and then he blew up when he read the line, 'I feel that the whole structure of the military encourages a callous attitude toward human life.' That was sophomoric to say, I'll admit it now, not really true. Jordan then said, 'You don't understand. I've been in battle, I've seen men die.'"

Jackson and I were removed from our jobs as soon as we submitted our C.O. applications, stripped of our security clearances, shunned by many colleagues. "People treated me like I was somebody dying in a hospital," Jackson remembers.

There followed a battery of personal interviews, interviews with one's commander, a chaplain, a psychiatrist and a lawyer (in the Army, but not the Navy). Each interviewer submitted a written report with a recommendation to approve or reject the application. These interviews were the sternest test of the entire C.O. process since there was no way of knowing how hostile the questioner would be or what he would ask, although every C.O. applicant did prepare some response for what was considered the ultimate trick question— "Wouldn't you have fought against Hitler?" This was considered a trap because, in order to qualify as a conscientious objector, one had to be opposed to "all war," and not just Vietnam. The Hitler question was like a time bomb ticking throughout the application process; answering in the affirmative would presumably scuttle an application and result in a plane ticket to Saigon. So many applicants responded to the Hitler question by saying it was a hypothetical from another time and another war and therefore could not be answered.

"During those interviews," I tell Jackson, "I felt like my whole life was hanging in the balance."

"The worst was the shrink," he says. "I spent a half hour with him and he wrote up some descriptions of me that left me pissed as hell when I got a copy of his report."

Next came weeks of waiting while the application worked all the way up the chain of command, each headquarters adding its own recommendation for either approval or rejection, until the application finally reached Washington. Jackson's totaled twenty-seven pages by then and mine sixty-three, which was indicative of our confidence in having it approved.

"I felt I was going to get out," Jackson says, "although I wondered if they were going to fuck me over in some legalistic way, since I was not a member of any pacifist sect."

"I felt much more uncertainty than you did," I say. "I was always afraid that my application would be handled differently because of my grandfather. That's why it was so long; I thought it had to be one of the best C.O. applications that the Army had ever received. But I still never had any confidence that it would be approved; I was in doubt until the moment when I heard it was."

"I was extremely lucky," Jackson adds. "It was a class-based decision. I was from a good university, I knew how to use regulations and how to express myself."

"Plus we were officers," I inject, "and they didn't want such officers around."

"Plus we were officers. Right."

We were indeed lucky. As Myra MacPherson notes in her massive study, *Long Time Passing: Vietnam & the Haunted Generation:* "In-service conscientious objector applicants were met with intimidation. . . . Still, C.O. application rates zoomed almost 400 percent in the Army from 1967 to mid-1971. Countless other would-be applicants . . . never showed up in statistics because they were harassed and discouraged when they tried for C.O. status."[1]

Discouragement enough was provided by the high rejection rates for military C.O. applications until late in the Vietnam War. The first year when the Navy approved more than half of its C.O. discharge applications was 1970, the year of Jackson's application, when 63 percent of 577 applications were approved. The first year when the Army approved more than half of its C.O. discharge applications was 1971, the year of mine, when 58 percent of 1,525 applications were approved.

Jackson and I were among the 7,493 conscientious objectors discharged from the military during Vietnam. There were 3,275 C.O.s from the Army, 2,087 from the Navy, 1,779 from the Air Force, 352 from the Marines. We became partners in nonviolence with 172,000 conscientious objectors recognized by their draft boards, and countless others who should have been, but were not.

A few of our views on the war and that time have changed in the passing years, Jackson and I agree. We no longer consider those in the military to be the enemy, as we once did. But we still hold the belief that the best way to ensure peace is to not participate in war.

Period. As John F. Kennedy once said, "War will exist until that distant day when the conscientious objector enjoys the same reputation and prestige that the warrior does today."[2]

I ask Jackson one last question as it nears midnight, a question whose answer I can anticipate. But I still feel compelled to ask anyway, to put things in perspective, sum up.

"How would you rank becoming a C.O. with other things you've done in your life?"

"I would put it at the top of the list, I truly would," Jackson says. "I feel privileged to have had that opportunity. I'm glad I did it. It was a historical moment when I felt alive, when choices really mattered."

"I have always felt," I add, "that if I never did anything else worthwhile in my life, at least I did this. I took a stand once for what I believe."

21

In the Wake of the Six-Day War

HE FREEWAY KEEPS WIDENING, adding new lanes every few miles, this vast swath of asphalt, soon twelve lanes across. I see the first glimpse of Manhattan in the distance, several silhouettes on the horizon, the brute towers of the World Trade Center, the timeless elegance of the Empire State Building. The highway is now lined with tank farms and chemical plants, the eerie glare of halogen lights, clouds of of industrial discharge, foul smells, New Jersey hell.

I exit at The Meadowlands, former wetlands now covered with acres of parking lots, Giants Stadium, a coliseum, a horse race track, industrial parks. I spend the night in the high-rise condominium of Jane Hennessey and Chuck Adams, a Virginia friend, now an executive with a worldwide hotel chain. There is takeout Chinese to eat in the hectic New York fashion, while a FAX spits out messages from corporate headquarters in Hong Kong.

The next morning, I play New York City commuter, boarding the 8:30 A.M. bus to Manhattan. The bus revs up onto a freeway, then slows amidst the monstrous flow of traffic being funneled into the Lincoln Tunnel. We come out of the tunnel and head up a labyrinth of ramps attached to the Port Authority Bus Terminal. The bus pulls to a stop and we passengers file off without a word.

The bus terminal is New York at its most bizarre, the city as it might be seen by Fellini, a vast expanse containing a riot of people, executives and office workers rushing to their skyscrapers, the destitute milling about with no place else to go, assorted crazies, screamers, dealers. A voice over the loudspeaker makes announce-

231

ments that no one seems to notice, the words echo off cold floors, hard walls, a din. Even the New York City streets seem an escape.

I start walking up Eighth Avenue. It is seventeen blocks to the offices of "60 Minutes," a considerable hike, but I have not walked Manhattan streets in more than a decade so I want to take in the scene on these broad sidewalks. This is not an appealing route; it is workaday New York, no skyscrapers, just low-rise brick buildings, offices of people who cannot afford better, small shops, little groceries, restaurants run by families, often immigrants.

I turn onto West 57th Street, proceed a few blocks, enter a nondescript office tower, not the flashy CBS corporate headquarters known as "Black Rock." I get off the elevator, enter the reception area for "60 Minutes," say "I'm here to see Mike Wallace," take a seat on the couch, and wait.

How many of my Sunday evenings have been spent watching the product of these offices, I think to myself, America's long-running morality play. "60 Minutes" has become our real-life "Bonanza," with Mike Wallace and his cohorts roaming the globe as their Ponderosa—good guys in trench coats meeting the newsmakers, confronting the wrong-doers, although there have been times when they go after targets not of their stature, scam artists, petty crooks, cheats, people certain to squirm under the full glare of CBS. Still, I keep watching, along with millions more, maybe not every week, but many. I continue to wonder who will get skewered this time.

I am escorted down a long hallway leading straight to Mike Wallace's office. I can see him hunched over his desk, his face as familiar as my own in the mirror. We wait outside his office for a moment. I notice Morley Safer in his office next door. A nearby secretary answers her phone with "Ed Bradley's office."

Wallace motions me in, shakes hands while still seated at his desk, the Hudson River over his shoulder, industrial New Jersey beyond. He is cordial, soft-spoken, friendly, but harried, and suffering from a killer cold, Mike Wallace with the sniffles, hardly the commanding presence glimpsed so often on TV.

Wallace apologizes for having to finish a radio commentary before he can view the special on Israel that he did with my grandfather. Then his mind skips ahead to later this day, his next destination, his next story, Dallas.

"Am I going out of La Guardia or JFK tonight?" he asks assistant Trent Gillies.

"La Guardia."

"Good."

I am led past a blackboard which keeps a tongue-in-cheek countdown on the days left until Mike Wallace's retirement, now numbering over two thousand days, and a chart nearby that tracks the current location of the "60 Minutes" correspondents, the traditional office sign-out sheet, only this one happens to list:

Safer	NY
Wallace	NY
Reasoner	Germany
Bradley	NY
Kroft	NY/London
Vieira	NY

I enter a small screening room. A huge Sony television dominates the far end of the room. Chairs are strewn about in random disorder. I take a place at a folding table set up on a riser, moving aside a yellow legal pad on which it is written, "Show tapes to lawyer," the notation underscored several times.

Wallace rushes in after a while, plops down in a chair, props his feet up and remarks, "I haven't seen this in a long, long time. Jesus, this was twenty-two years ago."

The lights dim, the film begins. "How Israel Won the War" flashes across the screen, along with "A CBS News Special," this broadcast on July 18, 1967, my grandfather's sixty-seventh birthday.

Mike Wallace appears on the screen, outfitted in khaki, a baseball cap on his head. He is seated on sandbags, his eyes squinting in the Mideast sun, deep blue water behind him as he intones, "This is Mike Wallace. This is where the war began, at Ras Nasrani, 20 miles north of Sharm El Sheikh, overlooking the Strait of Tiran at the head of the Gulf of Aqaba."[1]

I feel my pulse quicken, my anticipation grow.

"In six days the war was over. How did Israel do it? Israel, roughly the size of New Jersey, was surrounded by an Arab world 50 times its size: 14 Arab divisions against five Israeli. But Israel's air

S. L. A. Marshall and CBS-TV correspondent Mike Wallace in the Middle East during filming of 1967 special on the Six-Day War. Courtesy S. L. A. Marshall Military History Collection, University of Texas at El Paso.

power wiped out this advantage in an hour and 20 minutes, from 7:45 to 9:05 a.m. . . . . In this report we will see the battlefields, and hear from the men who fought the war. My colleague on this broadcast, CBS News Military Consultant, General S. L. A. Marshall."

The camera pulls back to show Wallace and Marshall surveying some battlements. "Here you see another reason for Egypt's great fall," Marshall says. "They were mixing up two things—the idea of mobility based on armor, and the idea of position warfare. Have you noticed for instance that there are no defensive positions in Israel?"

"Over in Israel," Wallace repeats.

"That's right. They don't get confused. Everything is mobility and fire-power."

An eerie chill comes over me. I feel a rush of many emotions, excitement, pride, remorse, morbid fascination. This is the grandfather of my strongest memories. I have spent months on his trail now, traveled coast-to-coast, asked his friends and foes alike what they think of him, shifted through the evidence he left behind. And yet here he is on the screen, alive again, responding to questions from Mike Wallace. I feel an urge to pose a few questions of my own: "Let's go over where you were in World War I and when, the true story for once, places and dates. And what prompted that figure on men not firing their weapons in World War II? Did you have any computations in your field notebooks at all? And what ever happened to your notebooks anyway?"

Wallace and Marshall are shown interviewing a commander in the Israeli Air Force, then Wallace is interviewing some Israeli pilots, shockingly young pilots. Then Marshall and Wallace are bouncing along in a jeep, Wallace behind the wheel, before they stop along the road to Jiradi, where one of the crucial battles was fought.

"General Marshall," asks Wallace, "what about the quality of these Egyptian trenches?"

"Well, they're not hasty trenches," Marshall replies. "They've been long in the making. They're revetted with bricks, made of bricks, mud and straw. Otherwise, the normal shifting of the dune would promptly cover in the trench work. However, they're completely impractical."

"Why?" says Wallace.

"Well, for one thing, it's a straight-running trench and one man could get in with an automatic rifle at the end of it and can enfilade everybody that's in here. And the other thing is the height of the trench and the parapet. If you stand up, you might just as well not have a trench."

"Because you can be hit from here on up," says Wallace, motioning at his waist.

"That's right. But if you stoop down to where you've got protection, then you cannot see over the top of the trench. So it's badly engineered from any point of view."

The two move about the battlements, with pieces of Egyptian weaponry picked up and examined, commentary and critique provided by Marshall, a scene that seems slightly staged, a little too convenient.

"You just found all that stuff there?" I ask Wallace.

"That's right. It was there as we found it."

Captured Egyptian generals are soon interviewed by Wallace in the film, then Israeli generals are interviewed by Wallace and Marshall.

"It's amazing," I remark after a while, "to get both sides discussing the war so soon after the battles."

"This was," Wallace nods, "a wonderful, wonderful piece."

Wallace is soon summoned for an urgent call from the State Department. I watch the rest of the film alone, surprised by the seriousness of this documentary, so different from the flash-and-dash of TV today. All the Israeli principals have consented to interviews and speak with candor, General Moshe Dayan, General Itzhak Rabin.

But whenever my grandfather comes on, I focus on him. I examine his movements, assess his speech, look for any hint of advancing senility, what several of his friends noticed after his heart attack. But I see no such evidence. My grandfather springs out of the jeep, clambers around battlements, climbs hills, has no apparent trouble keeping up with a man almost twenty years his junior. And this is occurring only a few months after he had completed an extended tour through the war zone in Vietnam, and at an age when many men tour through the local golf course in electric carts.

So perhaps this notion of advancing senility may not wash.

Maybe that does not explain his behavior back then, the outbursts, the peevishness, the fictions presented as realities. But then again, maybe it does. My grandfather had admitted to his brother that he had been trying to fight off senility for years, and sometimes lost the battle. Which led Burt to conclude that maybe senility had not washed over Sam at once, but instead had the distinct ebb and flow of the tides.

Burt had seen evidence of this in 1964, when the two brothers spent weeks traveling through England, West Germany, Belgium, France, and Spain. As Burt recalled in a letter to me: "Sam took his time, but his stamina was good. His mien was magisterial amidst an assemblage of U.S. generals attending a luncheon in Heidelberg hosted by the commander of U.S. Forces in Europe. His discourse was cogent and his inquiries sharp on successive occasions whose numerousness and range you would, I believe, find impressive if I undertook to list them. In contrast, Sam repeatedly made known his status as a general to persons casually encountered—stewardesses, room clerks, and the like. A honeymooning couple aboard an airport bus in Paris looked puzzled by his narrative of winning a battlefield commission. He volunteered the story of his military career to two touring lady schoolteachers having a nightcap in a Paris bistro. And so on. These things, though small, were worrisome to me."

Burt's observation makes me think it was unlikely that my grandfather would exhibit senility when the CBS-TV cameras were rolling, or when he was interviewing troops in Vietnam. He would have tried like hell to rally himself for such performances, and besides he was dealing with subjects he knew so well. So that was probably when he was at his best, still self-assured, his old self.

The film is now winding toward its conclusion. Wallace and Marshall are standing at a former Syrian strong point, a hill laced with trenches where hand-to-hand combat broke out, causing significant casualties in a battle between small outfits. Ninety men were killed only weeks before at this very place where two Americans now converse.

Wallace says to Marshall: "I don't imagine that anybody, certainly no foreigner, has gotten as thorough a briefing as you have in the last two or three weeks here in Israel. And there are one or two points that I'd like to clear up that I believe that you know something about. One is the number of Israeli planes left behind to cover Israel at the time of the first air strikes on Monday morning."

"Well," says Marshall, "there were 12 planes left behind to cover the whole State of Israel. And they did not take the air immediately when the assault was made on Egypt. Then when the time came to put up a defensive screen, only 8 of them went up, and that left exactly four planes as a reserve."

"Isn't that a little foolhardy?"

"We would think so. I would think so. Looking back even now, I think it's a little foolhardy, but it is what is called a 'calculated risk' by the Israelis."

"The other point that you've made a couple of times over the past two weeks, General, is that 8 o'clock in the morning, 7 to 8 o'clock in the morning, is the worst time to start a war, and yet the Israelis did that. Why?"

"Well, the other fellow is bound to be up and awake, going about his rounds. There's bound to be maximum visibility, a good chance to see you coming on, and 8 o'clock is considered therefore, one of the worst possible hours, if not *the* worst. And I think that's the reason, one of the reasons, that they chose it."

"Perhaps another reason is that they knew that the people at the United Nations would be fast asleep in New York, and that they'd be able to move before they could get the Security Council together."

"I know definitely that was one of their calculations."

The film closes as Wallace sums up and signs off. The lights come back on, but I remain in my seat. I linger in the screening room, reflecting on what I have just seen, impressed once again by another bravura performance by my grandfather, much as I had been by his work in World War II, only this totally different. He displays his insider's knowledge of what went on during the Six-Day War, but also the knack for making that come alive for the viewer. The man had a gift, a definite gift. And suddenly I feel strangely wistful, wishing that that was all I knew about my grandfather.

I walk back to Mike Wallace's office, am welcomed inside, have the door shut behind me. It is my chance to ask a few questions of the great inquisitor, this weird role reversal, Mike Wallace seated behind the office desk this time while I get my notebook out. I do not think I have ever felt quite this odd, doing what I do. This thought passes once I start into my question about Wallace's impression of S. L. A. Marshall.

"I want you to be aware of the fact that I didn't know him that well—other than this one time we worked together," Wallace says. "I found him to be no-nonsense, professional, serious, and genuinely helpful to me."

Wallace proceeds to talk about the show with no prompting: "I was assigned this special. We were in Israel within just a few days of the war's end. Now, I'm no military authority, so I turned to an authority. And Slam Marshall had the entrée to the Israelis at the highest levels. He was also highly regarded by the military in the United States. And he also had that rare capacity to not only make things clear but also interesting. We went from one end of the battlefields to the other, this special was put together in a huge hurry."

"Did you feel the competition?" I ask, voicing that common journalist's concern. "Or did you have it knocked?"

"We had it knocked," Wallace says. "In those days, CBS News did not compete with anybody but CBS News. We had great foreign correspondents then, Winston Burdett, Daniel Schorr, the late Charles Collingwood."

"I wonder if you and my grandfather were up all night partying, then working all day. I have heard that is what he did in Vietnam."

"I don't have that kind of reputation."

"Did you notice any signs of aberrant behavior from him, any huffiness, braggadocio, fits of pique?"

"Slam Marshall was a character, but that comes with the territory. He was a general officer taking sometimes controversial positions, he believed what he believed, he stood his ground. But, as to him coming across as peevish or arrogant, I did not get that feeling. I did not know that much about military matters—I had been a communications officer in the Navy—so this was a voyage of discovery for me."

"Did you notice anything in particular about his health? Did he act like a man who had had a heart attack a few years before? Did you have to slow down any because of him? I mean, he was sixty-seven when this was filmed."

"He was sixty-seven?" Wallace replies. "He did not seem sixty-seven. I'm seventy-one myself now and he certainly did not come across as that old. We responded to the energy in each other. It didn't occur to me that he was an older person. I'm surprised to learn he was sixty-seven."

"Is it possible," I ask, "to put this special in context with all the thousands of other pieces that you've done?"

"I'm very proud of it. It is a document, for Chrissake. That thought came back to me when I watched it for the first time in a long time this morning. It is an extraordinary document."

Wallace proceeds to pull out some of the program's reviews. "A first-class, wholly absorbing documentary," says one. "Excellent teaming of Mike Wallace and S. L. A. Marshall, unique and imaginative, knowledge of Marshall gave the show additional depth," says another. And a third review comments that "this special reprise of the war is the result of the Israelis lifting their ban on interviews with top military officers, the ban lifted for S. L. A. Marshall."

Wallace's office is small, crowded, clearly inhabited by a working journalist. It is not some ceremonial habitat for a network star. Wallace's back is to the river view; he faces the hectic activity inside "60 Minutes." His bookshelves are crowded with volumes on current history, his Zenith TV looks old enough to be sold by the Salvation Army, his typewriter stand supports an aging manual straight out of "The Front Page."

Wallace's work space also shows his intense pride in his long career, but with a sense of humor about it, too. Eleven Emmy awards are tucked here and there, in the bookshelves, on ledges, a table, this matter-of-fact part of the decor. There are photographs of Wallace relaxing in tennis togs, but also being hustled off the floor of the Chicago Democratic Convention in 1968, strong-armed by heavies. There is an inscribed photograph of Nancy Reagan, a framed Newsweek cover with a photograph of Wallace, several cartoons that mention "60 Minutes," an ad that proclaims, "The four most dreaded words in the English language: 'Mike Wallace is here.'"

Our conversation turns to the relationship between Marshall and the Israelis, how that opened doors for the special.

"The Israelis respected him, they admired him," Wallace says.

"He had done that book on the 1956 war, *Sinai Victory*. That showed his perspective."

I am well aware of Marshall's fondness for Israel and the Israelis, his steadfast support for the Jewish state, his willingness to champion the cause, make speeches, raise money. And the Israelis recognized his efforts. In 1961, Marshall was made an honorary fellow of Bar-Ilan University, the American-sponsored university in Israel, and a scholarship there was established in his name. In 1962, Marshall was awarded Israel's Medallion of Valor at a Los Angeles dinner presided over by former President Harry S Truman. Among the eleven recipients of the Medallion of Valor that evening were Gen. Omar Bradley, Jack Benny, Van Cliburn, and Sol Hurok.

Marshall's brief acceptance speech before the distinguished assemblage included these words: "Now, about Israel, I here repeat what I have said over and again to all who will hear me: I support Israel because I love my own country and because common sense tells me that that little lighthouse over there is a vital part of our own free world security. We don't give Israel anything. We get back full value for what we invest in this magnificent hope. And buying bonds is never enough. This thing is like the old-time religion. To be happy with it, you go full-length, dunking yourself in all the programs of Israel's upbuilding—I mean every program."[2]

This relationship was of benefit to both the Israelis and to Marshall. But I still find myself wondering if his extraordinary entrée after the Six-Day War was the result of the Israelis knowing that he was sympathetic to their side, or because they genuinely respected the man and his work, if it is possible to separate such things. So I ask Wallace.

"Absolutely, the Israelis respected him," Wallace replies.

"I have one final question," I say. "What, if anything, did you learn from your experiences with S. L. A. Marshall?"

"You know as well as I do that a reporter is no better than his sources," Wallace says. "S. L. A. Marshall was a superb source for me in the understanding of military matters. I came to a fuller understanding and appreciation of that particular war, and of the pressures, strains, and strategies of a military operation in battle."

Wallace does not close there. He adds one last comment, "And I liked him as a person."

22

Questions of Fairness

I T IS A LONG HIKE to the offices of *American Heritage,* another long
hike over these Manhattan streets, maybe a couple of miles, but I
am in no particular hurry. It does not matter at all when I arrive.
Because I will not be meeting with anyone at *American Heritage,* not
the editor, not the managing editor, no one. I am being shut out of
their offices. I am being given the Big Media Snub.

I had hoped things would be otherwise. I have met with
S. L. A. Marshall's critics whenever I can, Roger Spiller on my newspaper research trip, later David Hackworth, then Albert Garland
and Harold Leinbaugh on this trip. I have corresponded with Charles
White, too. I have thought it was my duty to hear them out, share
some of what I have found, get their reaction, in the spirit of fairness. I
am a firm believer in letting those on the other side have their say.
That seems one of the most basic tenets of American journalism.

So I intended to meet with the editors of *American Heritage.* I
thought there were things we could discuss in person, even if we had
already exchanged several letters in the past. The article in *American
Heritage* had set off the Marshall controversy. The editors should be
interested in any new information I had uncovered. I am a fellow
journalist, not some media-baiting critic.

I had written Richard Snow, *American Heritage's* managing editor, from the road and proposed a brief meeting when I got to New
York: "After all the correspondence that has passed between us—and
with my father, for that matter—I thought it might be intriguing for
us to meet face-to-face and have a short discussion."

242

But when I called Snow from New Jersey to set up such a meeting, he said, "I'm not going to be meeting with you, on the orders of my editor."

"Why?" I asked.

"I'm not going to tell you. It's in my letter."

"But I'm not at home to receive the letter—do you think perhaps you could read the letter to me?"

"No . . . . Well, all right."

Snow left the line for a time, then came back and practically spit out the words of a letter that concluded: "My editor has asked me not to see you. He feels we have been extremely open, have spent an enormous amount of time responding to your letters and calls, and that, in the end, your intent has been hostile and destructive. We simply can no longer trust in your good faith."

"OK," I said.

We hung up.

I wish I had been shocked by *American Heritage*'s decision, but I was not. It fit their pattern of behavior with their article and afterward. Every time that common journalistic practice, or even basic fairness, seemed to dictate a certain course of action, the editors at *American Heritage* did just about the opposite.

They wrote a Letter to the Editor of the *Seattle Post-Intelligencer* saying that my series on S. L. A. Marshall included "nothing to put a dent" in their article. The newspaper published *American Heritage*'s entire letter without comment, as it should. Fair enough. I was prompted to write a Letter to the Editor of *American Heritage*, enumerating six errors of fact and fifteen misleading statements in their article—errors that included the work performed by Marshall's unit in World War I, the Army school he was attending at the end of the war, the extent of his newspaper experience after the war, his father's occupation. I set forth such misleading statements as there is "no indication" that Marshall did "company-level interviews" during World War II, and that Marshall perpetuated "a peculiar hoax" with *Men Against Fire*, an assertion directly contradicted by even the magazine's primary research source, historian Roger Spiller, who told me, "I know what 'hoax' means. That's why I didn't say that."

And *American Heritage*'s response to all this? The editors refused to publish my Letter to the Editor. Too long, they said. So, I wrote a shorter Letter to the Editor that conformed to the length the editors proscribed. They refused to publish my second letter. As editor Byron Dobell wrote to me, "You have entered a zone of discourse that puts you in another world as far as I am concerned." A "zone of discourse?" "In another world?" What happened to a publication's responsibility to correct its mistakes?

American Heritage did not print a correction. A subsequent issue instead included an "Editors' Note" which began, "Since publishing the Marshall story, we have learned. . . ."[1] This coy phrase implied the editors had been doing additional research that led them to discover: The work performed by Marshall's unit in World War I, the Army school he was attending at the end of the war, and his father's occupation. No source of such information was cited.

So maybe my letters to the magazine did contain harsh words. I was frustrated by their shoddy research on an article that called a historical figure's reputation into question. Yes, he was my grandfather, but it was more than that. American Heritage had not insisted that the author of its article do any original research in the Marshall collection in El Paso, instead depending on Spiller and Leinbaugh, that approach confirmed by managing editor Snow over the telephone: "Spiller had, I believe, been to El Paso or in touch with El Paso, as had Leinbaugh [he had not been to El Paso]. We relied on them." Nor did American Heritage contact any members of Marshall's family to verify the many personal details in the article. "We didn't go to the family," Snow told me, "because that didn't seem an important step to take at the time. . . . in the story of Leinbaugh's quest and Spiller's scholarship, we felt we had the story." Which were just some of the reasons why I had told the editors that their article made me "ashamed to be part of the same profession."

And it was not as if I had no direct knowledge about how such national publications should operate. I worked at Sports Illustrated in New York as a researcher during one college summer and my job was doing the kind of thorough fact-checking that should have caught the errors and misleading statements in American Heritage's article. Sports Illustrated insisted that every fact be corroborated by two independent sources. No detail was too minor to get right. Long-distance calls were to be placed to the principals in a story if that was what it took to clear something up. Tedious work at times, but absolutely crucial. The magazine's reputation demanded nothing less.

S. L. A. Marshall typing his notes in the field in Europe during World War II, probably 1944. Courtesy S. L. A. Marshall Military History Collection, University of Texas at El Paso.

There would have been little point in trying to discuss such thorough research procedures with the editors of *American Heritage*, not after all the flaws I discovered in their article. Especially after editor Dobell had even admitted to the *New York Times*: "All we said was that Marshall's hypothesis [in *Men Against Fire*] was not backed by interviews. We don't know what the truth is. Marshall may or may not have been right."[2] Never mind that *American Heritage* had promoted its Marshall article on the cover with, "DID OUR SOLDIERS FIGHT POORLY IN WW II?" The answer, according to the editor, was: "We don't know what the truth is."

Still, I did not intend to rehash this when meeting with the editors of *American Heritage*, or replay our past correspondence either. I wanted to discuss something new, something I heard on this trip, something I thought the editors would want to respond to—what was said to me by *American Heritage*'s former editor in chief.

Now, I stand on the sidewalk of Fifth Avenue gazing up at the imposing edifice where *American Heritage*'s editors go about their work. This nine-story building appears to have been a bank at one time, maybe a mercantile exchange, something moneyed, substantial, establishment. Forbes Publishing is headquartered here, with its *Forbes* magazine and *American Heritage* in this imperial structure, massive pillars, windows at street level of reflective black glass, revolving front doors permanently locked shut, a small sign directing visitors to a side entrance, TV cameras monitoring the sidewalk.

Maybe, I think, someone inside the building is watching me on a TV screen inside right now, wondering who is that guy on the sidewalk writing into what looks like a reporter's notebook. What is he up to out there, does he have some business with us, is he going to come inside?

I keep thinking how strange this is, and how humbling. I am part of the media, make my living by having my words published; it is so routine that I give the process little thought. But now I am being taught what it is like to be shunned by the media, my words denied publication, my request to meet an editor declined. I am relegated to standing on the sidewalk outside looking in. Maybe all of us in the media should have this experience to remind us how the public often feels, and to remind us that we are part of the public, too.

My thoughts shift to my second day on the road in Oregon, my first interview of the trip. It had been a perfect September day, cloudless, hot, a light breeze blowing down from the jagged peaks of the Wallowa Mountains, this great alpine place in the northeastern corner of the state, "the Switzerland of America." I had come to the summer home of Alvin M. Josephy, Jr., western historian, expert on American Indians, author of more than a dozen books, and for twenty years, one of the top people at *American Heritage*: Senior Editor, Editor in Chief, Member of the Editorial Advisory Board.

I talked for almost five hours with Josephy, a sturdy, seventy-four-year-old man in a western shirt with pearl snap buttons, some resemblance to the late actor Joseph Cotten, his silver hair brushed back from a strong forehead burnished by summer sun, a prominent nose, kindly eyes behind tortoise shell glasses. We sat on the deck of Josephy's cabin at a table with fresh wildflowers under a cottonwood tree; we shared a marvelous lunch of chicken stew and fresh salad prepared by his wife; we hiked up to the ridge line where we looked down on a vast western panorama, peaks coming right down to the blue waters of Wallowa Lake, and in the distance, the Seven Devils Mountains on the edge of Hells Canyon and the Snake River.

But mostly, Josephy and I talked about *American Heritage* and S. L. A. Marshall. Josephy first met Marshall during World War II, when Josephy was a sergeant in the Marine Corps, a combat veteran of the Pacific Islands campaigns, winner of the Bronze Star. He had come to know Marshall better in later years, considered him a friend, a man whose work he "greatly respected." Josephy enlisted Marshall to write *The American Heritage History of World War I* and he had been the book's editor, matters of pride for him.

"I thought that was a very good book," Josephy said. "If I wanted to give someone a single book on World War I, it's as good as any I could find. It was well-researched, well-written. I doubt there were any mistakes in there. . . . Slam was a pro."

Our conversation moved to the present, when Marshall has gone from respected author at *American Heritage* to disparaged subject of an *American Heritage* "exposé." I brought out copies of my lengthy correspondence with the magazine and asked Josephy to read through the letters. I wanted his opinion because the magazine's reaction had prompted some self-doubt. I wondered if my anger at the way the article was done had warped my professional judgment, turned me into a belaborer of unimportant points.

Josephy read slowly, deliberately. I waited.

"This is a very good letter," Josephy finally said. "You got 'em with that last line. That's what stung them."

"I guess I don't remember the last line."

Josephy handed the letter back to me and I read the letter's conclusion, my reference to Dobell's admitting that *American Heritage* did not know whether or not Marshall was right about firing problems. "It is my belief," I had written, "that *American Heritage* should have known that—at least—prior to publishing an article that would call S. L. A. Marshall's reputation into question. That *American Heritage* went ahead with publication anyway says far more about the magazine than its article says about S. L. A. Marshall."

I also pulled out the issue of *American Heritage* with the Marshall article and Josephy combed through that, although he did not get past the first page before his ire started to rise. He read aloud the subheading on the first page of text: "Slam Marshall, who is regarded as one of our great military historians, looked into the heart of combat and discovered a mystery there that raised doubts about the fighting quality of U.S. troops. But one GI thought he was a liar . . . "[3]

Josephy looked up at me and said, "'Thought he was a liar'— that's what does it. A character assassination is implied there. The magazine gets on Leinbaugh's side by doing it that way. The magazine's proper role should be to say this is one guy saying this, but instead, it took his side. It agreed with him on the flimsiest of evidence."

I asked Josephy to read the separate "Letter from the Editors," something he had overlooked. Here, the editors explain how they came to publish the Marshall piece, what they describe as "a complex and troubling process" because "there was the uneasy sense that there might be something unseemly in revealing the frailties of a vanished colleague." The editors ultimately conclude that it was "a good story" and go ahead, but allow as how they "were not entirely comfortable with their role in telling it."[4]

"Jesus!" Josephy exclaimed, incensed by this editorial hedging.

Then he continued, "They should have backed off, they should have presented this as a new perspective on Marshall. My reaction is that they could have done this a different way. They tried to demolish his reputation, but it's very hypocritical. To say he wrote 'books of lasting value' when you're now saying he's a 'liar'—who's going to believe him after that?

"And he did NOT defame soldiers, maybe the soldiers in Leinbaugh's unit, but not all infantry soldiers. To this Marine, what Slam wrote came so close to the truth that I never thought he defamed anyone—based on the observations I had, what I saw myself. During the Guam landing, thirty-two of us got off a landing craft and twenty-six of us were hit walking across the reef. I saw a guy go out of his head into panic on the beach, and two of the guys had to wrestle him down. I never saw people freeze and couldn't fire. But I did see people get scared. And some people did fire, some did not."

Josephy was upset by this point. The rustle of the cottonwoods did not calm him, nor did the rush of the nearby stream.

"The main point," he emphasized, "is that this is character assassination by the author and the magazine. It was not a judicious handling of the subject in my opinion. I read the *New York Times* on this and it stung me. Then I read the article in *American Heritage* and I felt it was not handled in a scholarly way. The magazine simply became a party to the accusation."

Josephy's anger finally subsided, gave way to sadness. He had devoted two decades of his working life to *American Heritage*, had had such responsibilities there until his voluntary retirement in 1979. He had seen the magazine sold to Forbes, had watched the changes there with growing disappointment, and finally there had been this "character assassination" of S. L. A. Marshall. Josephy had tried to sum that up with growing frustration, until he finally said, "There's a veneer of history now at *American Heritage*, but that's all."

Many weeks later, I can still hear Josephy's words echoing in my mind as I stand outside *American Heritage*.

23

Sunday in the Country

I LINGER IN THE NEW YORK AREA for several days. Winter suddenly arrives, a severe storm riding the jet stream. Temperatures drop into the thirties, torrential rains fall, high winds cause several deaths, killer tornadoes cut through the South and the East. It is a week before Thanksgiving, and I feel growing apprehension about trying to make it across the country this time of year. Snow has started to fall around the Great Lakes.

I take a Sunday drive up the Taconic State Parkway, once such a marvel of a road, this scenic highway that was begun in 1940 and featured picnic tables with design work by one Franklin D. Roosevelt. The setting is still bucolic as I head north away from New York, rolling hills, forests, farms. I enter the town of Catskill, not far from a Hudson River bridge with a perfect name, the Rip Van Winkle. Because this town where my grandfather was born appears so unchanged.

The 1886 bank on Main Street still has golden doors and a golden eagle perched at the crown of the building. The brick firehouse still has "A. M. Osborn Hose Co. No. 2" painted above the garage doors. I cross Catskill Creek, then drive up Division Street, where the Marshalls lived when my grandfather was born, still not the better part of town, a steep street lined with big rambling houses, now in various stages of disrepair. "We were not poor in Catskill," my grandfather remembered once, "we just had no money."

I try to find the brick plant where Caleb Marshall had worked and discover an old bricked-up hulk of a building beside the creek.

But a utility worker tells me no, the brick plant was torn down years ago. Then she utters the lament of preservationists everywhere: "All the most important buildings have been turned into parking lots." This seems horrendous overstatement in a town so untouched by time, but then she rushes off and brings back a calendar filled with historic pictures of "Catskill Remembered." And her comment no longer seems so overdrawn. The Catskill Armory. Gone. The Smith House Hotel. Gone. Catskill High School. Gone. St. Patrick's Academy. Gone. The Saulpaugh Hotel. Gone. Time no longer seems so benign in this town with fewer than 5,000 folks.

I still leave Catskill with a sense of accomplishment, and completeness. My little Sunday drive in the country turns into a 235–mile trek, but I have now visited all the places where my grandfather was at crucial times in his life. I have looked at the houses where he lived, have walked sidewalks he walked, have seen what he saw, or at least what is left of it now. And all these places have helped me bring him back to life, a figure from my memory transported to this street or that square, a new connection with my family past.

I head back to New York City and spend time in Scarsdale with Susan and Sanford Sacks. Three decades ago, I sat in Susan's classroom in seventh and eighth grade, social studies with a social conscience. She was unlike any teacher I had had before, relentlessly challenging, frightfully tough, an absolute perfectionist, but also young and pretty. I was thirteen, that awakening time, and I was touched by Mrs. Sacks and her views. Truth was, I had a crush.

We were, I suspected, the only supporters of John F. Kennedy in her classroom that year. I argued his position in a class debate and what I said fell mostly on deaf ears. This was suburban Cleveland, where there were broad lawns and Republican views. But I did not stop arguing for Kennedy in class. I came home from school with a mission, to convince my parents to vote my way. I had a Kennedy campaign poster plastered on my bedroom door, his image many times larger than life, and I never missed a chance to tell my mother and father what a great man Kennedy was, what changes he would make, how his positions made such sense. I was insufferable, but they listened patiently, although when November came, they made it quite plain that they were not about to vote for a Democrat. But I still had learned an important lesson, although I did not recognize it until much later. Mrs. Sacks had shown me for the first time that my parents' way was not the only way to think.

We kept in touch over the years. I even grew accustomed to calling her Sue instead of Mrs. Sacks. We had had a chance meeting on the streets of New York when I worked at *Sports Illustrated,* and we had a reunion in Seattle last summer when Sanford was attending a convention.

Now, I pull into the driveway of the Sacks' large brick house perched on a hillside, surrounded by trees, the upstairs hallway filled with framed posters from various protests in the 1960s where Sue marched. We have another grand reunion, more reminiscences, more reflections on the influence that teachers can have on their students' lives. Sue, now fifty-two, has gone on to become the director of education programs at Barnard College. She is still young-looking, still dark-haired and pretty, still committed to liberal activism after all these years, social justice, equality, and peace.

We sit alone in the dining room on the last morning of my visit and we talk over coffee about what we remember when she was my teacher and I was her student. Time and again, Sue keeps coming back to my grandfather. That is what she remembers most about me.

"I didn't know anything about your family," Sue says. "The only person I knew about was your grandfather. I didn't meet your mother, I don't think I met your father, I can't remember meeting your folks. I have no recollection of that—which is kind of unusual. But I clearly remember your mythical and very real relationship with your grandfather. You wrote about it, you talked about it, plus you were a good writer.

"It was so salient. A lot of people love their grandparents, but it's more of an attachment than as a role model. I don't remember anyone else having a grandfather as a role model, on a pedestal. My grandparents certainly weren't my role models. Intellectually, my father was; he was a great reader, arguer. My mother was a psychiatric social worker; she was very compassionate. But my grandfather—I wrote to him every week, until he died at age eighty-six; that was the kind of relationship we had.

"Yours was so different. I have a very clear vision of your grandfather as a shining knight to you, a role model. In seventh and eighth grade, you were already showing talents like his; that identification was so clear. It was a real, living, bonded connectedness for you—not some abstract. It was so real."

What Sue says is not startling to me, but important confirmation. So much of my journey has centered on memory, sorting through what people say happened in hopes of arriving at a reasoned approximation of what actually did. Witness the legendary Liberation of Paris, the stark differences between Westover's account and Marshall's. I do not want to be guilty of similar excesses, over-dramatizing my early relationship with my grandfather, in order to make sense of the great hurt I bore for years.

I pack up my things at Sue's, load up the car. We pose for pictures, trading cameras, then a few snow flurries start to fall as we embrace.

I am heading west soon after that, glorious west at last, west toward Seattle. Actually southwest into New Jersey, but that is close enough. I have turned the last corner of the country on my trip.

24

Eisenhower's Biographer

THE DARKNESS LENGTHENS, the weather worsens while I make my way west. These November days bring a new sense of urgency to all I do, and homesickness too, especially as Thanksgiving nears. Everything seems more acute now, the stops, the time, my emotions, everything that is except the vast stretches of highway that still lie ahead.

I blitz through Fort Indiantown Gap in Pennsylvania, where I was first introduced to the Army at ROTC summer camp. The cluster of white clapboard buildings, our barracks, our mess hall, sits deserted at this time of year, but I can still hear echoes of 1968, that summer of tumult and discontent. Robert Kennedy had been murdered, students were marching in the streets around the world—and I was suddenly in uniform, my Mustang consigned to a distant parking lot, the bumper still wearing a Eugene McCarthy sticker. Indiantown Gap was my boot camp. I had fired every individual weapon in the Army arsenal, thrown a hand grenade, taken off my protective mask in a tent filled with tear gas, peeled potatoes on K.P. I had done fairly well, all things considered, even won an overblown commendation for a platoon newspaper that another student editor and I had produced. But at Indiantown Gap, I also felt the first stirrings of disquiet over the role I was soon supposed to play.

I race into Carlisle, Pennsylvania, intent on finishing my work here in the day and a half before Thanksgiving. This is the last archive I must search, the U.S. Army Military History Institute, the last place to discover S. L. A. Marshall's missing field notebooks. The institute's bibliography describes its Marshall holdings: "For World War II . . . numerous notes of interviews and correspondence with participants are available concerning operations of the 82nd and 191st Airborne Divisions in Normandy and the Ardennes."

I rush through eleven boxes of Marshall material at Carlisle, but no such notes are to be found. There are plenty of field notebooks all right, but all from later wars, Korea, Israel, Vietnam. And I am left feeling the same disappointment that I felt in Washington when I had visited the Office of the Army's Chief of Military History, carrying a copy of Marshall's 1958 letter saying he donated his field notebooks to that office. Marshall's section in the card catalog there seemed so promising, with individual cards for his field notes from the Gilbert and Marshall Islands campaigns in the Pacific, the 82nd Airborne's operations in Normandy and General Omar Bradley's campaigns in II Corps. But the librarian came back and said that all these catalog cards had absolutely nothing to back them up in the stacks. I tried to be polite, but I still said how incredible it was that such important historical documents could be misplaced or lost. Perhaps, she offered, they were shipped to Carlisle.

But that is not the case, I now confirm. And the Carlisle archivists point fingers of blame back at Washington. The Office of the Chief of Military History was shunted about that city during the mid-1970s, its vast holdings moved to three different locations. Carlisle's archivists have long suspected that materials were lost during the moves. David Keough, one of the archivists, even brings forth a transmittal slip for a "Combat Interview Index, Dept. of the Army, Adjutant General's Office, 2 Sept. 48" that is said to contain "2,000 combat interviews" with "the testimony of 8,000 front-line officers and soldiers."

I look up at Keough and exclaim, "This is it! This may not be Marshall's field notebooks, but it's the next best thing—all the interviews he would have done himself or probably read when he was theater historian. These are the interviews on which he drew his conclusions for *Men Against Fire* and they're far more extensive than anyone has reported."

"There's only one problem," Keough responds.

"What's that?"

"This came to the archives from Washington by itself. You noticed it mentions 244 pages of supporting materials. Well, not a page of those supporting materials ever arrived here."

"What happened to them?"

"We have no idea."

I encounter other disappointments at Carlisle. A massive two-volume interview with Marshall is included in the materials, part of an Army program of "oral history" debriefings of general officers instituted in 1970 at the direction of General Westmoreland. The Marshall interview was first opened to researchers only a few months ago and I plunge in with great hopes. But it proves to be a rambling bullshit session conducted in 1973 and 1974, with softball questions served up by an admiring lieutenant colonel and Marshall running on, Cate inserting herself into the dialogue in an attempt to focus the colonel's questions or keep her husband approximately on track, no easy task since he is drinking through some of the sessions.

The man I knew did not drink during the day, and certainly not when he had important work to complete, or so it seemed that summer I lived in his home. He had cocktails to unwind after long hours at the typewriter and the drinking sometimes extended late into the night, especially when there was an audience. So I am not prepared to encounter my grandfather drinking heavily during this final interview with his beloved Army, this chance to reflect on his life and work. Instead, it includes this painful passage to read:

"BG Marshall: Hey, will you mix me another, or have I had too much?

"Mrs. Marshall: I think you better slow down.

"BG Marshall: I haven't been drinking all afternoon. Well, at any rate . . ."

My time at Carlisle is one disappointment after another. Then I meet Stephen Ambrose, the biographer of Eisenhower and Nixon who is visiting professor at the Army War College. Keough mentions that Ambrose would be interested in talking to me about S. L. A. Marshall and I welcome the opportunity, aware of the praise his work has garnered from many quarters, including Hugh Sidey, Time's longtime Washington correspondent, who has said: "If there is a better historian at work on the events and personalities of our time than Stephen Ambrose, that person has not been discovered."

Ambrose, a handsomely chiseled man in a blue wool shirt and

President Dwight D. Eisenhower and S. L. A. Marshall, Jan. 10, 1961. Courtesy S. L. A. Marshall Military History Collection, University of Texas at El Paso.

khaki pants, welcomes me into his office, where the raw material of the third and concluding volume of his Nixon biography covers every flat surface. I have barely sat down before Ambrose starts offering stalwart support for the work of S. L. A. Marshall, particularly *Night Drop*, his 1962 account of the paratroop attack immediately preceding D-Day.

"Damn that book holds up!" says Ambrose, gesturing toward a copy of *Night Drop* in the bookcase across the room. "You can stand on the bridges in Normandy with that book and it all springs to life for you. I am in the process of compiling an oral history of D-Day for publication on the fiftieth anniversary. I have made several trips to Normandy for that book and I have taken to using *Night Drop* as my guide to that country instead of Michelin. I am a fan of *Pork Chop Hill, Men Against Fire,* but *Night Drop*—*Night Drop* is the great monument."

"You're aware," I inject, "that there are some problems with *Men Against Fire.*"

"Clearly, Marshall overstated his case in *Men Against Fire,*" Ambrose replies. "But Marshall is still such an important figure, a towering figure among military historians. Spiller [the Army historian at Leavenworth] goes too far; he is not fair to Marshall. Spiller says, for example, that Marshall never acknowledged his debt to [Ardent] du Picq [a nineteenth-century French soldier-historian]. But that is not true. Marshall acknowledged his debt to du Picq in a letter to me and I was just an obscure twenty-five-year-old grad student." [Spiller wrote in an article: "Du Picq was not alone in being rejected by Marshall as an intellectual forebear; Marshall recognized no one as his equal on the subject of men in battle."][1]

"Then," I say to Ambrose, "you do not believe this controversy has done much damage to Marshall's reputation?"

"Slam Marshall's place in military history is secure," he emphasizes. "He has suffered the curse of having too much adulation at one point. That's why this controversy is tending toward bitterness, rather than scholarship. He oversold himself, but some of his critics are as guilty of bad overstatement.

"*Men Against Fire* is a very valuable book, even if it is wrong by some factor. It was a shock to practicing soldiers and military historians. Clearly, we were not getting the fire we thought. So corrective steps were then taken. Marshall had more impact on infantry training than any other man. And in Korea and Vietnam, there is not any question there was a higher rate of fire. This is one area where Marshall had more impact than any individual. He was the pioneer here—and the prophet has to overstate his case."

We adjourn for lunch in the war college cafeteria. I tell Ambrose what happened between my grandfather and me during Vietnam.

"That goddamn war!" he spits out.

Ambrose talks of his long opposition to the war, and how that kept him from undertaking a biography of Nixon after he had finished his two-volume biography of Eisenhower. It seemed such an obvious follow-up, people said. But Ambrose balked, fearful that his intense opposition to Nixon's conduct of the war might color his ability to bring a historian's perspective to the man's life. Ambrose tells me how his research instead gave him a begrudging admiration for Nixon as a historical figure, if not as a person.

I am immediately struck by similarities between Ambrose's journey with Nixon and my journey with my grandfather. What happened during Vietnam breeds such bitterness when considering both men. Ambrose himself notes the parallels, inscribing a copy of his new Nixon book: "SLAM—A man not unlike Nixon, sometimes less than careful with the truth, a man of great passion (often misplaced and inappropriate) yet a man who did great things."

25

Days of Thanksgiving

THANKSGIVING DAWNS CLOUDY AND COLD, with a couple of inches of snow on the ground. I look out my motel room at this white world and wonder how far I will get on the road this day. Cleveland had been my hope, then the car spins out on the motel driveway, a worrisome reminder of its terrible traction. But the clouds start to clear as I am leaving Carlisle, and then the sun comes out, blindingly bright. My apprehension about snow fades, my spirits rise. I take comfort in being part of the Thanksgiving parade on the highway, while the Pennsylvania countryside presents endless Christmas card scenes, the gently rolling Alleghenies, handsome farmhouses with smoke rising from the chimneys, livestock crowded around old barns, snowy rural roads still awaiting the morning's first tire tracks.

I pass around Pittsburgh, soon cross into Ohio. A blizzard blows in near Youngstown. The Ohio Turnpike turns white, I switch on my lights, slow to forty-five miles per hour. The going gets rough, then rougher. There is not enough traffic to keep the pavement wet. The blizzard continues unabated.

I finally exit the Interstate in the Cleveland suburbs at Chagrin Boulevard, a street that is Memory Lane for me. I pass the Dairy Queen where we used to gather after high school baseball games; the jewelry store where I worked my first real job; Orange High School and Moreland Hills Elementary; Mill Creek Lane where we Marshalls lived. I soon enter Chagrin Falls. Snow covers the triangle park surrounded by old brick buildings in the center of town, tall evergreens and the bandstand are turned white, and yellow Christmas lights are blinking, the entire scene looking as it did in "The Gathering," that heart-rending TV movie, starring Edward Asner, about a fateful family reunion during the holidays.

I am feeling misty-eyed myself by the time I arrive at the home of Jim and Janet O'Hara, two high school classmates. Janet had been my first love back in eighth grade, Jim a teammate on the baseball varsity. The aroma of roasting turkey greets me at the front door, beers are brought forth, and football is on the TV. Four generations soon gather around the Thanksgiving table, we bow our heads, a blessing is said. And there is no one more thankful than I am, warmed by the welcome of a family during a holiday far from home.

The next morning, I leave to see Dr. Raymond Waggoner, my grandfather's best friend, who is visiting his son outside Columbus for Thanksgiving. I am lulled by the passing farmland of Ohio, its small towns called Congress and Pleasant Home. My mind drifts back to my previous visit with Waggoner eight months ago in Ann Arbor.

He and my grandfather had been such good friends, a relationship that had endured for four decades, through crises and normalcy, countless long conversations and shared bottles of Scotch. Waggoner was the one who had first diagnosed Ives' multiple sclerosis and had gone on to provide counsel through the many stages of her illness. Of Waggoner, my grandfather once wrote: "More than all other things put together, my close friendship with Ray Waggoner had steadied me through some trying years. He knew me better than I understood myself. I have never had a friend more considerate, painstaking and unfalteringly loyal, nor one whose genius was more handsomely cloaked in native modesty."

I could see the aptness of my grandfather's description even in two hours with Waggoner. He was eighty-seven and had a distinguished career as a neuropsychiatrist—chairman of the University of Michigan's Department of Psychiatry, president of the American Psychiatric Association, among many achievements. But he made no more of that than the fact that he had been out on his tractor that morning, clearing some brush in the woods around his house.

Waggoner turned out to be the sort of animated gentleman who gives old age a good name. A smallish man in a dapper three-piece suit, Waggoner had a kindly face, sympathetic eyes behind bifocals, plump cheeks, a wide chin, an impish grin. He radiated brisk good health. His mind was as sharp as a barber's straight razor.

Waggoner had been my grandfather's closest confidant, but no one involved in the Marshall controversy had bothered to solicit his memories. This was a mistake. For Waggoner told me how Marshall had come to him upon his return from World War II, seeking explanations for a strange phenomenon that he had noted during the war—the failure of soldiers to fire their weapons in combat.

"He wanted to know why," Waggoner recalled. "And in that book of his, *Men Against Fire,* there are a number of things we discussed. He distinctly said 'very few men'—I remember 'very few'— actually fired their rifles. He came to me and Dave—Dave Boyd was a professor, my first assistant—and we talked to him about these questions. I don't remember exactly what the questions were any more. But I can remember the great deal of emphasis Sam put on the fact that these men did not fire frequently like they were supposed to do. So we told him a lot about how the mind works, how people react to stress. I can't think of a much more stressful situation than being in the front line of an army engagement."

"How many times did you talk to him about these things before he wrote *Men Against Fire?*"

"A couple times, probably three times, I'm not sure."

"But it was obvious to you that he was looking for explanations for something he really didn't understand?"

"That's right. What he wanted to do was find out what the emotional reaction would cost an individual, how it would cause him to react."

"Did he think this problem with firing was going to be considered a startling finding?"

"Yes, I think he did. I think he thought that people wouldn't believe it."

Marshall had discovered a phenomenon that was also suggested by questionnaires distributed to some American infantrymen during the war. In a study published in 1949 (two years after *Men Against Fire*), social scientist Samuel Stouffer wrote that among these combat soldiers in Europe, "65 percent of them . . . admitted that on at least one occasion they had been unable to perform adequately because of extreme fear, whilst 42 percent admitted this happened more than once."[1] There is no evidence that Marshall knew of Stouffer's study, but their work recognized the same problem.

The most memorable moments of my visit with Waggoner had come after I had put away my notebook. We were seated in Waggoner's basement study, cool and dark as a cave, the walls lined with leather-bound volumes, and he had asked whether I thought 3:00 P.M. was too early for a drink. I said I didn't think so, and Waggoner brought out tiny bottles of Tanqueray, along with glasses filled with ice. I hadn't eaten since breakfast and the gin did its work quickly, producing that warmth and haze. I soon felt closer to Waggoner and to my grandfather as I sat in a room where the two of them often sat and talked and drank.

So, after a time, I brought out a copy of my grandfather's letter disowning me, which Waggoner knew nothing about, then watched as he read it. Waggoner laughed, startling me. Waggoner laughed again, then said, "Boy, he was really giving it to you, wasn't he! This sounds just like Sam!"

But when he finished the letter, I told Waggoner about how I had always wondered whether my grandfather had written the letter himself, since both he and Cate had signed it. So Waggoner read through the letter again, commenting as he went, "It sounds like Sam, it looks like his typing, until this last page, this part about your not being welcome in their house again. That sounds like Cate."

Waggoner took another sip of his Tanqueray, fell silent.

"It's something," he finally said, "that you're interested in defending your grandfather's name after receiving a letter like that. I would think that when all this stuff started coming out about him, you would have thought he had it coming."

"I'm not sure I really started out on this to defend him," I said. "I just wanted to find out what the truth was."

"You know, I think if your grandfather had thought the way you did about Vietnam, he probably would have done exactly what you did. Because when he believed in something, he went after it all the way."

No one else had ever said such a thing to me. No one else had even suggested it. And certainly no one in the family. Waggoner's words provided a new sense that I was part of a real family tradition, the willingness to act on belief.

Now months later, I leave the Interstate north of Columbus, travel along the Olentangy River to a development in what must have been woodlands not long ago, now manicured lawns and country estates. Ray, Jr., greets me at the door of his huge home; he is a child psychologist at Harding Hospital, a man who reminds me of Clark Kent, with that earnestness. His father and I shake hands warmly, then we all walk to the study where we sit in wing chairs, a plush Oriental rug at our feet.

I ask Waggoner again about the impact of my grandfather's size on his character. Some have said that this is too simplistic, this rationale of a short man trying so hard to be bigger. But Waggoner is not among those skeptics: "With Sam, there is no question that his size affected him. He wanted to be a little Napoleon."

We also discuss Charly Jones and my conclusion that my grandfather could not have been there when he was killed. Which surprises Waggoner because he says he remembers discussing the death of a World War I buddy with Sam.

"I had the feeling he was emotionally disturbed by what happened," Waggoner says. "The amount of emotion he showed made me think this was real."

"That intense reaction could have come because he felt so guilty about what happened," Ray, Jr., adds. "That he should have been there and he wasn't."

"But I still have a hard time," I say, "trying to understand how someone would lie about such a thing."

"I don't think it's lying," the elder Waggoner says. "It's an attempt to establish selfness, what a recent book I read described as 'a thirst for approval,' the tendency to build a better feeling about how accomplished you've been. It's not real lying. Lying, in my opinion, is a direct attempt to change facts, rather than to exaggerate them. Would you agree, Ray?"

"What this gets to, though," his son replies, "is motive. Why would he do this?"

"It was something he really believed when he said it," the elder Waggoner says. "I don't think there is any question about a Napoleonic effect here. And I don't think there's any question about Sam's need to bolster his masculinity, but farther than that, I can't go. I never had the idea that Sam felt insecure. I thought he was frustrated by his size."

I return to the road. Ohio gives way to Indiana on a day the color of slate. I make one brief stop in Indianapolis at Fort Benjamin Harrison, site of the Defense Information School, where I spent two dreary winter months in 1970. There was challenging work in military journalism here and it was also where I gave that historic final talk in the public speaking course, a twenty-minute oration entitled "What It's Like to Smoke Marijuana." And not just talk, a sound-and-light show, my portable stereo brought from my apartment, speakers set up some distance apart, classic grass songs played with explication to a standing-room-only crowd, Jefferson Airplane, Rolling Stones, the Beatles, how different these songs would sound when stoned. And when I finally finished my tour through the strawberry fields, someone should have pulled my Army file right then and there. Instead, there was sustained applause and I was later named an Honor Graduate of the Defense Information School.

I speed into Lafayette for an appointment with Gunther Rothenburg, a Purdue professor of military history. He is one of a half dozen such civilian professors around the country, someone who has been at it for three decades and now draws three hundred to four hundred students a semester to his classes at Purdue.

Rothenburg turns out to be a bearded character in quasi-military garb, a sixty-seven-year-old former infantryman in World War II and Korea who has closely followed the Marshall controversy. We have been sitting together for no more than three minutes when he refers to Leinbaugh as "the lunatic," leaving little doubt about his own sympathies.

"Your grandfather was becoming an American hero," Rothenburg says. "Then it was as if someone had found out that Santa Claus has AIDS. When you really look at *Men Against Fire*, it is a very small little study, a modest work; it made sense to many people. His other books were generally well received, some almost best sellers. And Marshall defended the Army when the Army had few defenders. His contribution to the United States Army—its spirit, its institutions—were considerable.

"When I met him, he was a living legend, a very important, but real person. To find out later that he was like the Wizard of Oz was a real shock. That caused some people to turn against him. I did not. There are valuable things he did, things valuable by themselves. If he fell short of the ideal that people had about him, he is certainly not the first person to be that way."

These days of endgame on the road have taken on the quality of a speeded-up movie, hit-and-run visits with people, long stretches doing seventy-five on the Interstate. I make Chicago early the next morning, so numbed by the driving that I am oblivious to having entered another time zone. I awaken Larry Heinemann and have to apologize. He is far more cordial than most friends would be in a similar situation.

I have gotten to know Heinemann over the last several years, this acclaimed Vietnam writer, winner of the National Book Award for *Paco's Story*. Last June, we had spent an extraordinary weekend in Port Angeles, Washington, when Heinemann brought together a group of Vietnam vets and Soviet vets from the war in Afghanistan, a time of shared brotherhood, pledges of never again exchanged, combat tortures laid bare in 180-degree Indian sweat lodges, then cleansed away in the icy waters of the Strait of Juan de Fuca. Heinemann has always impressed me as someone who is a combat vet's sort of vet, tested, tough-talking, but eloquent, sensitive, a bear of a guy solid at the core.

Sunlight streams into Heinemann's study through a skylight, reflects off wood floors painted red. He sits at his writing desk with the hula lamp, I sit in an easy chair. We sip our coffee and our Sunday morning conversation centers on Vietnam.

I summarize the experiences I have had on my trip, especially with Vietnam vets and those who opposed the war. I tell him how angry I was to find that ribbon with "Not in Vain" at the Wall.

"To say 'Not in Vain' at the Wall is really wishful thinking; it shows how unrealistic remain our attitudes about that war," Heinemann says. "It is troubling to think that, twenty years ago, we Vietnam vets were the goats. Now we're looked up to for a lot of the wrong reasons. Reagan reasons. The men of our generation who didn't go—that part of the story has simply not been told."

"Did you ever think of not going yourself?"

"That subject never came up," Heinemann replies. "I came from a family of four boys and three went into the service. I remember trying to stop my brother from going on a second tour to Vietnam. I even went to a well-connected attorney in Chicago, trying to get strings pulled so he wouldn't go. 'I want to know who to pay and how much,' I told him. 'Our family has done enough.'

"But when he came back from his second tour, my reaction was to protest. I had seen the pictures in *Stars & Stripes* of guys lying in front of ammunition trains and I'm thinking to myself, I have a lot of resentment, but also envy and jealousy. Because it was clear to me anyway, and I would have thought it was clear to most other people too, this war was just bullshit. The war in the field was obviously going sour by the time I was in Vietnam [1967] and we would go out there and come upon this old, abandoned French equipment that had been there since 1954, and it was made clear to us that if this happened to the French, then what in the hell were we doing here in the field. I had an officer then whose name was Erik Opsul. He said, 'I've lost enough men' and I said, 'Right' and so we didn't do ambushes or take chances. Opsul had, I think, a very educated attitude about the war."

Heinemann talks about his welcome home from the war, getting married to Edie his first week back in the States. He talks of the years afterward: "I have tremendous feelings of survivor's guilt. Twenty years later, I still can't shake them. I also had the attitude that nobody I would run into would have behaved any differently . . . the war was a complicated, contradictory, paradoxical event."

This is an opening I have been seeking to ask Heinemann about those of us who took different courses during those days and how, even now, we seem to go our separate ways, that estrangement I had felt at the Wall. I ask Heinemann if he is ever approached at readings by those who took stands against the war.

"Every once in a while, they do, and often they say they haven't told anybody about what they did," Heinemann says. "It's a funny thing—the guys who didn't go, even those who took C.O. stands, seem to feel guilty when they come up to me. But I hasten to tell them they have nothing to feel guilty about. Those who stood against the war had some courage, too. Now they're shut out. We Vietnam vets—we've had the stage to ourselves. As a group, the men of this generation are schizophrenic. There's this dilemma about what we all did in the war. We've got to resolve this, and not fall into who was right and who was wrong. We're all old enough, thoughtful enough, philosophical enough to talk about it."

We continue to talk about it a while longer, in Heinemann's upstairs study and later around the dining room table over turkey sandwiches with Edie. This brief conversation about our choices during Vietnam affects us both, as we acknowledge outside. It is a modest start, but at least a start, on what Heinemann has described to me as our generation's "unfinished business."

26

The Wreath

THIS MAY BE THE STRANGEST MOMENT of the entire trip. I am
nearing St. Louis, searching through the radio when suddenly the
voice of a radio preacher starts reciting questions: "Are you on a
consistent search for knowledge? . . . Are you asking questions? . . .
Are you listening for answers? . . . Will you commit yourself to doing
what is right, regardless of the price?" I cannot help but smile.
Maybe this is when you know you've been on the road too long—
that moment when radio preachers start to speak directly to you.

The Mississippi River looms, wind gusts whipping up white-
caps, sand bars exposed to the November sun. The river through
here is the color of mud, wide and meandering as it cuts the country
in half. I feel a swelling of accomplishment, crossing this American
landmark. This is my sixty-eighth day on the road and I have now
put almost 10,000 miles behind me. Just ahead is this trip's third
reunion with my father, no longer viewed with the old apprehension, not after El Paso and what we shared there.

I drive through the St. Louis suburbs and find my father's apartment, my first visit here. We hug at the door and he wants to hear
all that has happened since Charlotte.

We head to the golf course after an hour. It is 76 degrees in St.
Louis, an all-time high for this date, so we want to do something
outside in the warm weather, even if it is blustery. Tonight is supposed
to be much colder. Tomorrow, the reports say, there may be snow.

"This is where I play," my father says, as he parks the car.

It is a municipal course, hilly, well kept, heavily used, with a

269

portion of the course reserved for those who like to practice their chip shots, as my father does. My father always seems to talk on the phone about having just played some golf and I had always assumed that meant he had played an actual game, probably nine holes. But now I see he does not really play golf, he practices golf, a discovery that leaves me feeling sad somehow.

We get golf balls out of the trunk, we grab a couple of nine irons and take turns chipping toward a small tree. My father has a fine swing and lofts the ball smoothly; many of his shots land close to the tree. I have not picked up a golf club in ten years, and with no regret; I would rather sweep the garage than play golf. But my layoff from golf has worked wonders, I am not thinking about what I am doing and several balls I hit land in the general vicinity of the tree.

"Nice shot," my father says, his voice registering my surprise.

We go pick up the balls, then repeat the process. Several of my father's friends from the golf course stop by after a while. Introductions are made, hands shaken.

"This is my son, the writer," my father says. "You know the one I told you about."

"Oh, right," the old men say.

I have never seen my father like this before. These past few years, we have had our whirlwind visits, usually in Seattle, but always my father by himself, looking a little grayer, a little heavier, but not that different from our last visit. But our time together has always been just us, not with his friends, or at least golfing acquaintances, old men whiling away time, trading chitchat about how well they are stroking the ball today, sharing tales of what they have heard lately from their children, and maybe a picture of the grandchildren.

My father has never seemed quite as old to me as he does talking to these men on the golf course. I feel like I am in one of those movies starring Art Carney or Burt Lancaster where they play old guys in that bittersweet way. I have known that my father is getting old, of course. He is sixty-eight, after all. I have known that in my head for some time, but I have never felt it in my heart until right now.

The next morning, we are up early and it is cold as promised, probably 30, although not snowing yet. I tell my father that I want to visit my mother's grave on the way out of town. I ask him for the name of the cemetery. He says he cannot remember. We have to consult the Yellow Pages.

"Oak Grove Cemetery," my father finally says, after searching through the listings. "I think that's it."

My father gets in the car with me and I give him a ride to the corner drugstore.

"I'm sorry I couldn't stay longer," I say, "but I am really getting anxious to get home."

"Oh, I understand."

The cemetery turns out to be only a few miles away. I stop at a florist's shop across the street, get out of the car, and discover it has not opened yet. I stare at the door, disappointed. But a woman inside comes to the door and opens it.

"Can I help you?" she asks.

"I had hoped to buy a wreath for my mother's grave, maybe a Christmas wreath or something. I'm sorry to bother you. I'm from out-of-town. I don't get to St. Louis very often."

"We have some very fresh Christmas wreaths in that semi trailer over there. I'd be happy to get you one, if you don't mind holding the stepladder."

"Certainly. I appreciate your help."

Her name, she tells me climbing the ladder, is Cecelia Pyatt and she apologizes for not making it up the ladder any faster, what with being sixty-nine-years-old. I tell her that I hope I can get up a ladder this fast when I am sixty-nine. She pulls out a beautiful wreath with a red ribbon bow and passes it down to me. I take it in my hands, already starting to feel that I am losing control of my emotions. I am not accustomed to dealing with cemetery wreaths.

I drive across the street and stop at the cemetery office to get directions to my mother's grave.

"I haven't been here since her funeral," I say to the woman in the office, for some reason.

"You'll have no trouble finding it," she says. "It's right by the woods."

I drive over in that direction. The cemetery is hilly, quite pretty, absolutely deserted on this frigid morning.

I park the car and start to walk up the hill, leaves crunching under my feet. Suddenly, the setting does start to become familiar, this rise, the trees just beyond, and memories come roaring back, the shock, the pain.

The phone had rung at 3:00 A.M. in our apartment in Germany. We were startled from sleep. I walked to the phone in the hallway. I heard my father's voice on the line.

"Your mother is dead," he said.

"What? . . . How?"

"She shot herself."

"She what?"

"She shot herself. Committed suicide."

The next thirty-six hours were hell. I went to the Frankfurt airport carrying emergency orders that stated "Death of Mother," entitling me to a standby seat on one of the military charter flights. By the time I finally left Frankfurt, I was exhausted, and then there were all those hours crossing the Atlantic to think about my mother.

She had been such a good mother—that was the role to which she had devoted her life, cook, chauffeur, cleaner, in the 1950s' suburban housewife mold. Holidays were her forte, countless hours expended in making the house a magical place, what the rest of us too often took for granted, the roasts, the decorations, the presents, nothing left to chance. She had a certain perfectionist bent, this conservative, reserved, almost prim woman; she was a stern taskmaster, making sure we attended to homework and chores, or allowances would not be earned. Yet, sometimes, she broke out of the mold in astounding ways, using an eyedropper to feed several baby bats that my brother and I had found; attending to the tiny creatures hanging upside down from a stick across a mixing bowl, until they died after days of her intensive care. Or the time I hit a home run in high school, my only home run of countless baseball summers, and I had crossed the plate in my moment of great triumph, only to be enveloped in a hug and kiss from my mother who had rushed out of the bleachers, much to my embarrassment. And the rest of the time, she was the center of calm in the kidstorm, tending to scrapes, bruises, and crazy escapades of three children and a pointer named Cookie.

I sat on that plane across the Atlantic and wished I could remember seeing my mother smiling more, laughing more, saying something other than "Wait 'til your father gets home and hears

John Marshall with his parents, Nancy and Sam Marshall, outside the White House in a 1956 visit to Washington.

about this." But mostly, what I kept thinking about was my own guilt about not understanding what this thing called a "nervous breakdown" was, or the bouts with depression that came afterward. Why couldn't Mom just snap out of this, lighten up, I remembered thinking during one brief visit home. There were many things I should have recognized, or read about, or something. Sure, this all happened after I went off to college, the marital problems, her collapse, her slow and hesitant semirecovery. But it seemed frightfully predictable, if I had only taken the time to think about it, how she had given everything of herself to be a wife and mother, only to have her marriage crumble, her children rebel, then leave home, first me, now Sam, soon Shannon. My mother must have felt so terribly alone, finally dying three days before her birthday, less from a gunshot than a broken heart.

When the plane made it back to the States, it was the middle of the night and I was a zombie. Then there was a bus ride to a civilian airport, where I spent the rest of the night trying to sleep on airport seats in my rumpled uniform. I grabbed another standby flight that morning, made it to St. Louis, and soon found myself in the midst of a household filled with people battling their own private guilts, people teetering on the edge, angry, hurt, bitter, including my grandfather, what was destined to be the last time I ever saw him, the two of us talking about writing on the living room couch.

One of the first things I had done in St. Louis was take my uniform to the dry cleaners. They said it could be finished the next day and I told them I did not want it back that fast. I wanted them to keep it several days. I was not about to wear a uniform to my mother's funeral. I was preparing my conscientious objector application by then and her suicide only strengthened my resolve to leave the Army. "The fact that my mother shot herself in the head has deepened my total abhorrence of weapons and the violence to which they inevitably lead," I later wrote in my C.O. application.

Now, I have reached that place in the cemetery where we all sat in front of the casket, still so numb that almost no one managed to cry. But I am crying now. I look down at the simple bronze headstone on my mother's grave and read:

Mother
Nancy P. Marshall
Mar. 4, 1923
Mar. 1, 1971

I start sobbing uncontrollably, weeping in a way that I never have wept in my entire adult life, my hands covering my face, my chest heaving. I let the sobs flow out of me, years of grief. I do not try to stop myself. I sob until the sobbing finally stops by itself, half a minute, a minute, I don't know.

I go back to the car and get the wreath. I set it up just above my mother's headstone, pushing the wire stand into the ground. I go back to the car and get the camera and then come back and take a few pictures. The camera helps pull me together. I get some distance. I start to think I should have made this visit before.

But then I think of something else and go back to the car once more, rummaging through my leather valise for the envelope from the film store. I search through the photographs until I find what seems like the right picture of Thatcher. He is smiling at the beach, a baseball cap tilted back on his head, looking boyish, too cute.

I walk back to my mother's grave and start to lose control all over again.

"This is your grandson," I say, holding the picture facing the ground. "This is your grandson you never got to see."

I am sobbing again, but blurt out, "He's a very happy boy."

I affix his picture to the wreath after that, using a couple of paper clips, wedging it beside the bright red bow.

I stand at my mother's grave for a few more minutes, feeling a sense of peace and calm come over me at last. I think this may be the most important thing I have done on this odyssey, something I have needed to do for years but never recognized—mourn the loss of my mother and what she will never get to see, the adult I have become, the family I am so fortunate to have, the lives we live, the love we share.

27

Racing December

THE UNDULATING HILLS OF MISSOURI now wear their winter brown, the trees are stripped of their leaves. It is that brief respite between the seasons in the Midwest, fall definitely gone, winter coming on, the landscape and the people bracing for the worse weather sure to arrive soon. I know this place and this time. I leave the Interstate at Columbia, home of the University of Missouri, where I received my master's degree in journalism. But the detour here is brief. This school never touched me in the way that the University of Virginia did, and I want to keep moving west.

I soon cross the Missouri River, which is taking a slow turn south at the base of a towering bluff. Then, there are more hills, more low lazy hills, part of Harry Truman Country, this timeless land of plain-spoken truths, towns named Oak Grove or Sweet Springs or Pleasant Green, lodgings called Atlasta Motel or OK Motel. There is a sense around here that the 1950s represented progress enough. Motel rooms still go for "$14 and Up," some still try to lure travelers with billboards promising "Direct Dial Phones."

I skirt Kansas City, swing north on the bypass, late afternoon by now, rush hour starting to build. I leave the freeway and head to Fort Leavenworth, another meeting ahead with Army historian Roger Spiller, but so much changed now.

Back last spring, I was the newcomer to all this, here to interview the most important figure in the Marshall controversy, the historian who provided the aura of scholarship for the *American Heritage* article. Spiller, who has degrees from Southwest Texas State and

276

Louisiana State University, turned out to be a phlegmatic figure with a walrus mustache, a pleasant enough fellow, my own age, helpful to me, and I felt somewhat in awe of the way he knew more about my grandfather than I did. We had spent many hours together over two days, and I had taken exhaustive notes on all that Spiller had to say, his dissection of the *American Heritage* article, his disagreements with what it and Leinbaugh alleged. "Some of it is flat wrong," Spiller told me.

Now, I have come back to Spiller after seeing things that Spiller has not seen, interviewing people he has not interviewed, including historians of national stature—Frank Vandiver, Alvin Josephy, Stephen Ambrose—who have told me of the high regard they still have for the work of S. L. A. Marshall. And I have come to a different view of Spiller as one who hitched his own reputation to Marshall's star, just as David Hackworth did. Spiller had started the S. L. A. Marshall guest lecture series at Leavenworth, had edited some of Marshall's Leavenworth lectures, and had published them in 1980 with his own name on the cover and an admiring introduction in which he referred to Marshall as "the premier American writer on the man in combat."[1] Spiller returned to the subject in 1984 when he wrote the entry on Marshall in the *Dictionary of American Military Biography* (for which Spiller served as editor). The five-page entry on Marshall shows Spiller with some lingering awe for Marshall ["he may have spent more time under fire than many riflemen."],[2] but turning more critical, a position that will intensify in the following years with Spiller's research and publication of Marshall articles in a British military journal and finally *American Heritage.*

A Marshall biography seemed where Spiller was heading, but no longer. Spiller, like Hackworth, had once idolized Marshall. Then, confronted with his flaws, he had done a complete about-face on Marshall, as if he had been personally betrayed by a man who was not that same hero anymore. "His work has lost the trust I once placed in it," Spiller declared in a letter to me. "I could not do a book on a man who seems to have built his professional career on a contempt for ideas, those who valued them, and the readers who advanced that career. This contempt was especially brought home to me by the Hackworth book, but I think that this was what I had seen in the files at El Paso that so startled me."

I pull into Leavenworth in late afternoon, then find Spiller in his basement office at the U.S. Army Command and General Staff College. I rush in, intent on sharing some of my discoveries from the trip, what Ambrose had said to me about Marshall's letter to him on du Picq, this direct rebuke to what Spiller had published. But this and other matters I mention prompt almost no reaction from him. He strikes a pose of Olympian disinterest. He has written his last words on S. L. A. Marshall, Spiller insists.

I leave after an hour, without taking any notes. There is no debate on Marshall, no research give-and-take. I get nowhere with Spiller. I walk up the steps, return to my car. It is past 6:00 P.M. and I should check into a motel. But I do not want to spend the night in Leavenworth. I have had my fill of the military. I do not want to stay someplace where roadway signs warn of "Captains Crossing." I want out. There are no more forts I must visit, no more military types I must interview. I am finished with all that.

I make it another sixty miles before finally stopping in Topeka, road-weary, totally beat. The next day dawns bright and unseasonably warm. Progress west is swift, effortless.

I am making such great time that I am lured off the Interstate by a sign for the Kansas Vietnam Veterans Memorial. The memorial is in the central park of Junction City, another granite wall inscribed with names, 758 Kansans killed, 38 Kansans still missing. But what strikes me most is a poem at the base, one written by a veteran killed in the war, one that describes the war as "insane." And I think how extraordinary this is in the town that is home to Fort Riley. And I think of future generations of Kansans, farm boys, salt of this rich earth, and hope that perhaps this view of the Vietnam War as "insane" will take seed with them.

Back on the highway, Kansas soon flattens out, turns desolate, the daunting landscape of the Great Plains. Billboards provide welcome diversion. America's first helicopter is ahead in Goodland, America's first two-story Kentucky Fried Chicken is in Hays. But what causes me to leave the Interstate is a startling apparition first glimpsed from afar, St. Fidelis Church, the "Cathedral of the Plains," a soaring Romanesque structure that seats 1,100, an inspiring testament to the faith of a small community of Volga-Germans who took refuge here after fleeing conscription in the Czar's Army.

I press on. It is a long haul to Denver. I doubt I can make it tonight. I am starting to tire already. But I cross into Colorado at 3:00 P.M., buoyed by being back in the West again. I can feel the pull of Denver now, adrenaline kicking in after coffee's caffeine had long since quit, all common sense shot, Denver luring me on. I arrive in Denver in the crush of rush hour, my nerves raw, my body numb, after 550 miles on the road. I somehow make it through the traffic to the apartment of an Army friend, Dick Young.

I spend a sleepless night on the floor on what only looks like a mattress, a depressing prelude to the day I have dreaded ever since I left Seattle, this December day when I must cross the Rocky Mountains, or try to cross the Rocky Mountains. It is frosty this morning, but clear, no hint of snow in the weather forecast. I am encouraged, but wary. I know how fast this can change in the mountains.

I set out. The sun warms. The weather holds. I turn west on Interstate 80 at Cheyenne, having made Wyoming in remarkable time. I head into the Rockies, climb to Laramie, climb some more toward Rawlins. The pavement is perfectly dry, but all the surrounding countryside is covered with snow, high plateaus, distant peaks, now bright white in the midday sun. And there is little traffic, a few trucks, even fewer cars, causing me to speed up to 80 miles per hour through the Rockies, then 85, even 95 for a time.

I cross the Continental Divide at mid-afternoon, coming down now from 7,000 feet. I pass Rock Springs, then pull in for gas in Little America, a huge truck stop and motel complex. I could stay at Little America, I have made great progress on this day, but I can't stop here. I am intent now on making it all the way through the Rockies in one road race of a day.

The sunset soon produces a fireball directly in my eyes, making it so difficult to see that I wish I had stayed in Little America. Then darkness descends and the temperature plummets to 15 degrees. The Interstate starts to snake through canyons, large patches of snow and ice cover the roadway. I slow down, tighten my grip on the wheel, swear at myself for not stopping sooner.

The snow finally disappears from the road. I relax slightly, continue on, cross into Utah. I speed down from the mountains, make Ogden, 600 miles after Denver.

I awaken far earlier than I would like the next morning. I have that road rhythm now, that anxious edge. I see windshield visions even when I try to sleep. I am back on the Interstate before 8:00 A.M., loaded down by a trucker's breakfast of steak 'n eggs, what seemed a great way to start one of my last days on the road.

I speed along Interstate 84 again, the same Interstate I had traveled my first day of the trip, and I flash on what I felt then, all that uncertainty. I remember that traveler on the Oregon Trail, his words immortalized at a highway rest stop, musings about why people undertake long treks, their questions of whether it will all be worth it, and in what way.

Now, I have at least a tentative answer. There have been so many memorable moments for me on the road, encounters with people who have touched me, times of honest emotions and shared truths. I had set out in search of my grandfather and to find out, as best I could, whether he was a fraud. I have come to conclude he was not. His work stands, not perfect, but solid, important, even historic. He left a definite mark on military history and the Army he so loved.

But my grandfather was a flawed person, as we all are, as even he admitted in a speech I discovered: "There is no such thing as 'a truly great man,'" he wrote. "All men are fallible. All are prone to make serious error, to take occasionally hasty judgement and to overlook important detail."

My great dilemma on this trip has been trying to determine what matters more with a life, what it accomplishes or the way it is lived. This is a longtime debate—the books or the writer, the paintings or the artist, the statecraft or the politician. This is the same dilemma that historian Stephen Ambrose had confronted with Richard Nixon—trying to understand the real person, contradictions and all, flaws and all, someone neither hero nor villain. I have arrived, hopefully, at the same reasoned perspective on my grandfather as I near the end of my journey.

My grandfather had written in his memoirs that he wanted to be "rated not by what I wrote, but how I lived." But I am not sure I believe that, not when most of what he wrote still stands, while much of the way he lived deserves criticism, definite criticism. I am not about to excuse his excesses, the needless carelessness he sometimes brought to his life. He hurt people, he hurt himself, especially in his later years when he became so rigid, mistaking honest disagreement for personal affront, turning vindictive, even cruel. So many of his longtime relationships were shattered, with friends, with family.

My grandfather remains a fascinating, contradictory character to me, inspiring in some ways, exasperating in others. At the end of the unedited manuscript of his memoirs, he sums up his life by citing what he calls "the greatest compliment" he had ever received in his seventy-two years. It had come from Cate who recently told him, "I have never known you to be afraid of anything." What a strange comment this is for him to cite in conclusion, but what an insight into his character. Even then he was still trying so hard to prove something . . . himself.

We are so different. Vietnam brought that out. What I have found on the road has only reinforced that. There are some things I hope people may say about me toward the end of my life, but among them is not: He was "not afraid of anything." I have been afraid, and do not mind admitting it.

Still, this journey, born amid my lingering anger and ambivalence about my grandfather, has brought me to the point where I can honestly say I forgive him for what he did to me. I still deplore it, but I forgive him now. Finally.

It is too late now for him to know that, of course, too late for Cate. Which is a terrible shame. I have often found myself bedeviled on the road by thoughts of what might have been. If only my grandfather or Cate had, at some point, said those difficult, but simple words—"I forgive." Or if I myself had said that to them. How many years of family animosity and distance might have been avoided. What family experiences might we all have shared, holidays, reunions, marriages, births, indelible family memories lost forever, all for the want of forgiveness. Family should matter more than the politics of the moment, as several people have told me on this trip. Family, despite the inevitable troubles and disappointments, should somehow endure. And forgiveness, the true expression of love's selflessness, may be what is needed most in families. Words can wound, but words can also heal. If people will try them before it its too late.

The Rockies are behind me at last, the Continental Divide too. I continue to make my way along the highway. The Northwest is just up ahead, Idaho, then Oregon, and Washington now only a day away. I am nearly home.

Epilogue

WHEN I ARRIVE BACK IN SEATTLE, Anne's embrace is even better that I had imagined, all these months and miles away. I have missed her more than I will ever be able to say.

I sneak into Thatcher's room, stand beside his crib and am amazed. He looks so grown up, twice as big as when I left. He is facing the wall, humming softly to himself, a blissful little melody. Then, he flips over and looks up at me. "Daddy!" he screams as I bend down and take my son into my arms.

The Christmas tree goes up early at our house in Seattle. The holiday is celebrated with the joy of a family reunited, comforting rituals, new togetherness.

Weeks and months pass and I begin to see increasing evidence that S. L. A. Marshall's reputation has started to rebound. The most zealous partisans in the Marshall controversy—his critics, his fans— have their say, then fall silent.

More detached voices are heard in the controversy's wake, voices of reason rather than anger. Gen. William E. Dupuy, the commander of the First Infantry Division in Vietnam and later the commander of the Army's Training and Doctrine Command (TRADOC), writes a strong defense of Marshall's finding on firing for *Military Review*: "Marshall was on to something more important, whether he interviewed 500 companies or none. That 'something'— the long-standing challenge of bringing a very high percentage of infantry soldiers (and others) effectively into battle at crucial moments. . . . the problem of battle participation is not trivial, nor

282

can it easily be dismissed on the basis of alleged deficiencies in research."[1]

TRADOC itself finally publishes Maj. F. D. G. Williams' book on Marshall for distribution within the Army, especially to Army schools and libraries. The 137-page SLAM: The Influence of S. L. A. Marshall on the United States Army goes through its first printing of 2,500 copies and a second printing is ordered, based upon strong demand and positive response.

Two young Turks in military history, American Eliot A. Cohen of Harvard and Englishman John Gooch of the University of Lancaster, write a 1990 book that draws heavily on Marshall's work in Korea. Military Misfortunes: The Anatomy of Failure in War devotes an entire chapter to the defeat of the U.S. Eighth Army which Marshall recounted in The River and the Gauntlet. Cohen and Gooch describe Marshall as "perhaps the greatest of all American combat historians and the author of the most important studies of combat in this phase of the Korean War."[2] They praise Marshall's post-combat interview technique as "one of the most striking methodological innovations in the study of military history."[3]

But nothing that Cohen and Gooch write catches my attention quite like their description of the approach which Marshall brought to his study of the Army in Korea, the same approach he used in Vietnam, as my interview with General Westmoreland confirmed. Cohen and Gooch write: "In public Marshall leaped to the defense of the GIs and their commanders in Korea. In private—in letters and classified reports—he scourged the Army he held responsible for the needless losses of November and December 1950."[4]

S. L. A. Marshall's "important discoveries" are also cited in Geoffrey Perrett's 1991 book, There's a War to Be Won: The United States Army in World War II. Perrett spotlights Marshall's post-combat interview technique, emphasizing its crucial contribution to both the history of the war and to those soldiers interviewed. "Combat historians . . . would get to the survivors of firefights and battles to show them where they had been, describe what they had done and turn the reconstruction of combat into a collective act of memory and catharsis," Perrett writes. "What had become obscure became knowledge, what had been mystifying became obvious. The actors finally understood their parts and could measure their performance."[5]

Finally, I talk to John Keegan, widely considered the pre-eminent military historian of this day. The Englishman is in the midst of an American interview tour for his latest book, a history of the Second World War. Keegan had called *Men Against Fire* a "masterpiece"[6] in his *Face of Battle* and had once described Marshall as "a genius." He says he is not about to renounce those descriptions now, despite the controversy.

"I think Marshall's influence is enduring," Keegan tells me. "S.L.A. Marshall is a very major figure, largely because of *Men Against Fire*. That is an extraordinary book, a teaching aide in the writing of military history. You cannot disregard it. Anyone who is not aware of what S.L.A. Marshall said is ill-equipped to be a military historian."

The passing months bring word of several passings. Harold Leinbaugh, prime mover behind the Marshall controversy, dies suddenly of cancer only four months after our meeting in a Washington cocktail lounge. The Harpers in Atlanta also succumb, first the general, then Mrs. Harper. And Betty Marshall, Burt's wife, one of the most charming people I met on my trip, dies of cancer in Washington. And Sally Jacobs, my father's second wife, also dies of cancer after the two of them wage a truly valiant struggle together, best friends to the end, despite all their difficulties in the past.

My father dies a year later. I am alone at his hospital bedside for the last five days of his life. He cannot speak, or respond to my words and embraces in any way. But at least we have said what we needed to say to each other during our time together in El Paso.

And Anne and I are standing in the kitchen not long after my return from the road when she says quietly, "I'm pregnant again." Our second child is born on September 13, 1990, another marvel, our little girl. We do not choose a name from my mother's family this time, not after all I have learned on my odyssey. Our daughter may not be another Sam exactly, but she is: Samantha Aimée Marshall.

Thatcher nicknames her Lee-Lee, for no reason we can fathom. But, combined with her initials, it does turn Samantha into our own little SLAM.

Notes

Bibliography

Notes

Prologue

1. S. L. A. Marshall, "On Being Commissioned," in *The Last Refuge: Three Public Addresses in the Spring, 1969* (Detroit: Author, 1969), 14.
2. Richard Halloran, "Pivotal S. L. A. Marshall Book on Warfare Assailed as False," *New York Times*, Feb. 19, 1989, 1.
3. S. L. A. Marshall, *Men Against Fire: The Problem of Battle Command in Future War* (Gloucester, Mass.: Peter Smith, 1978), 53.
4. Frederic Smoler, "The Secret of the Soldiers Who Didn't Shoot," *American Heritage* 40, no. 2 (1989): 40–44.

1. Detroit Years

1. S. L. A. Marshall, *Battles in the Monsoon* (New York: Morrow, 1967), 12.

2. Setting Out in September

1. "Milestones," *Time*, Dec. 26, 1977: 58.
2. Lawrence Feinberg, "S. L. A. Marshall, 77, Dies, Noted Military Historian," *Washington Post*, Dec. 18, 1977, sec. B, 4.
3. Robert D. McFadden, "S. L. A. Marshall, Historian, Dies," *New York Times*, Dec. 18, 1977, 1, 45.
4. Joe McGinniss, *Heroes* (New York: Pocket, 1977), 34.

3. Liberating Paris

1. S. L. A. Marshall, "How Papa Liberated Paris," *American Heritage* 13, no. 3 (1962): 93.
2. Ibid., 99–100.
3. Ibid., 97.

4. Under Fire

1. John Keegan, "The Historian and Battle," *International Security* 3, no. 3 (Winter 1978/1979): 145.
2. Smoler, 43.
3. Roger J. Spiller, "S. L. A. Marshall and the Ratio of Fire," *RUSI Journal* 133, no. 4 (1988): 68.
4. S. L. A. Marshall, "Bringing up the Rear" (unedited manuscript for published book, library of the Univ. of Texas at El Paso): 243.

5. Military Heritage

1. S. L. A. Marshall, *The River and the Gauntlet* (New York: Warner, 1989), 227.

6. El Paso Roots

1. Ernest Hemingway, *A Farewell to Arms* (New York: Scribners, 1929), 196.
2. S. L. A. Marshall, *Bringing up the Rear* (San Rafael, Calif.: Presidio, 1979), 14.
3. Paul Fussell, *The Great War and Modern Memory* (New York: Oxford Univ. Press, 1977), 181.
4. Maj. George Wythe, *A History of the 90th Division* (N.p.: 90th Division Association, 1920), 62.
5. Ibid., 158.

7. Research Partners

1. Col. David H. Hackworth, *About Face: The Odyssey of an American Warrior* (New York: Simon and Schuster, 1989), 564.

8. Uncharted Territory

1. *Trainfire: Department of the Army Pamphlet No. 355-14* (Washington, D.C.: Department of the Army, 1958), 4.
2. Caryn James, "Gregory Peck Enters The 'Tribute Stage,'" *New York Times,* Apr. 12, 1992, sec. 2, 16.
3. S. L. A. Marshall, *West to Cambodia* (New York: Cowles, 1968), v.
4. "Who's Retiring?" *Newsweek,* Aug. 15, 1960, 75.
5. Ibid., 76.

11. A Protégé's Allegations

1. Hackworth, 756.
2. Ibid., 575.

3. Ibid., 580.

4. Capt. Daniel P. Bolger, "Hackworth—'Hard-Charger Turned Sour,'" *Army*, June 1989: 85.

5. Hackworth, 617.

6. Ibid., 807.

7. S. L. A. Marshall, syndicated newspaper column on Col. David H. Hackworth, Los Angeles Times–Washington Post News Service, July 10, 1971.

8. Hackworth, 585.

9. Ibid., 571.

12. Westy & Slam

1. David Halberstam, *The Best and the Brightest* (New York: Fawcett Crest, 1973), 655, 675.

2. Gen. William C. Westmoreland, *A Soldier Reports* (New York: Da Capo, 1989), 305.

3. Ibid., 422.

4. Ibid., vii–viii.

5. William G. Effros, ed. *Quotations Vietnam: 1945–1970* (New York: Random House, 1970), 84.

6. Ibid.

7. Ibid., 92.

8. Ibid., 93

9. Ibid.

10. Neil Sheehan, *A Bright Shining Lie: John Paul Vann and America in Vietnam* (New York: Random House, 1988), 717–18.

14. The Demise of Coats & Ties

1. *Cavalier Daily*, student newspaper at the Univ. of Virginia, Charlottesville. Articles cited from the school year of 1965–66 were found in bound volumes kept in the newspaper's office, Newcomb Hall.

2. Ibid. Articles cited from the school year of 1968–69 were found on microfiche in the university's Alderman Library.

15. Rising Star

1. Maj. F. D. G. Williams, *SLAM: The Influence of S. L. A. Marshall on the United States Army* (Fort Monroe, Va.: United States Army Training and Doctrine Command, 1990), 28.

2. S. L. A. Marshall, *Island Victory: The Battle of Kwajalein Atoll* (Washington, D.C.: Infantry Journal, 1945).

16. Tempting Trouble

1. Marshall, *Bringing up the Rear*, 15.

2. S. L. A. Marshall, *The American Heritage History of World War I* (New York: Dell, 1966), 398.

3. Harold P. Leinbaugh and John D. Campbell, *The Men of Company K* (New York: Morrow, 1985), 282.

17. Bedrock for a General

1. Lewis H. Lapham, "Case Study of an Army Star," *Life*, Sept. 1970: 54–68.

18. Elegy at the Wall

1. Andrew Melnykovych, "21 Years Later, Mills Vet's Name Engraved on Wall," *Casper (Wyo.) Star-Tribune*, Oct. 3, 1989, 1.

20. Brothers in Conscience

1. Myra MacPherson, *Long Time Passing: Vietnam & the Haunted Generation* (New York: Signet, 1985), 402.

2. Dr. Laurence J. Peter, *Peter's Quotations: Ideas for Our Time* (New York: Bantam, 1989), 516.

21. In the Wake of the Six-Day War

1. "How Israel Won the War," CBS telecast, July 18, 1967. All references to the telecast come from the transcript and are used with the permission of CBS. The transcript is:

© CBS Inc. 1967
All Rights Reserved.
Originally broadcast on July 18, 1967
over the CBS Television Network.

2. S. L. A. Marshall, prepared acceptance speech on the occasion of receipt of the Medallion of Valor from Israel, Nov. 18, 1962. Speech included in the archives of the S. L. A. Marshall Military History Collection in the library of the Univ. of Texas at El Paso.

22. Questions of Fairness

1. "Editors' Note," *American Heritage* 40, no. 6 (1989): 12.

2. Richard Halloran, "General's Grandson Says Gunfire Thesis Is Backed," *New York Times*, July 3, 1989, sec. A, 8.

3. Smoler, 37.

4. "Letter from the Editors," *American Heritage* 40, no. 2 (1989): 5.

24. Eisenhower's Biographer

1. Spiller, "Marshall," 66.

25. Days of Thanksgiving

1. Samuel A. Stouffer, *The American Soldier: Combat and Its Aftermath* (Princeton: Princeton Univ. Press, 1949), 192.

27. Racing December

1. Roger J. Spiller, ed., *S. L. A. Marshall at Leavenworth: Five Lectures at the U.S. Army Command and General Staff College* (Fort Leavenworth, Kans.: U.S. Army Command and General Staff College, 1980), iv.

2. Roger J. Spiller, ed. *Dictionary of American Military Biography* (Westport, Conn.: Greenwood, 1984), 739.

Epilogue

1. Gen. William E. DuPuy, "Insights," *Military Review*, July 1989: 96.

2. Eliot A. Cohen and John Gooch, *Military Misfortunes: The Anatomy of Failure in War* (New York: Free Press, 1990), 72.

3. Ibid., 40.

4. Ibid., 186.

5. Geoffrey Perrett, *There's a War to Be Won: The United States Army in World War II* (New York: Ballantine, 1992), 520

6. John Keegan, *The Face of Battle* (New York: Penguin, 1978), 71.

Bibliography

Atkinson, Rick. *The Long Gray Line: The American Journey of West Point's Class of 1966.* Boston: Houghton Mifflin, 1989.

Baritz, Loren. *Backfire: A History of How American Culture Led Us into Vietnam and Made Us Fight the Way We Did.* New York: Ballantine, 1986.

Bolger, Capt. Daniel P. "Hackworth—'Hard-Charger Turned Sour'" *Army,* June 1989: 85.

Cavalier Daily, student newspaper at the Univ. of Virginia, Charlottesville, 1965–66, 1968–69.

Cohen, Eliot A., and John Gooch. *Military Misfortunes: The Anatomy of Failure in War.* New York: Free Press, 1990.

DuPuy, Gen. William E. "Insights." *Military Review* (July 1989): 96.

"Editors' Note." *American Heritage* 40, no. 6 (1989): 12.

Effros, William G., ed. *Quotations Vietnam: 1945–1970.* New York: Random House, 1970.

Feinberg, Lawrence. "S. L. A. Marshall, 77, Dies, Noted Military Historian." *Washington Post,* Dec. 18, 1977, sec. B, 4.

Fussell, Paul. *The Great War and Modern Memory.* New York: Oxford Univ. Press, 1977.

Gioglio, Gerald R. *Days of Decision: An Oral History of Conscientious Objection in the Military During the Vietnam War.* Trenton, N.J.: Broken Rifle, 1989.

Gregg, Richard B. *The Power of Nonviolence.* New York: Schocken, 1970.

Hackworth, Col. David H. *About Face: The Odyssey of an American Warrior.* New York: Simon and Schuster, 1989.

Halberstam, David. *The Best and the Brightest.* New York: Fawcett Crest, 1973.

Halloran, Richard. "General's Grandson Says Gunfire Thesis Is Backed." *New York Times,* July 3, 1989, sec. A, 8.

———. "Pivotal S. L. A. Marshall Book on Warfare Assailed as False." *New York Times*, Feb. 19, 1989, 1.

Heinemann, Larry. *Close Quarters*. New York: Penguin, 1986..

Hemingway, Ernest. *A Farewell to Arms*. New York: Scribners, 1929.

"How Israel Won the War." CBS telecast, July 18, 1967.

James, Caryn. "Gregory Peck Enters the 'Tribute Stage.'" *New York Times*, Apr. 12, 1992, sec. 2, 16.

Keegan, John. *The Face of Battle*. New York: Penguin, 1978.

———. "The Historian and Battle." *International Security* 3, no. 3 (Winter 1978/79): 145.

Lapham, Lewis H. "Case Study of an Army Star." *Life*, Sept. 1970: 54–68.

Leinbaugh, Harold P., and John D. Campbell. *The Men of Company K*. New York: Morrow, 1985.

"Letter from the Editors." *American Heritage* 40, no. 2 (1989): 5.

McFadden, Robert D. "S. L. A. Marshall, Historian, Dies." *New York Times*, Dec. 18, 1977, 1.

McGinniss, Joe. *Heroes*. New York: Pocket, 1977.

MacPherson, Myra. *Long Time Passing: Vietnam & the Haunted Generation*. New York: Signet, 1985.

Marshall, John Douglas. "A Grandson's Search for the Truth." *Seattle Post-Intelligencer*, May 30, May 31, June 1, 1989, 1.

Marshall, S. L. A. *The American Heritage History of World War I*. New York: Dell, 1966.

———. *The Armed Forces Officer*. Washington: Department of Defense, 1975.

———. *Battle at Best*. New York: Jove, 1989.

———. *Battles in the Monsoon*. New York: Morrow, 1967.

———. *Bringing up the Rear*. San Rafael, Calif.: Presidio, 1979.

———. *Crimsoned Prairie: The Indian Wars on the Great Plains*. New York: Scribners, 1972.

———. "How Papa Liberated Paris." *American Heritage* 13, no. 3 (1962): 5–7, 92–101.

———. *Island Victory: The Battle of Kwajalein Atoll*. Washington, D.C.: Infantry Journal, 1945.

———. *The Last Refuge: Three Public Addresses in the Spring, 1969*. Detroit: Author, 1969.

———. *Men Against Fire: The Problem of Battle Command in Future War*. Gloucester, Mass.: Peter Smith, 1978.

———. *Night Drop*. New York: Bantam, 1963.

———. *Pork Chop Hill*. New York: Jove, 1986.

———. Prepared acceptance speech on occasion of the receipt of the Medallion of Valor from Israel, Nov. 18, 1962. Speech included in the archives of the S.L.A. Marshall Military History Collection in the library of the Univ. of Texas at El Paso.

———. *The River and the Gauntlet.* New York: Warner, 1989.

———. *Sinai Victory.* New York: Apollo, 1967.

———. Syndicated newspaper column on Col. David H. Hackworth. Los Angeles Times–Washington Post News Service, July 10, 1971.

———. *West to Cambodia.* New York: Cowles, 1968.

Melnykovych, Andrew. "21 Years Later, Mills Vet's Name Engraved on Wall." *Casper (Wyo.) Star-Tribune,* Oct. 3, 1989, 1.

"Milestones." *Time,* Dec. 26, 1977: 58.

Moon, William Least Heat. *Blue Highways: A Journey into America.* Boston: Atlantic–Little, Brown, 1982.

Norman, Michael. *These Good Men: Friendships Forged from War.* New York: Crown, 1989.

O'Brien, Tim. *The Things They Carried.* New York: Penguin, 1991.

Perrett, Geoffrey. *There's a War to Be Won: The United States Army in World War II.* New York: Ballantine, 1992.

Peter, Dr. Laurence J. *Peter's Quotations: Ideas for Our Time.* New York: Bantam, 1989.

Seidenberg, Willa, and William Short. *A Matter of Conscience: GI Resistance During the Vietnam War.* Andover, Mass.: Addison Gallery of American Art, 1991.

Sheehan, Neil. *A Bright Shining Lie: John Paul Vann and America in Vietnam.* New York: Random House, 1988.

Smoler, Fredric. "The Secret of the Soldiers Who Didn't Shoot." *American Heritage* 40, no. 2 (1989): 37–45.

Spiller, Roger J., ed. *Dictionary of American Military Biography.* Westport, Conn.: Greenwood, 1984.

———. "S.L.A. Marshall and the Ratio of Fire." *RUSI Journal* 133, no. 4 (1988): 63–71.

———. *S.L.A. Marshall at Leavenworth: Five Lectures at the U.S. Army Command and General Staff College.* Fort Leavenworth, Kans.: U.S. Army Command and General Staff College, 1980.

Stouffer, Samuel A. *The American Soldier: Combat and Its Aftermath.* Princeton: Princeton Univ. Press, 1949.

Trainfire: Department of the Army Pamphlet No. 355-14. Washington, D.C.: Department of the Army, 1958.

Tuchman, Barbara W. *Practicing History.* New York: Ballantine, 1982.

Westmoreland, Gen. William C. *A Soldier Reports.* New York: Da Capo, 1989.

"Who's Retiring?" *Newsweek,* Aug. 15, 1960: 75–76.

Williams, Maj. F. D. G. *SLAM: The Influence of S. L. A. Marshall on the United States Army.* Fort Monroe, Va.: United States Army Training and Doctrine Command, 1990.

Wolff, Geoffrey. *The Duke of Deception.* New York: Penguin, 1986.

Wythe, Maj. George. *A History of the 90th Division.* N.p.: 90th Division Association, 1920.